DISCARD

Teaching

MATHEMATICS

How can mathematics be taught effectively?

What are the key issues in mathematics teaching today?

This handbook provides a comprehensive introduction to teaching mathematics in primary and secondary schools. It brings together the latest standards with authoritative guidance, ensuring that readers feel confident about how to approach their role as a teacher.

The book explores the context of the subject of mathematics and brings readers up to date with key developments. It places the mathematics curriculum in the context of whole-school numeracy issues and it introduces readers to key areas such as:

- planning and classroom management;
- assessment, recording and reporting;
- information and communication technology;
- investigative mathematics;
- equal opportunities, special needs and differentiation;
- Key Skills and alternative mathematics qualifications;
- being an effective maths teacher;
- personal and professional early career development for the early stages in the career.

This practical and accessible book will give beginning mathematics teachers a solid and dependable introduction to teaching the subject. The book is absolutely grounded in the realities of teaching and offers practical and relevant advice, as well as plentiful ideas to stimulate thinking and teaching.

Pamela Cowan is the tutor for PGCE Information and Communications Technology/ Computing and Mathematics at Queen's University Belfast. She is the Pathway Co-ordinator and tutor for all Masters modules in e-learning, and is also a member of the Teacher Education Partnership Group for e-learning.

Teaching Series

Teaching

MATHEMATICS

**A HANDBOOK FOR PRIMARY AND
SECONDARY SCHOOL TEACHERS**

Pamela COWAN

Routledge
Taylor & Francis Group

LONDON AND NEW YORK

TRS

First published 2006
by Routledge
4 Park Square, Milton Park, Abingdon, Oxon OX14 4RN

Simultaneously published in the USA and Canada
by Routledge
270 Madison Ave, New York, NY 10016

Routledge is an imprint of the Taylor & Francis Group

© 2006 Pamela Cowan

Typeset in Palatino by
Florence Production Ltd, Stoodleigh, Devon

Printed and bound in Great Britain by
Bell & Bain Ltd, Glasgow

British Library Cataloguing in Publication Data
A catalogue record for this book is available from
the British Library

Library of Congress Cataloging in Publication Data
A catalog record for this book has been requested

ISBN10: 0–415–33517–5
ISBN13: 978–0–415–33517–1

41.95   0013386432   2/5/08

Contents

Acknowledgements

My sincere thanks are extended to everyone who helped and encouraged me in the production of this book. I trust that you will recognise small parts of yourself in the words I have written.

1 Learning to teach

Introduction

This chapter aims to provide the reader with a broad overview of teaching in general to set the scene for the rest of the book, which deals with teaching mathematics. The process of teaching is highly complex and therefore to become an effective teacher is a great achievement. There are a number of 'steps' to help you reach this goal, so these steps will be the focus of this chapter. The best analogy to describe 'becoming a teacher' is that it is like a journey – one that lasts a lifetime, provides a wide variety of experiences and offers numerous 'great wonders' along the way. This book will focus on the early stages of your journey. It aims to guide you through Initial Teacher Education, securing your first post and introducing you to the requirements of Induction and Early Professional Development. From there, you should have the confidence to continue your journey of professional development with the support, advice and friendship of your colleagues.

Learning outcomes

At the end of this chapter you should be able to:

- describe the processes involved in teaching;
- list the qualities of a 'modern and effective' teacher;
- state the areas of competence to be developed as part of becoming a teacher.

What is teaching?

Teaching is more than just the delivery of strings of words to the listener: teaching must be meaningful to be remembered; it must be coherent to be understood; it must be planned to be continuous, and it must be enjoyed to be sustained for the rest of one's life.

In its broadest sense, teaching occurs in a variety of places. Through watching other people's actions, we are taught the basic skills needed to deal with everyday situations. For example, when shopping, we see others lifting their groceries and putting them in a trolley or basket; we notice people taking polythene bags and selecting their own fruit and

vegetables; we observe queues forming at the checkout tills; we watch people paying by cash, writing cheques or using their credit cards, and we see people returning their trolleys to the trolley park to get their monetary deposit back. No one teaches us *how* to shop – we are taught by our peers and we learn by imitation. We are all teachers (and learners) in the supermarket. Similarly, by listening to other people, we are taught new vocabulary, new ideas, new information about the world around us and other countries. So does that mean newsreaders are teachers too?

We also teach ourselves about safety and dangers through personal experiences. How many times have you touched a shiny metal kettle when it has just boiled, or the hob when it has just been turned off, or a live wire? Probably just the once! Although we cannot always see the danger, we are aware that it exists and normally take the necessary precautions.

So teaching takes a variety of forms. Sometimes it is the demonstration of certain skills and physical activities (think of PE or ICT); often it is verbal communication in the form of exposition: learning facts and dates in history; frequently, it is through discovery (in science); and it may also be through problem-solving in mathematics. Sometimes, the teaching is planned and organised in advance (in school), while other times it occurs quite naturally (through playing, going for walks, participating in activities or hobbies).

In this book we are focusing on the planned and organised process of teaching. This is not to say that informal teaching should not occur in the classroom – a good teacher will be effective in both the formal and informal process of teaching, with the latter often going unnoticed by most pupils.

The processes of teaching

The National Curriculum is a statutory framework outlining the subjects to be addressed by all schools at Key Stages 1 to 4 (the compulsory years of schooling). It aims to provide depth and breadth in curriculum subjects, in addition to encouraging the development of the 'whole child' through the cross-curricular themes. Schools are therefore guided by the National Curriculum on the range of subjects to include at each Key Stage. Within each subject, a scheme of work is planned for each academic year to ensure continuity within and across Key Stages. The Scheme of Work provides a yearly plan of the topics to be covered that academic year. It is composed of Units of Work which offer a more detailed breakdown of the criteria to be addressed by the teachers. These Units of Work contain series of lessons, which are usually topic-based. For each series of lessons, the teacher develops his or her own individual lesson plans with the key lesson objectives or learning outcomes collectively meeting the criteria outlined in the corresponding Unit of Work.

Delivering a lesson

In every lesson and for every series of lessons comprising a topic, a teacher goes through a sequence of steps to ensure that all the criteria outlined in the Unit of Work are met and that there is continuity and progression within and between lessons. These steps are:

- planning and preparing the lesson(s);
- presenting the lesson, taking account of classroom management issues;

- assessing the pupils to determine the effectiveness of the lesson;
- reviewing and evaluating the lesson(s).

This process is cyclical. After each lesson, the reviewing and evaluating step will inform the teacher's approach to the next lesson, thereby feeding into the planning and preparation stage. At the end of a topic, the teacher reviews the series of lessons to ensure that all the criteria outlined in the Unit of Work have been addressed to the required level of proficiency. This review often takes the form of pupil assessment in order to ensure that learning has occurred.

Planning and preparation

It is a surprise to many people that planning and preparation is often considered to be the most important part of the lesson, particularly when there are no pupils involved in this step. A solid, detailed and thoughtful approach to lesson-planning is required to ensure that the teacher minimises the opportunities for disruption and confusion. By focusing on a limited number of criteria in each lesson, the teacher can develop the pupils' understanding of the topic over a period of time. Normally, the basic or core skills within the topic are taught, practised and then developed further. Through the teacher's own understanding and knowledge of the subject matter, this pedagogical approach to the material can be adopted to cover the content to the required level. Planning constitutes a sequencing of the order in which the content domain for each lesson will be addressed in the classroom.

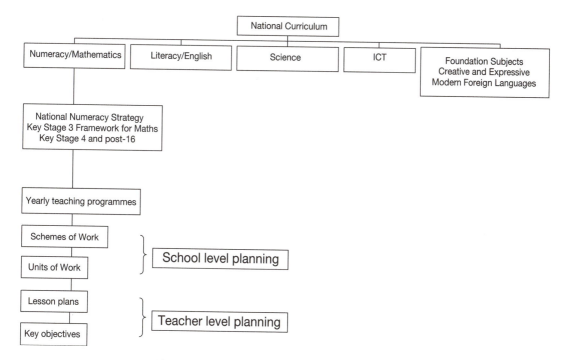

Figure 1.1 Structure of the National Curriculum

It also includes the identification of the most appropriate teaching strategy for the delivery of the lesson and the range of resources needed to assist in the delivery.

Preparation is the gathering together of the resources needed in a lesson. Each lesson will have its own specific requirements, although it can be assumed that textbooks, whiteboard markers or chalk, and overhead projector (OHP) or data projector and laptop connected to an interactive whiteboard will be needed in every lesson. In the context of maths, for example, preparation may entail finding visual aids and graphics calculators, and creating worksheets for the introduction and/or presentation phase of each lesson. Additional preparation may include writing key formulae, criterial attributes or notes on an overhead transparency (OHT) or on the board prior to the pupils arriving in the room, bringing a class set of protractors or compasses to the room, or preparing a demonstration using a piece of mathematical software to facilitate an explanation or encourage discussion.

Classroom management and discipline

The level of planning and preparation has a strong impact on the success of the lesson in achieving its aims and consequently the level of classroom management needed within the lesson. An interesting, well-structured, organised and clearly explained lesson will offer little opportunity for pupils to become disengaged, confused or bored. As a result, classroom control will be maintained with relative ease. The majority of classroom management problems in a mathematics lesson result from:

- teachers 'talking at' the pupils, thereby curtailing any mathematical discussion, instead of encouraging them to participate in the lesson;
- pupils becoming confused due to an ill-prepared delivery of the content of the lesson, including skipping steps in a calculation;
- pupils becoming bored as the lesson has been pitched either too high or too low for their mathematical ability;
- pupils being unable to complete the textbook/worksheet exercises due to a mismatch between the material taught and that addressed in the exercise/worksheet;
- pupils lacking confidence in their mathematical ability.

In the chapters that follow, advice on dealing with pupil misbehaviour is offered in terms of the least-to-most intrusive strategies. In all cases, teachers need to be aware of the school's discipline policy so that the correct sequence of events is adhered to during the assignment of sanctions.

Assessment

There are two main forms of assessment: formative and summative. Formative assessment provides information on a continuous basis throughout the duration of the course or module and is achieved through a combination of formal and informal strategies. The most common forms of formative assessment are:

- questioning the pupils in class;
- marking classwork exercises;
- marking homework exercises;
- grading project work, investigations, practical activities;
- end of topic tests or school examinations.

The results of formative assessment in mathematics lessons are used to inform the teacher of the pupils' progress and to assist in the planning of subsequent lessons. Problems that arise in classwork or homework exercises must be addressed in the next lesson, otherwise further progression in the topic cannot be achieved.

Summative assessment is used to summarise the pupils' achievements to date, normally against the National Curriculum levels. These are usually the formal examinations such as end-of-Key Stage tests, GCSEs and AS and A levels. The results also provide information about the pupils, although in this instance it is not used to inform subsequent teaching, but instead may be applied to subject or career choices for the pupil. Summative assessment is reported for each pupil, whereas formative assessment tends to focus more on the overall achievement of the whole class or subgroups within the class.

What are the purposes of assessment?

Effective assessment techniques offer 'feedback for learning'. In mathematics, higher-ability children are more able to learn from written feedback on their maths homework assignments or examinations than lower-ability children, so the type of feedback offered to the class should take account of this (Assessment Reform Group, 1999). Younger children and less able mathematicians should be taken through the solution to the questions on test papers or homework questions via discussion with the teacher who can offer reasons and explanations why a certain methodology was used. For higher-ability classes, it will often be sufficient to highlight the pupil's error on his or her homework or exam script. Once highlighted, these pupils are more likely to understand the mistake made and remember it for future questions, or they will have the interest and confidence to approach the teacher directly for further clarification if the problem remains unclear.

Who benefits from assessment?

Assessment offers information to three different groups of people: pupils, teachers and parents. The feedback to pupils has already been discussed – pupils receive regular, informal information about their learning and level of achievement through their performance in class and in homework assignments. Teachers obtain information about their teaching through the responses of the pupils to questions and the pupils' performance in classwork and homework. Based on this feedback, the teacher can decide whether he or she needs to recap on the existing material, or to move on to new material. The informal feedback in class also indicates whether the pace of the lesson and the depth of coverage of the content are suitable for the ability of the pupils. Parents obtain information about their children through the comments offered by teachers in homework books and also via test scores, grades and comments on term reports. Based on this information, parents can determine whether their child is making good and steady progress at regular intervals during the year, or whether he or she is underachieving in the class.

Reviewing and evaluating

Teachers must adapt to changing circumstances in the classroom on a daily, weekly, monthly, term and even yearly basis. No two classes behave in the same way, so no two lessons will feel the same, regardless of the fact that the same content is being covered in them. Teacher–pupil interactions differ with different personalities within the class, with different levels or mixes of ability, and even with different times of the day. As mentioned earlier, teaching is a journey, a continuous learning experience for everyone, including the teacher. Therefore, at the end of each class, teachers should ask themselves the following four questions:

- What did I learn from this lesson?
- How would I teach it differently in the future?
- What worked well and why?
- What didn't work and why?

Based on the responses to these questions, a teacher can plan an effective follow-up lesson to address any issues that may have arisen and to make good use of the most appropriate pedagogical teaching techniques for the class. For example, some maths classes may be relatively quiet in general, and the pupils may prefer to work individually or in pairs, practising examples and reinforcing the use of particular formulae and techniques. Other classes may dislike completing exercises and drill-and-practice work, and respond more favourably to problem-solving scenarios and practical maths that is contextualised in the real world. Based on this knowledge, the maths teacher can maximise pupil performance by preparing lessons that use the preferred learning disposition of the pupils (or at least by offering a range of activities addressing the same content through a variety of approaches). More information about Learning Dispositions is available from Johnston (1997) and her Learning Combination Inventory (LCI) (www.letmelearn.org/).

Task 1.1 The LCI and your approach to teaching
Read the information on the letmelearn website about Precise, Sequential, Technical and Confluent learners. Determine your own learning disposition. How does this influence the way you approach and plan your maths lessons? Are you excluding any other types of learners by assuming this style in every lesson? Can you think of alternative ways of teaching some topics to provide a variety of experiences that favours every preferred learning disposition?

Becoming a modern and effective teacher

What are the qualities of a modern and effective teacher? First, think of a teacher from your own school days who you admired and highlight what made him or her so special in your opinion. Clearly, qualities such as that teacher's personality – friendliness, approachability, rapport with the pupils, his or her dedication to teaching, and knowledge and enjoyment of the subject – will be some of the first things that probably spring to mind. You might also say that that teacher was never cross with the class and always made the work very easy. So how did that teacher achieve all of these characteristics with so much ease? And, more importantly, how can you achieve them in your classroom too?

Modern and effective teachers enjoy their work. They like to put their subject in a context that will engage and encourage their pupils to feel the same emotions in the classroom that the teacher feels. In the context of maths, teachers will use examples from everyday life to explain concepts, to practise skills, to establish a purposeful learning environment, and to develop an enthusiasm for the subject in their pupils. The use of resources such as ICT, videos, simulations from the workplace or from sports all add to that extra enjoyment and interest for the pupils. They subconsciously notice and respect the teacher who puts the extra effort into his or her lessons, introduces topics through situations arising from the news or on television, brings maths to life. Modern teachers are constantly reviewing and updating their methods of teaching, looking for opportunities to make maths more interesting and relevant to their pupils, and finding ways to develop higher-order thinking skills such as problem-solving and investigations. They adopt new strategies with a positive disposition and share ideas and advice with other teachers.

Effective maths teachers are well prepared, highly organised and logical in their coverage of the material on the syllabus. They plan and schedule their time effectively to ensure that all the required material is covered in good time for tests or examinations, and they also build in opportunities for revising work covered earlier in the year before using it in another context. They encourage pupils to make connections between topics, plan a variety of experiences, use practical work as well as theoretical approaches where possible, and ensure that pupils experience success in reaching their expectations in terms of achievement. Effective teachers of maths rarely need to use a range of disciplinary strategies in their classrooms because they plan lessons that are suited to the pupils' ages, abilities and interests, so that feelings of boredom and confusion are seldom experienced. These teachers also address common misconceptions during the phases in their teaching, and so pupils understand how to work mathematically and with accuracy, thereby reducing the opportunities of 'failure' that so often result in a dislike of the subject.

The teacher competences

There are three main areas of teaching competence that should be addressed during Initial Teacher Education (ITE). In *England* these are:

1 professional values and practice;
2 knowledge and understanding;
3 teaching, which includes the themes of Planning, expectations and targets; Monitoring and assessment; Teaching and class management.

The document *Qualifying to Teach* is available in downloadable format from the DfES website at www.dfes.gov.uk, or from the Teacher Training Agency (TTA) website at www.tda.gov.uk/upload/resources/pdf/q/qualifying-to-teach.pdf. Readers are advised to refer to the detailed breakdown of each of these competence areas regularly during ITE.

The *Teacher Education Partnership Handbook* outlines the Competence model for ITE in *Northern Ireland*. It has five categories for development:

1   understanding the curriculum and professional knowledge;
2   subject knowledge and subject applications;
3   teaching strategies and techniques, and classroom management;
4   assessment and recording of students' progress;
5   foundation for further professional development.

The reader is advised to consult the website for the Department of Education (DENI) at www.deni.gov.uk/teachers/car_dev/teph.pdf, the Northern Ireland Network for Education (NINE) at www.nine.org.uk/, or the General Teaching Council for Northern Ireland (GTC(NI)) www.gtcni.org.uk, for a more detailed breakdown of each of these areas.

Teacher Education Partnership in *Scotland* is governed by the General Teaching Council (GTC). It is also a competence-based model with four sections:

1   subject and content of teaching;
2.1 communication and approaches to teaching and learning;
2.2 class organisation and management;
2.3 assessment;
3   the school and the education system;
4   the values, attributes and abilities integral to professionalism.

The reader is advised to consult the website at www.gtcs.org.uk/ or www.scotland.gov. uk/library/documents_w3/git-00.htm for the Guidelines for ITE Courses in Scotland.

The General Teaching Council in Wales is currently reviewing their teacher competency model Circular 13/98 which advocated four main areas of competence:

1   knowledge and understanding;
2   planning, teaching and class management;
3   monitoring, assessment, recording, reporting and accountability;
4   other professional requirements.

This document is available from the GTC website at www.wales.gov.uk/subieducation training/content/circulars/1398/1398-contents-e.htm. However, readers are encouraged to monitor this website for the revised version due to be published in 2006.

Literacy, Numeracy and ICT in ITE

Additional assessments have also been introduced for the award of Qualified Teacher Status (QTS) in England. From February 2001, all new entrants to the teaching profession are required to have passed the QTS Skills Tests in Literacy and Numeracy, regardless of their teaching discipline. From 2002, passing the ICT Skills Test is also a requirement for QTS. If you have completed ITE and have secured a teaching post but have not passed your QTS Skills Tests, you may only teach as an unqualified teacher for a maximum of five years (TTA, 2003). Induction will not commence until you have passed the tests and achieved QTS. Forty test centres currently exist across England and the student teacher is required to register at one of these centres for each test. Initially, an upper limit of four attempts at each Skills Test was defined. However, following considerable pressure from the education community, students have been allowed an unlimited number of opportunities to take the test from September 2001. The reasoning behind student assessment in these three areas was included in the Green Paper in the context of *Better Training* as follows:

> The Government has set a demanding agenda for high standards. We are committed to giving teachers the training and support they need to do their jobs well and to progress in their careers. We propose further changes are needed to make initial teacher training more flexible and more rigorous and to ensure that all newly qualified teachers have the skills they need.
>
> (p. 43)

The tests are designed to ensure that newly qualified teachers can use their literacy, numeracy and ICT skills in the wider context of their professional role. The tests are of 45-minute duration and are equivalent to Key Skills level 2–3 in terms of their 'standard'. No exemptions exist for teachers of specialist subjects such as English, mathematics or ICT/Computing. The tests are computerised, which facilitates immediate feedback to the candidate at the end of the test period.

The Numeracy Skills Test

This test comprises questions on mental arithmetic, general arithmetic, practical applications of measurements, basic algebra, handling and using statistical information. Calculators are permitted in all sections apart from the mental arithmetic questions. All questions are set in the context of teaching.

The Literacy Skills Test

This test contains the categories of spelling, punctuation, grammar and comprehension. All sections are contextualised in an educational setting. Students with English as an additional language or candidates with special needs such as dyslexia are offered extra time to read and complete the tests.

The ICT Skills Test

The content categories in this test include gathering information for professional use, handling information, presenting information, communication and operation. Familiarity with applications software for spreadsheets, databases, word-processing and presentations is covered in these broad descriptions, as well as skills in file management, internet searching, e-mailing, connecting and setting up ICT equipment and the security of data.

Additional information on test content and sample skills tests can be downloaded from www.tta.gov.uk/training/skillstests. A series of books entitled *Achieving QTS* is available from Learning Matters (www.learningmatters.co.uk), which may assist you in your revision prior to the tests.

Table 1.1 Summary of ITE requirements

England	Wales	Northern Ireland	Scotland
3 areas of teaching competence	*4 areas of teaching competence*	*5 areas of teaching competence*	*4 areas of teaching competence*
1 Professional values and practice 2 Knowledge and understanding 3 Teaching (which includes the themes: Planning, expectations and targets; Monitoring and assessment; Teaching and class management)	1 Knowledge and understanding 2 Planning, teaching and class management 3 Monitoring, assessment, recording, reporting and accountability 4 Other professional requirements	1 Understanding the curriculum and professional knowledge 2 Subject knowledge and subject applications 3 Teaching strategies and techniques, and classroom management 4 Assessment and recording of students' progress 5 Foundation for further professional development	1 Subject and content of teaching 2.1 Communication and approaches to teaching and learning 2.2 Class organisation and management 2.3 Assessment 3 The school and the education system 4 The values, attributes and abilities integral to professionalism
3 Skills tests for QTS	*No skills tests*	*No skills tests*	*No skills tests*
• Literacy • Numeracy • ICT			
Newly qualified teacher has QTS (qualified teacher status)	*Newly qualified teacher has QTS (qualified teacher status)*	*Newly qualified teacher is called a BT (beginning teacher)*	*Newly qualified teacher has TQ (a teacher qualification)*
Academic entry requirements • GCSE Mathematics grade C • GCSE English grade C • GCSE Science grade C (for primary or KS2/3 courses) • a UK degree (for postgraduate courses)	*Academic entry requirements* • GCSE Mathematics grade C • GCSE English grade C • GCSE Science grade C (for primary or KS2/3 courses) • a UK degree (for postgraduate courses)	*Academic entry requirements* • GCSE Mathematics grade C • GCSE English grade C • GCSE Science grade C (for primary or KS2/3 courses) • a UK degree (for postgraduate courses)	*Academic entry requirements* • GCSE Mathematics grade C • GCSE English grade C • GCSE Science grade C (for primary or KS2/3 courses) • a UK degree (for postgraduate courses)
Placements • Minimum of two schools • 32 weeks for 4 year UG programmes • 24 weeks for 2–3 year UG programmes • 24 weeks for all secondary and KS2/3 PG programmes • 18 weeks for all primary PG programmes	*Placements* • Minimum of two schools • 32 weeks for 4 year UG programmes • 24 weeks for 2–3 year UG programmes • 24 weeks for all secondary and KS2/3 PG programmes • 18 weeks for all primary PG programmes	*Placements* • Minimum of two schools • 32 weeks for 4 year UG programmes • 24 weeks for 2–3 year UG programmes • 24 weeks for all secondary and KS2/3 PG programmes • 18 weeks for all primary PG programmes	*Placements* • Minimum of two schools • At least 30 weeks for UG programmes • At least 18 weeks for all PG programmes (primary and secondary)
Use of mentors in schools for main assessment of students during placements	Use of mentors in schools for main assessment of students during placements	University tutors complete main assessment during placements.	Use of mentors in schools for main assessment of students during placements
More information at www.tta.gov.uk/training/qtsstandards/index.htm	More information at: www.wales.gov.uk/subieducationtraining/content/circulars/1398/1398-contents-e.htm	More information at: www.deni.gov.uk/teachers/car_dev/teph.pdf	More information at: www.scotland.gov.uk/library/documents_w3/git-00.htm

The structure of this book

This book is divided into four main sections:

Part I: Setting the scene for teaching mathematics;
Part II: The 'bigger picture' in teaching mathematics;
Part III: In the maths classroom;
Part IV: Personal and professional development.

Part I examines the twofold nature of mathematics through considering 'teaching for understanding' in the context of the theories of learning. It also reviews the National Curriculum and the National Strategies for Numeracy and Key Stage 3 as a backdrop for the further ideas on teaching mathematics offered in subsequent sections.

Part II of the book looks at the 'bigger picture' in teaching mathematics, and initially addresses the concept of being an effective teacher in terms of planning and preparing effective lessons, establishing a positive learning environment and using resources. The issues surrounding effective classroom management and working with pupils are introduced before attention is directed towards two key areas that assist teachers in reducing the levels of misbehaviour in their classrooms: dealing with misconceptions in maths and the role of ICT in the maths classroom. By understanding the common misconceptions experienced by pupils, teachers can address these at an early stage in their teaching and therefore minimise the opportunities for 'failure'. The use of ICT engages pupils and also facilitates the use of mathematical techniques for solving problems normally beyond the pupils' grasp.

In Part III, 'In the maths classroom', the reader is guided through a series of ideas for lessons, highlighting the types and range of teaching styles available across the maths curriculum. Separate chapters are devoted to teaching mathematics in the primary school, the use of investigations and problem-solving with a specific focus on GCSE coursework, and Key Skills at A level. Inclusion has resulted in increasing numbers of children with learning difficulties being integrated into the normal classroom. Chapter 13 is dedicated to assisting pupils who have special educational needs, including the mathematically gifted students. Finally, this section concludes with information on assessment.

In the final section of the book, Part IV – Personal and professional development – the reader is offered advice and guidance on applying for jobs, the interview technique and securing your first teaching post. This stage leads directly to professional development – Induction – and the requirements of Early Professional Development before moving on to consider how you can plan for your Continued Professional Development.

Part I

Setting the scene for teaching mathematics

2 Teaching for understanding: mathematical knowledge or enquiry

Introduction

How were you taught maths in primary school? Did you learn number sequences by songs or rhymes such as Ten Green Bottles? Did you play with scales and counters or pretend you were working in a shop? What changes occurred when you entered the post-primary maths classroom? Did your teacher relate maths to other subjects such as science or geography? Or were you prepared for 'the exams'? Was more time spent *using* maths or *practising* mathematical skills?

This chapter aims to highlight the reasoning behind the viewpoint that mathematics is twofold: a body of knowledge and a mode of enquiry. In the first part of this chapter an overview of the various learning theories is offered before focusing on the writings of Bruner and Gardner to exemplify the dual nature of mathematics.

Learning outcomes

At the end of this chapter you should be able to:

- recall various theories of learning;
- make links between these theories and the teaching of mathematics;
- discuss why it is important to teach the skills and concepts in maths as well as mathematical problem-solving.

The theories of how children learn

Learning is not a new phenomenon; over the years research into how pupils learn has resulted in the formation of many teaching paradigms. This section aims to introduce the reader to the key findings of educational psychologists that guide the pedagogical approaches used in classrooms today.

Skinner

Skinner (1974), the psychologist, adopted a behaviourist approach to his research where animals were 'taught' to complete various activities through the use of positive reinforcement

– the rewarding of compliance with food or treats. Using this method, he established power over the animals, acting as 'the controlling agent' or 'master' giving instructions. Skinner averred that in the classroom, such positive reinforcement would ease the management and discipline problems being experienced by teachers. By encouraging the teachers to focus only on the good behaviour in the classroom and ignoring occurrences of misbehaviour, the pupils would realise that attention is only given to those who act in keeping with the teacher's requests. This theory and its implementation through the use of 'learning programs' or teaching machines was the first instance of ICT in the classroom. Nowadays, it has been surpassed by the drill and practice programs on the internet and on CD-ROMs, or the use of Integrated Learning Systems (ILS) such as Successmaker. The computer can monitor each stage in the pupils' work, giving feedback and interacting with the pupils as they complete the work on screen. Unfortunately, this behaviourist approach deals only with the low-level skills of recall and the application of well-rehearsed algorithms. There is little opportunity for contextualising the calculations in everyday life or building social interactions or discussions into the work. Perhaps the most familiar application of behaviourism experienced by a high proportion of the population is the rote learning of multiplication tables in primary school.

Task 2.1

List three examples of a Skinner approach from your own experiences of education to date. How successful were they in achieving their aim? What were the difficulties?

Piaget

Jean Piaget was also a psychologist who focused on the two basic elements of how children learn: their mental stages in development and their intellectual skills. He highlighted the importance of understanding when and how children are ready to learn as this plays a pivotal role in the types of teaching and learning experiences used in the classroom. The progression from sensory-motor intelligence as demonstrated by babies and very young children (up to the age of two years old) into the concrete stage typical of the pre-school and primary school children as they try to make sense of the world around them illustrates the need for 'play' and opportunities to 'discover' as part of the learning process. Much of the primary school maths taught today involves the use of physical objects and open-ended activities to promote investigation and discovery by doing.

Later, from the age of about 12 years old, the concrete operations become replaced by the more formal and abstract thinking processes required in adult life. A typical example of abstract thinking in maths is algebra – where numbers are replaced by letters and solutions to problems move from being a simple number to a set of solutions represented by an inequality.

Alongside these cognitive developments, the children's intellectual skills are also expanding. From an early age, pupils master the language needed to communicate and understand what is happening around them such as larger/smaller and higher/lower. Then they form concepts and reasons to explain what they see and do – answers to the *why* and *how* questions. Next, pupils move to the stage where symbols and icons are used

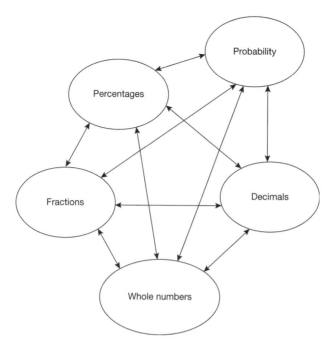

Figure 2.1   The links between fractions, decimals, percentages and probabilities

to represent their interpretations of the world – a mathematical language develops and finally logical thinking occurs through the use of Boolean algebra and induction.

In terms of teaching, Piaget believes in strategies whereby the pupils are actively involved in a discovery environment in which interactions with the environment, their teacher and their peers facilitate the learning process. From the hands-on experiences, the pupils develop schema to remember the connections between prior experiences and the new learning. Assimilation of these new learning experiences with the old increases the interconnectedness of the schema and updates them for later use in other situations.

Task 2.2

Create a spider diagram to illustrate the interconnections between other main areas of mathematics such as graphs, measurement or algebra and their sub-themes.

Vygotsky

Lev Vygotsky was interested in the idea that learning, when properly organised, allows for mental development. However, he questioned the sole measurement of what a pupil can do alone in a test environment as being a true representation of that pupil's ability. He maintained that educators should give pupils hints and prompts to see how far they could be led. Often pupils working in pairs or collaborating as a group achieve much more than each individual would achieve alone. Clearly, this form of collaboration is progressing the mental development of many of the group's participants. Vygotsky (1978) defined the zone of proximal development as:

> The distance between the actual development level as determined by independent problem-solving and the level of potential as determined through problem-solving under adult guidance or in collaboration with more capable peers.
>
> (p. 86)

He declared this zone as the range within which the instructions of adults could have the greatest impact. Van der Veer and Valsiner (1991) posit that two levels of a child's development can be determined: that which the pupil can do alone and the level which he or she has the potential to achieve. The actual development is the level of development of a child's mental functions which has already been completed as demonstrated in tests, while the proximal development refers to those functions that have not yet matured – the mental processes that are currently in embryonic state. Imitation has an important role to play in bridging the gap between the actual and proximal developmental levels. Children are excellent imitators, copying the actions of others well beyond the limits of their personal capabilities. Through working with others, interacting with people and the environment, children can progress quickly through their zones of proximal development, making learning rapid and effective.

Within the mathematics curriculum, activities such as problem-solving, collaborative groupwork, investigations, exploring real-life scenarios, role play, discussions and many more, offer pupils the opportunity to co-operate with their teacher and peers to make the transition across their current zone of proximal development and into a higher one.

Task 2.3

List instances in your maths career where you have benefited from working as part of a team on a project/assignment or revision topic. Why was the collaboration effective? Were you a mixed-ability group or all of equal ability? What additional qualities were brought to the group or surfaced during your collaboration?

Bloom's Taxonomy

A number of taxonomies and heuristics also exist which impact on the approaches teachers use in the classroom. Bloom (1956) noted three domains of learning: cognitive, affective and psychomotor. In Bloom's Taxonomy, learning is broken down into a hierarchy of mutually exclusive categories. In the cognitive domain these were classified as: knowledge, comprehension, application, analysis, synthesis and evaluation. However, Bloom recognised the limitations of this approach, declaring:

> It might lead to fragmentation and atomisation of educational purposes such that the parts and pieces finally placed into the classification might be very different from the complete objective with which one started.
>
> (Bloom, 1956, pp. 5–6)

This fragmentation conflicts with the current emphasis on integrative, holistic systems in which any part belongs to a greater whole, sharing reciprocal relationships with other parts. The differences between the classroom-based tasks of school mathematics and the real-life mathematical problems of the outside world highlight the artificial nature of the classroom context and its learning styles.

Task 2.4

List examples of maths in other subjects such as geography, science, music or art. How could you use these examples to engage your pupils in the cognitive, affective and psychomotor domains.

Polya heuristic

Polya (1945) revived the idea of a heuristic – the art of discovery. Whereas Euclid and Descartes attempted to promote approaches to mathematics centred on discovery and invention, these approaches did not translate well into the school curriculum. Polya, however, reformulated and illustrated these ideas in such a way that teachers could implement them in the classroom. He recognised that mathematics in its neat and finished state hid the messy and imaginative process that underpins all mathematical enquiry. The demonstrative reasoning typical of 'finished' mathematics is usually all that is taught in schools. However, Polya (1966) argued that mathematics teaching should also promote the plausible reasoning skills used to solve the problem:

> If the teaching of mathematics gives only a one-sided idea of the mathematician's thinking, it totally suppresses those 'informal' activities of guessing and extracting mathematical concepts from the visible world around us. It neglects what may be the most interesting part for the general student, the most instructive part for the future user of mathematics, and the most inspiring part for the future mathematician.
>
> (pp. 124–125)

Polya (1966) viewed mathematics as consisting of information and 'know-how'. Problem-solving techniques need to be illustrated and discussed with pupils in an insightful way by their teachers. Textbook exercises currently in use in classrooms fulfil the pedagogical function of teaching pupils to use algorithms to solve highly structured problems, whereas non-routine, ill-structured problems are needed to develop pupils' problem-solving skills.

Papert and Logo

Papert and his colleagues at the Massachusetts Institute of Technology (MIT) developed Logo in the late 1960s with the aim of revolutionising education. Papert (1980) envisaged the computer as a tool to think with and is normally associated with the constructivist movement. Using Logo allows the pupils to make the transition from the concrete to the abstract by facilitating the reverse operation too. By taking an abstract idea, pupils could use the turtle graphics facility to test their hypothesis by viewing the concrete feedback given on-screen. This environment assists the pupils in editing and manipulating their ideas as they re-structure their own thinking about the problem under investigation.

Papert (1971) firmly believed that pupils should 'do mathematics rather than merely learn about it'. Learning is 'constructed' through a variety of experiences and solving problems in context. Parallels are easily identified between the four-stage Polya heuristic: *understanding the problem, devising a plan, carrying out the plan* and *looking back,* and the four stages in Logo programming: *identifying the variables, writing the program, running the program* and *debugging.* Good problem-solving habits such as decomposing the problem are promoted through the use of Logo, as is the idea of means–end analysis (Newell and Simon, 1972).

Task 2.5

- Polya's book entitled *How to Solve It* lists four stages in problem-solving. Do you agree with them?
- Investigate what is meant by 'means–end analysis'. How does this process fit with Polya and Papert?
- Investigate the term *constructivist* and the work of Papert.

Perspectives on teaching from other parts of the world

Most recent research into how children learn has offered a variety of alternative perspectives in terms of learning skills, information or facts, and has highlighted the benefits of allowing pupils the freedom to discover ideas or knowledge and to learn at their own pace, when ready. The next section highlights the different approaches towards teaching, using examples from the Netherlands, Italy and Guatemala.

Dutch RME

Over 30 years ago, work began in the Freudenthal Institute in the Netherlands to investigate the use of real-world mathematics, or 'realistic mathematics', as a teaching strategy. Out of this research, Realistic Mathematics Education (RME) was born. RME focuses on the growth of the pupils' knowledge and understanding of maths, with an emphasis on offering pupils problem situations which they can 'imagine'. The idea of 'imagining' the problems is not intended to restrict the contexts to 'real-world' issues, but can extend from the use of fantasy-world situations such as fairytales to the formal world of mathematics. The key to the approach is the requirement that the pupil can imagine the problem being real in his or her mind.

Clearly, this teaching strategy is a definite move away from the mechanistic approach traditionally used in maths education. Traditional maths teaching comprised the use of stand-alone skills development through drill and practice exercises. The content to be covered by the teacher was well defined and easily broken into small, manageable chunks of information with little or no links to existing mathematical knowledge. The use of fixed algorithms or procedures was taught to solve particular problems with minimal attention given to the explanation of why the strategy worked. Once the skills had been mastered, the context of the mathematical problem could be added. RME is almost the reverse of this process.

Instead of contextualised problems being introduced at the end of the learning process, RME uses context as the source of the problem and encourages the pupils to develop their mathematical tools and strategies while solving the problem. Pupils are therefore active participants in the process, creating schemes and developing models useful in solving the given problem. With encouragement, these schemes can be generalised in stages to allow pupils to use the same (or similar) approaches to solving similar or related problems. Eventually, these models give the pupils access to the more formal mathematical processes. To assist the pupils in bridging the gap between the informal approaches and the formal strategies, the models shift from 'models of' to 'models for', thus expanding the pupils' knowledge base to increasingly higher levels of mathematical understanding.

Freudenthal (1968) declared that maths education should not focus on maths as a closed system but on the process of mathematization as an activity. Treffers (1987) defined mathematization in the educational context as being vertical and horizontal. Vertical mathematisation was the process of making connections between concepts and strategies – re-organisation within the mathematical system. Horizontal mathematization was the process of encouraging the pupils to create mathematical tools to organise and solve the 'real' problem. Freudenthal (1991) summarised these two types of mathematisation as this: 'horizontal mathematization involves going from the world of life to the world of symbols, while vertical mathematization means moving within the world of symbols'.

Treffers (1987) identified the five characteristics of RME as:

- the use of contexts that are 'real' to the pupils;
- the use of models to allow for shifts to higher levels of understanding;
- the use of the pupils' own mathematical constructions;
- the interactive nature of the teaching process – a partnership between the pupils and the teacher;
- the entwining of various learning strands.

The Dutch model of teaching illustrates the initial openness in interpretation of the content to be taught in schools in the Netherlands. Teacher autonomy alongside school-based decisions was used to guide the breadth and depth of content coverage in maths. Recent trends in RME are encouraging teachers to focus on their continuing professional development and on how pupils' learning takes place in the classroom. There has been direct government guidance on the content of mathematics teaching in Dutch primary schools and the ideal level of attainment in mathematics to be reached by all pupils before leaving the primary school. Recently, there has also been a switch to allowing pupils to practise mathematical skills to reinforce learning, more attention being paid to differentiation by ability and redressing the gender imbalance between the high levels of attainment of boys and the low performance of girls in mathematics in the Netherlands.

Reggio Emilia

The Reggio Emilia schools in Italy are an illustration of the use of an open approach to teaching and learning for pre-school children. These are schools where the pupils are surrounded by their cultural heritage in the form of art, sculpture and architecture which act as inspiration to the children. Through being encouraged to explore and investigate, the children demonstrate the use of analysis, synthesis and evaluation at a much earlier age. Their development is accelerated and the children become engaged in meaningful activities, sharing ideas with their peers. The openness of the approach to teaching and learning allows teachers to build opportunities for interconnecting areas of the learning experience such as highlighting the role of maths in art, nature and science. Teachers provide the inspiration for the pupils and the children add the creativity. In-depth exploration and an unhurried ethos within the classroom allow pupils to maintain their focus and concentration when investigating new topics and therefore they produce their best work.

The classroom environment is also conducive to learning, being bright, spacious and airy with colourful posters and wall displays of the pupils' work and that of their teacher or experienced artists. Inviting materials are on display for the pupils to touch and use. Mess, noise and freedom are accepted as part of the process of learning, and making mistakes, non-conformity to approaches or risk-taking, and singularity are characteristics that are welcomed in the children. The teachers and the classroom environment provide the inspiration and engagement for the pupils, but it is the pupils themselves who use their imagination, curiosity and creativity to make it into the learning experience.

Rogoff

Barbara Rogoff challenges the conventional approach of age-related classrooms in favour of Open Classrooms where learning is initiated and guided by the child's interest and motivation. Much of Rogoff's thinking on Open Classrooms results from her research into the Mayan community in Guatemala where children learn in an apprenticeship-type model by helping within the home or local community. Young girls watch their mothers weave colourful and complicated patterns, and when they show a sufficient level of interest, they are given simple projects of their own to complete under the guidance of their mothers. Rogoff advocates that children's development is a result of the cultural processes to which they are exposed and by segregating children into specialist child-focused settings (schools) we are removing important opportunities for them to observe, learn and work alongside their elders in valued community activities. Open Classrooms provide a step towards the community-centred approach of learning. Within an Open Classroom, pupils learn by becoming engaged or interested in a task or activity being completed by a peer or an adult in the room. The adult then becomes their guide or instructor working alongside the pupil, showing and assisting him in developing a skill or helping him solve a problem. Through a process of collaboration, the pupils make connections with existing knowledge from previous learning experiences and so knowledge grows.

In Open Classroom schools, the parents of the children assist in the education process by contributing around 2–3 hours per week in the school. Rogoff et al. (2002) highlight the importance of attending to parents' understanding of children's learning in an Open Classroom environment as many parents have experienced a traditional schooling and are unaware of the expectations being placed on them in the new teaching and learning environment. Consequently, parents need to learn how to teach the pupils and the teachers must understand the parents' learning process in the Open Classroom environment to ensure successful outcomes for everyone involved in the school. The main features of an Open Classroom are:

- co-operative learning;
- multi-age classrooms;
- integrated curriculum;
- authentic learning;
- assessment in the context of the instruction.

The concept of Communities of Practice (CoP) sits well with the Open Classroom approach to teaching and learning.

Summary

As evidenced in the above examples, much of the learning is occurring in an unstructured, discovery-based situation. Pupils learn from more knowledgeable others (peers, teachers, parents) by enquiry, and at a pace and time that suits them. Interest and motivation is self-initiated so pupils do not become bored or disengaged in the work. They also experience a feeling of involvement in the community in which they are a member, whether they are weaving colourful patterns, finding out about local art or history, or assisting others in an extended project.

The twofold nature of maths

The next section uses two key learning paradigms – the work of Bruner and that of Gardner – to explain the twofold approach to mathematics teaching and learning. It should be noted, however, that other research in this area also exists and the reader is encouraged to review a range of perspectives.

The 'folk pedagogies' in teaching

The National Curriculum places great emphasis on the teaching of subject knowledge and the acquisition of basic skills. McLaughlin and Shepard (1995) make the case for eschewing the behaviourist model in favour of the development of higher-order skills:

> Much of the current instructional practice is based on the behavioural-learning theory from the early part of this [twentieth] century. According to this theory, learning occurs by reinforcement of low level skills that become the building blocks for more complex understandings. . . . In more recent decades, learning researchers have demonstrated that memorising the facts first does not lead automatically to an ability to analyse and apply what has been learned. Learning requires thinking.
>
> (p. 9)

Teachers spend their professional lives making inferences about children's minds from their responses in class, their homeworks, test scores and so on. However, little attention is paid to the well-wrought psychological theory available to guide their decision-making processes. Bruner (1996) posits that teachers' thinking is informed by one of a number of 'folk pedagogies':

> if you as a pedagogical theorist are convinced that the best learning occurs when the teacher helps lead the pupils to discover generalisations on her own, you are likely to run into an established cultural belief that a teacher is an authority who is supposed to tell the child what the general case is, while the child should be occupying herself with memorising the particulars.
>
> (p. 46)

Two folk pedagogies are of particular interest. The first stresses the acquisition of propositional knowledge by learning facts and algorithms for future regurgitation in tests. Bruner (1996) argues that this folk pedagogy is informed by a limiting behaviourist view of the learner as a passive recipient of information that can be 'looked up' or 'listened to':

> In effect, this view presumes that the learner's mind is a *tabula rasa*, a blank slate. Knowledge put into the head is taken as cumulative, with later knowledge building upon priorly existing knowledge. More important is this view's assumption that the child's mind is passive, a receptacle waiting to be filled. Active interpretation or construal does not enter the picture. The didactic bias views the child from the outside, from a third person perspective, rather than trying to 'enter her thoughts'. It is blankly one-way: teaching is not a mutual dialogue, but a telling by one to the other.
>
> (p. 56)

The second folk pedagogy recognises the child as a thinker, dismissing the third person perspective above for the first person perspective. It is less dismissive of the child's mind and ideas. Children arrive at school for the first time with a mathematical model (albeit a poorly developed one) of how numbers are manipulated. In this pedagogical model (constructivism), the school is responsible for the transformation of the child's naive model to a sophisticated state. Techniques such as classroom discussion, collaboration and negotiation are used in the context of maths to reveal and challenge the pupils' models of the world. By working alongside more knowledgeable others, these naive ideas are replaced by more accurate, mathematical concepts.

Bruner (1996) suggests that folk theories 'are best thought of as parts of a broader continent, their significance to be understood in the light of their partialness' (p. 65). Teachers are advised to offer pupils opportunities to use the discipline in question as a mode of enquiry, through access to discovery learning, but this should not exclude the learning of facts and algorithms – mathematics as a body of knowledge. Bruner (1960) claims that 'computational practice may be a necessary step towards understanding conceptual ideas in mathematics' (p. 29). It is familiarity with the basic mathematical concepts and skills that underpin the ability to solve problems.

Gardner's unschooled mind

In keeping with Bruner's second folk pedagogy, Gardner (1991) also believes that children enter school with a set of ideas and skills they have created to explain the world around them. It is these intuitive theories that often persist long after formal education has been completed. Gardner argues that these naive theories can be so firmly entrenched in the child's mind that they distort the child's thinking processes, so when faced with a problem unlike those encountered in the classroom, the child resorts to his or her naive and intuitive 'rules' despite the newly acquired knowledge. Clearly, teachers have a responsibility to address these misconceptions, challenge them, demonstrate their inadequacy and then show the pupils the correct way of representing the concept using facts or algorithms as necessary:

it should be possible – and it would be educationally effective – to have students directly confront the discrepancies between their intuitive theories and those that have been developed by the experts in the disciplines. Indeed, unless such confrontations take place, it is likely that the intuitive theories will continue to exist, potentially re-emerge and dominate once the expert theories are no longer supported by the trappings of school.

(Gardner, 1991, p. 91)

Types of learners

Gardner (1991) highlights three types of learners: the intuitive learner, the traditional learner and the disciplinary learner. The first uses the naive intuitions of a young child, the second succeeds in the drill and practice environment within school by 'playing the teacher–pupil game' and regurgitating the material covered in class with little understanding of why the method is used or how this knowledge can be applied in alternative situations. The third type of learner, the disciplinary learner, has a true understanding of the subject matter, being able to apply the knowledge and skills in novel and unfamiliar contexts. These learners can see beyond the disjointed facts and algorithms to the general principles underlying the concepts. Gardner and Boix-Mansilla (1994, p. 212) aver that schools should aim to produce disciplinary learners by 'teaching for understanding'. Gardner (1991) declares that the testing process is partly to blame for the lack of awareness of the hidden misconceptions. The current assessment and grading of children fails to ensure that an understanding of the taught topic(s) has been achieved and that the internalisation of the knowledge and skills has occurred so that it can be utilised in other contexts or newly posed problems.

While acknowledging the value of learning facts, algorithms and skills, Gardner (1991) counsels that this approach should be combined with strategies that ensure that children learn to use cultural tools to improve their 'understanding':

The successful student is one who learns how to use research materials, libraries, notecards and computer files, as well as knowledgeable parents, teachers, older students and classmates – in order to master those tasks of schools that are not transparently clear. In terminology that has recently become fashionable, intelligence is 'distributed' in the environment as well as in the head and the 'intelligent student' makes use of the intelligence distributed throughout his environment.

(p. 253)

Bruner (1996) referred to these materials and the access to more knowledgeable people as the child's 'cultural tools'.

In summary, both Bruner and Gardner acknowledge the need for teachers to use drill and practice in the classroom to undermine any resident misconceptions in the pupils' minds and to offer pupils opportunities to internalise the 'basics' before moving to the higher-level work associated with problem-solving. By addressing the 'body of knowledge' first, the pupils can reflect and self-evaluate their learning when they have to apply their understanding of the topic to a novel context. 'Maths as a body of knowledge' is designed to *supplement* the main role of maths – namely, 'maths as a mode of enquiry'.

Mathematics as a mode of enquiry

Active engagement in mathematics

In order to develop mathematical thinking and the ability to solve problems, pupils need to 'do' mathematics (National Research Council, 1989, 1990). The act of 'doing' mathematics incorporates such activities as 'solving challenging problems, exploring patterns, formulating educated guesses (conjectures) and checking them, drawing conclusions through reasoning, and communicating ideas, patterns, conjectures, conclusions and reasons' (National Research Council, 1989, pp. 1–3). Each of these activities involves the use of higher order thinking. Open-ended questions for which there is no single correct answer encourage responses that involve the development of problem-solving skills. Pupils benefit from the switch from drill and practice to explorations. The latter equips pupils with the ability to solve problems, communicate, reason and interpret, refine ideas and apply them in creative ways.

Modern learning theory

Bruner (1996) posits that 'acquired knowledge is most useful to a learner, moreover, when it is "discovered" through the learner's own cognitive efforts, for it is then related to and used in reference to what one has known before' (p. xii). Teachers should avoid, where possible, imposing modes of mathematical thinking on pupils; rather, mathematical representations should, ideally, be actively constructed from within. When children start school they possess a considerably developed, informal body of mathematical knowledge, augmented by thinking skills from everyday experiences (Bruner, 1996; Gardner, 1991). By encouraging the active participation of students in problem-solving and exposing them to situations requiring the use of reasoning and communication, qualities such as self-regulated learning and thinking may be developed. Bruner (1996) makes the case for 'seeing children as thinkers':

> Children, like adults, are seen as constructing a model of the world to aid them in construing their experience. Pedagogy is to help the child understand better, more powerfully, less one-sidely. Understanding is fostered through discussion and

collaboration, with the child encouraged to express her own views better to achieve some meeting of minds with others who may have other views.

(p. 56)

The wealth of information, knowledge and intuition brought by students when they start school should not be ignored. Lester and Kroll (1990) insist this socio-cultural mathematics background is a determining factor in the pupil's mathematical development. Hunt (1986) states:

Thinking beings solve problems by manipulating mental models of the environment, rather than trying out responses until they find one that works. They build these models by combining their conceptualisation of the problem with personal information about the world, abstracted from previous experience.

(Cited in Kulm, 1990, p. 77)

Lesh (1990) counsels that the primary goal of instruction should be the construction of new mental models rather than the addition of new facts. Pupils must be convinced of the need to reject old naive and intuitive models and adopt new ones. Lesh (1990) highlights the constructivist view of learning as:

- conceptual frameworks are constructed;
- conceptual growth is not simply incremental, but involves discontinuities and digressions;
- a range of conceptual models may be appropriate to a given range of events;
- conceptual frameworks are refined as the child develops, from concrete to abstract, from intuitive to formal, and from external to internal.

Schema theory

Schema theory models the mind as a graph consisting of a number of nodes that may or may not be connected to other nodes. A 'fragmented' graph has few connections, making it difficult to 'travel' from one node to another. As a pupil's proficiency develops, the number of nodes and connections between them will also increase. Typically, nodes will occur for the connections between fractions, decimals and percentages initially, with nodes for proportionality, enlargements and probability appearing at a later stage.

In cognitive psychology, human memory is viewed as a series of networks called 'schema' (Rummelhart, 1980; Marshall, 1988). Each schema consists of well-connected facts, features, algorithms, skills and strategies. These schema can be viewed as problem-solving vehicles, since they allow pupils access to strategies used in solving similar problems already encountered, the methods used to simplify particular procedures, and the routines for establishing targets. Marshall (1990) focuses on four types of knowledge needed for schema development: 'feature recognition knowledge, constraint knowledge, planning knowledge and implementation knowledge' (pp. 175–176). Clearly, parallels exist with Polya's four stages in problem-solving.

Metacognition

Modern learning theory charges the teacher with enhancing the pupil's metacognitive skills (Bruner, 1996):

> Modern pedagogy is moving increasingly to the view that the child should be aware of her own thought processes, and it is crucial for the pedagogical theorist and teacher alike to help her to become more metacognitive – to be as aware of how she goes about her learning and thinking as she is about the subject matter she is studying. Achieving skills and accumulating knowledge are not enough. The learner can be helped to achieve full mastery by reflecting as well upon how she is going about her job and how her approach can be improved.
>
> (p. 64)

Success in solving problems is largely dependent on the student's ability to utilise the mathematical knowledge and skills she possesses. Lester and Kroll (1990) suggest that higher order skills such as planning, evaluating, monitoring and regulating allow the pupils to marshal and allocate cognitive resources. Again, notice the links between these skills and the four Polya stages. The level of control and regulation (metacognition) distinguishes experts from novice, successful from unsuccessful problem-solvers. Poor control limits the effectiveness of the problem-solving (Kroll, 1988). However, attention to the metacognitive aspects of problem-solving, in both instruction and evaluation, significantly influences the pupil's capacity to solve problems (Campione *et al.*, 1989). This ability to reflect on one's own problem-solving ability is internalised slowly, but can be aided by dialogue with fellow pupils and teachers (Vygotsky, 1978). By mentoring others, pupils are able to monitor themselves, and by discussing alternative solutions with other pupils, internal dialogue or thought (Vygotsky, 1962) is encouraged (Wertsch, 1982).

Mathematics as a body of knowledge

Convincing arguments have been made in the previous sections for the inclusion of problem-solving in the process of teaching and learning – in particular, its value in distinguishing between what has been covered in class by the teacher and what the pupils actually understand. The 'body of mathematical knowledge' refers to the skills, concepts, strategies and techniques that are often taught before a pupil engages in the application of this knowledge in a real-life context or open-ended problem-solving situation. It is also the 'knowledge' assessed in formal examinations – the investigation of the existence (or otherwise) of the nodes and schema associated with the topic and their links to other areas of mathematics. From a teacher's perspective, the body of knowledge is defined by the National Curriculum, National Numeracy Strategy, Key Stage 3 Strategy and the GCSE, AS- or A-level syllabus or specification being covered with the class.

The National Curriculum for mathematics exemplifies the 'body of knowledge' deemed relevant and appropriate by the Government for the young people of today. The content is structured hierarchically so that skills and concepts can be revisited and extended as the pupils progress up the eight-level scale. Continuity and progression across Key Stages can also be assured, particularly during the transition from primary to post-primary education.

The next chapter will discuss the requirements of the National Curriculum, while Chapter 4 considers the National Numeracy Strategy and Key Stage 3 Strategy in detail. Chapter 12 will look at the post-16 mathematics provision in terms of Key Skills.

The main role of the drill and practice elements of teaching, typically covered in text-book exercises or worksheets, is to ensure that all pupils have internalised the basic skills and techniques that will be needed in the more complex examples occurring through the 'enquiry' mode of learning. By placing this mathematical knowledge in their long-term memory, pupils' short-term memory is freed up to focus on the strategies needed for problem-solving.

So what is 'teaching for understanding'? Quite simply, it is teaching that centres on student thinking, that focuses on powerful scientific and mathematical ideas, and that offers equitable opportunities for learning.

3 National Curriculum for mathematics

Introduction

Why do we have a National Curriculum? What is its purpose? What are the aims? Does it change the way maths teachers teach? What are the implications for the future? This chapter offers an overview of the place of mathematics in the National Curriculum for primary and secondary pupils in the UK. It introduces the terminology and policy requirements used in teaching mathematics and endeavours to offer a backdrop and context for the chapters that follow.

Learning outcomes

By the end of this chapter the reader should be able to:

- explain the structure of the National Curriculum in the context of mathematics;
- use the terminology of Programmes of Study, attainment targets, levels and level descriptions correctly;
- state the cross-curricular themes;
- describe the recent changes in the National Curriculum;
- highlight the main changes in the post-16 education.

Mathematics is the central tenet of all things scientific. Without mathematics, how would we have measured distance and time, navigated across the oceans, explained planetary motion, created some of the great wonders of the world, which are still visited today due to their sheer size and architectural beauty? In more recent times, mathematics has played an important role in technological advancements in engineering, the computer, in communications and data security such as encryption, to name but a few. Both in the past and in the present, the country's economy has depended upon the numerical abilities of its leaders. Initially, it was skills of bartering, sharing, exchanging, trading and taxing people. Nowadays, importing and exporting goods, stock market trading, dealing with other nations, taxing people and businesses, and distributing financial resources around government agencies are the advancements on the traditional skills already mentioned. Consequently, the diversity of applications of mathematics around us illustrates the need to ensure that the future population are well prepared for the increasingly complex, numerical lifestyle in which money can be transferred and invested online, computers can assist in engineering – the design and manufacture of materials, buildings and cars – and people can communicate from anywhere across the globe at any time using mobile phones.

For these and many other reasons, mathematics as a subject is recognised as a core skill across the world. As a result, simple activities such as counting and becoming familiar with the number system are introduced in pre-school classes, while basic numeracy skills such as addition and subtraction are dealt with in the early years of primary school before developing into the more complex representations of number in the form of algebra and geometry later in the school career. So how has mathematics education changed over recent years?

The Cockcroft Report (1982) *Mathematics Counts* highlighted the concerns revealed from extensive research into mathematics education and the skills of young people entering employment. A number of recommendations were suggested and much of the current emphasis being addressed via the National Numeracy Strategy indicates that there have been few improvements over the past two decades. Around the same time, the government decided to replace the old Certificate of Education (CSE) and General Certificate of Education (GCE) 'O' level examinations with a new single system of examinations to be taken by all students called the General Certificate of Secondary Education (GCSE). With the new examination came the changes resulting in the National Curriculum.

Changes in the National Curriculum in mathematics from 1989

The National Curriculum aimed to offer pupils a curriculum that:

- was balanced and broadly based;
- promoted spiritual, moral, cultural, mental and physical development;
- prepared them for the opportunities, responsibilities and experiences of adult life;
- included religious education and, for secondary school pupils, sex education

by offering a common curriculum for all 5–16-year-olds in compulsory schooling. These twelve years of schooling were subdivided into four Key Stages: Key Stage 1 spanning ages 5–7 years, Key Stage 2 addressing the needs of 8–11-year-olds, Key Stage 3 focusing on the first three years of post-primary education (age 12–14 years) and Key Stage 4 covering the content for General Certificate in Secondary Education (GCSE) examinations spanning ages 15 and 16. By using this structure, the National Curriculum became a coherent and continuous learning process where ideas were introduced in their simplest form during Key Stage 1 and then revisited in subsequent Key Stages with increasing levels of depth and sophistication. For example, currently Key Stage 1 pupils in mathematics should be able to understand the use of a symbol ($\square$) to stand for an unknown number, e.g. $6 = 4 + \square$ or $\square - 3 = 2$. On reaching Key Stage 2, these pupils progress to understand that a letter can stand for an unknown number such as $8 + a = 20$. While at

Key Stage 3, they should be using and understanding the conventional notation of algebra, i.e. $5c + 4c = 9c$ and $y \times y \times y = y^3$. In addition, pupils should be able to formulate, interpret and evaluate algebraic expressions; manipulate simple expressions, simplify, remove brackets and factorise as appropriate; use these techniques with a range of more complex expressions; and use the rules of indices and fractional values.

It is clear that progression within and between Key Stages is easily documented and a greater emphasis is placed on the continuity of subject coverage compared to the past. Although separate Programmes of Study (PoS) have always been offered for each Key Stage, prior to 1996 these were general and quite vague in terms of content. Since the Dearing Review, these Programmes of Study have undergone considerable changes, including an increased emphasis on the content and organisation of the information. Within each subject, 'areas' of content are highlighted with each 'area' matching the assessed Attainment Targets (ATs) for that subject. In the case of mathematics, there are four attainment targets: AT1 – Using and Applying Mathematics; AT2 – Number and Algebra; AT3 – Shape, Space and Measures; AT4 – Handling Data[1]. A typical Programme of Study at Key Stage 2 in Handling Data is included in Box 3.1, opposite.

Clearly, pupils in this Key Stage are expected to understand the basic principles of probability in terms of 'levels of certainty' and to make sensible estimates in terms of everyday activities. Basic statistical techniques are also evident in terms of collecting and recording data, and the use of the correct terminology (mean and range) during the analysis.

Task 3.1 Investigate the Programme of Study across Key Stages

To become an effective teacher you will need to be aware of your pupils' mathematical background and what mathematical experiences will lie ahead. Consult the relevant documentation to identify the progression across the Programmes of Study of Key Stages you will be teaching. The transition from primary to post-primary education is particularly important as pupils may be coming from a diverse range of primary schools.

Attainment Targets, levels and Statements of Attainment

From its inception, all National Curriculum subjects were subdivided for assessment purposes into a small number of Attainment Targets (ATs) set out in eight pseudo-hierarchical levels. Each AT had a number of performance criteria or Statements of Attainment (SoA) describing the type and range of performance that pupils working at that level should characteristically demonstrate. For example, in 1992 the SoA for Shape and Space, and Measures at level 4 were defined as shown in Box 3.2. Therefore, a pupil whose achievement in Shape and Space or in Measures could broadly be characterised by these SoAs was deemed to have mastered level four in Shape and Space or in Measures.

Box 3.1 Key Stage 2 Programme of Study for Handling Data

Handling Data

Collect, represent and interpret data

Pupils should have opportunities to:

a. Use data drawn from a range of meaningful situations, *for example, those arising in other subjects.*

b. Collect, classify, record, represent and interpret discrete numerical data, using graphs, tables and diagrams, including Venn, Decision tree and Carroll diagrams, pictograms, block graphs, bar-line graphs and line graphs with the axes starting at zero (initially with given intervals); explain their work orally or through writing and draw conclusions.

c. Interpret tables and lists used in everyday life, *for example, those found in a catalogue or road safety accident report;* interpret a wide range of graphs and diagrams, including a pie chart; create and interpret frequency tables, including those for grouped discrete data, *for example, birthdays;* use tallying methods, including the 5-bar gate.

d. Design an observation sheet and use it to record a set of data leading to a frequency table; collate and analyse the results; progress to designing and using a data collection sheet, interpreting the results.

e. Enter information in a database and interrogate it, using at least two criteria; use an appropriate computer package to produce a variety of graphical representations of the data.

f. Understand, calculate and use the mean and range of a set of discrete data, *for example, calculating the mean score of two teams that have played different numbers of games in order to compare their performance.*

Introduction to Probability

Pupils should have opportunities to:

a. Become familiar with and use the language of probability, including certain, uncertain, likely, unlikely, impossible and fair, by participating in games and other practical activities.

b. Understand possible outcomes of simple and random events, *for example, that buttered toast will fall with either the buttered side up or the buttered side down;* understand that there is a degree of uncertainty about the outcome of some events, while others are certain or impossible, *for example, it is*

- *certain to get dark tonight;*
- *impossible for a person to turn into a fish;*
- *uncertain whether or not it will rain tomorrow.*

c. Place events in order of 'likelihood'; understand and use the idea of 'fifty-fifty' or 'evens' and know whether events are more or less likely than this, *for example, know that if a die is thrown there is an equal chance of an odd or even number but the chance of getting a five is less than an even chance.*

(DENI, 1996a)

Box 3.2   Statements of Attainment for Shape and Space, and Measures

Shape and Space 4

Pupils should:

a.   understand and use language associated with angle;
b.   make simple two-dimensional and three-dimensional shapes from given information and know associated language;
c.   understand eight points of the compass; use clockwise and anticlockwise appropriately;
d.   specify location by means of co-ordinates (in the first quadrant);
e.   use a computer package to investigate position in terms of angle and distance;
f.   recognise reflective symmetry in a variety of shapes in three dimensions.

Measures 4

Pupils should:

a.   understand the relationship between units;
b.   understand the concept of perimeter;
c.   find areas by counting squares, and volumes by counting cubes, using whole numbers;
d.   make sensible estimates of a range of everyday measures in relation to everyday objects or events;
e.   understand and use the 24 hour clock.

(DENI, 1992)

National Curriculum assessment: pre-Dearing

All National Curriculum achievement was criterion-referenced – that is, the pupils either could or could not respond correctly to standard items addressing these SoAs. There were no difficult numbers or twists in the wording of the questions to confuse the students. To determine if a pupil had mastered a particular level in any AT, teachers were required to compile evidence. Normally, this took the form of simple pen-and-paper tests composed of items related to each of the SoAs. These test scores were then converted to levels through a series of '*n minus* rules'. For example, the '*n*−2 rule' required the pupils to demonstrate mastery of all but two of the SoAs at a level in order to be awarded that level. The '*n* rule', on the other hand, demanded evidence of mastery of all the SoAs before the level could be awarded. Many schools adopted the practice of recording mastery of an individual SoA by ticking the appropriate box in an elaborate pupil record sheet, as shown in Figure 3.1. If a pupil had been tested, then a diagonal line was drawn upwards from left to right; if the pupil had been assessed and had attained the level, then an additional line was included from left to right in a downwards direction to complete the X-shape.

Student name *Joe Smyth*   **Year** 8M

Measures

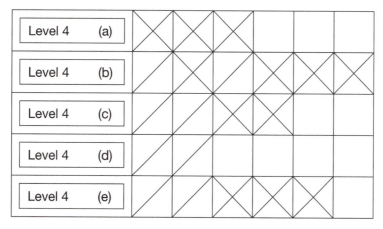

Figure 3.1   Assessment grid for each pupil

Dearing's curriculum reforms

Sir Ron Dearing's Interim Report (SEAC, 1993) acknowledged that this process of gathering and recording evidence against individual SoA was placing an unbearable burden upon classroom teachers:

> It is worth noting that the averagely successful pupil reaching level 7 during his or her eleven years at school would have been assessed by classroom teachers against some 700 SoA. A classroom teacher at Key Stage 1 with 35 pupils in his or her class who assesses all the class against all the SoA would make some 8,000 judgements.
>
> (para. 2.28)

Sir Ron Dearing's Final Report (SCAA, 1993) counselled that this atomistic approach to school-based assessment be replaced by a more holistic model in which the teacher's efforts centre on delivering the Programmes of Study appropriate to his or her pupils. As part of the 1993 Review of the National Curriculum, Dearing's remit was to 'slim down' the assessment framework so that the unwieldy procedures for assessing academic progress and recording evidence of pupil achievement could be eradicated. The myriad of SoAs was replaced by level descriptions and teachers were asked to make judgements of 'best fit' based on a pupil's performance in class tests, homework assignments, classroom discussion, school examinations and so on. However, it is important to stress that Sir Ron Dearing's strategy for slimming down the National Curriculum eschewed a simple reduction in the plethora of SoA for a 'clustering' process which schools interpreted as little

---

Box 3.3   *Shape, Space and Measures Level 4*

Pupils make simple two-dimensional and three-dimensional shapes. They understand and use language associated with line and angle. They know the eight points of the compass and understand the terms clockwise and anticlockwise. They use co-ordinates to plot points and draw shapes in the first quadrant. They understand the relationship between metric units. They find perimeters of simple shapes, find areas by counting squares and find volumes by counting cubes. They begin to make sensible estimates using standard units in relation to everyday situations. They understand and use the twelve and twenty-four hour clocks.

(DENI, 1996a)

---

more than a repackaging of the old SoA as level descriptions. For instance, the level description for level 4 in Shape, Space and Measures now reads as shown in Box 3.3.

Comparing the original SoAs for Shape and Space and Measures at level 4, it is clear that little of the content and terminology has changed, and it is therefore hardly surprising to find that teachers are breaking these levels descriptions into their component parts for the purpose of assessment.

The latest versions of the National Curriculum for mathematics can be freely downloaded from the QCA website at www.nc.uk.net.

Task 3.2   Progression within the level descriptions

- Choose your favourite topic in mathematics. In which AT is the topic assessed?
- Identify the key mathematical skills needed in the topic. Can you draw a line of development from the lower levels to the upper levels which address your chosen topic?
- Are the National Curriculum level descriptions truly hierarchical?

National Curriculum assessment: post-Dearing

Currently, teachers are required to make a holistic assessment of the pupils' attainment based on work in class, at home, test results and so on. This classroom-based measure is reported as a profile with the pupil's attainment in each AT recorded using the level descriptions of the eight-level scale. At the end of each Key Stage, the pupil takes a series of short pen-and-paper SATs (Subject Assessment Tests) from which the pupils' test performance can be converted into a National Curriculum level. Parents therefore receive information concerning their child's academic achievement in mathematics from two sources: the class teachers' judgement of the child's achievement (reported as a profile of levels – one for each AT) and the overall level awarded to the child in end-of-key stage national subject tests (reported as a single level). Should discrepancies occur between the level awarded by the teacher and by the test, the majority of parents will favour the test as the more reliable measure judgement hence undermining the role of the teacher in the assessment process. A further discussion on assessment issues will follow in Chapter 14.

Task 3.3 Familiarise yourself with the SATs

Choosing an AT of personal interest, browse the SATs for the levels you are likely to be teaching, i.e. primary school levels 2–5 or post-primary school levels 3–8. Map the content of the test to the relevant level descriptions and/or Programme of Study.

Current changes in education

The White Paper, *Excellence in Schools* (DfEE, 1998a)[2] extended the current goals of the National Curriculum to include an additional set of teaching priorities facilitating flexibility, breadth and balance across the subject areas. It advocated the incorporation of literacy, numeracy and key skills within each subject and encouraged the development of interest in citizenship; personal, social and health education; and in spiritual, moral, social and cultural education.

The three main issues are stated below:

1. The first task of the education service is to ensure that every child is taught to read, write and add up. But mastery of the basics is only a foundation. Literacy and numeracy matter so much because they open the door to success across all the other school subjects and beyond.

2. A good education provides access to this country's rich and diverse culture, to its history and to an understanding of its place in the world. It offers opportunities to gain insight into the best that has been thought and said and done.

3. There are wider goals of education which are also important. Schools, along with families, have a responsibility to ensure that children and young people learn respect for others and for themselves. They need to appreciate and understand the moral code on which civilised society is based and to appreciate the culture and background of others. They need to develop the strength of character and attitudes to life and work, such as responsibility, determination, care and generosity, which will enable them to become citizens of a successful democratic society.

(DfEE, 1998a)

The new basics? Literacy, numeracy and ICT in teaching and learning

In response to the requirements of improving literacy skills in the primary school, the government approved the introduction of the National Literacy Strategy (DfEE, 1998b) which outlined the scheme of work for 5–11-year-olds, to be completed during the Literacy Hour – a daily period of structured Literacy development lasting one hour per day.

The same approach was adopted for the 'Numeracy lesson' where pupils focus on specific learning objectives defined in terms of age and reinforcing continuity across the primary years. Five main areas are addressed: Numbers and the number system (called Counting and recognising numbers in Reception), Calculations (called Adding and subtracting in Reception), Solving problems, Measures, shape and space, and Handling data (for Year 3 upwards only). Since the scheme of work is presented in a 'sequenced' format, it is conceivable that teachers may feel obliged to begin a new topic or area of study, despite seeing their charges still struggling with the concepts presented in the previous sessions. Few teachers may have the confidence to abandon the Framework to assist their pupils in overcoming the problems for fear of becoming seriously out of step with the guidelines. The National Numeracy Strategy will be discussed further in Chapter 4.

A third recent addition to the teaching repertoire has been the incorporation of information technology into all curriculum areas (see *Connecting the Learning Society*, DfEEc, 1998)[3]. In the case of mathematics, this innovation was welcomed due to the wide range of skills-based educational software currently available for both primary and secondary pupils. New and exciting mathematical adventure programs now offer teachers the opportunity for developing strategic thinking and problem-solving skills, simulations help pupils to develop an appreciation of 'cause and effect' and a basic understanding of probability in terms of likelihood. Drill and practice software for number skills and mental arithmetic is disguised in 'fun' contexts which make the learning process enjoyable and motivating. Games with built-in levels of difficulty ensure that differentiation according to ability is offered to the less able and also the gifted members of the class without changing the program. The role of ICT in the mathematics classroom will be a recurring theme throughout this book and a chapter is dedicated to the pedagogical issues associated with this mode of teaching and learning in Part II.

The cross-curricular themes

In addition to the subject knowledge presented in the National Curriculum, broader and more diverse themes prevail *across* subjects that form part of the 'whole curriculum'. These six cross-curricular themes include information technology, economic awareness, health education, careers education (more recently renamed as careers education and guidance), education for mutual understanding (EMU), and cultural heritage (currently part of education for citizenship). Ideally, all six themes should be incorporated into subject teaching; however, some themes are more applicable to certain subjects than others. For example, health education and science are interrelated, information technology and mathematics overlap, EMU, citizenship and cultural heritage have distinct links to history and geography, and so on. The two cross-curricular dimensions are environmental education and the European dimension. Again, these issues should be discussed in a wide range of subject contexts. As part of the continued commitment to a curriculum that includes 'citizenship, personal, social and health education, and spiritual, moral, social and cultural development' (QCA, 1998), a number of review bodies have been created to offer recommendations in keeping with a policy of lifelong learning. These new changes are exemplified in the new curricula in England and Wales, and in the proposed Northern Ireland Curriculum Review.

Task 3.4 Integrating cross-curricular themes into mathematics

List the possible occurrences of each of the cross-curricular themes in the mathematical content of the Key Stage(s) you are teaching.

Review of qualifications for 16–19-year-olds

The Dearing Report (1996) highlighted the need to reduce the 'present high levels of non-completion and wastage in post-16 education' (p. 2) and to 'prepare young people for life in the widest sense' (p. 4). He viewed the youth of today as tomorrow's leaders and recognised their role of assuming 'responsibility for the quality of our society and civilisation' (p. 4). As a result, he declared 'Spiritual and moral values must therefore be an essential element in education.' (p. 4). More recently, these ideas have developed into the aims of the new curriculum and the development of citizenship across Key Stages 3 and 4. To assist in bridging the 'academic' gap between GNVQ and Advanced level qualifications, the Dearing Report initially recommended renaming the Advanced GNVQ to 'Applied A level' and to introduce a new 'half' A level called the AS level. In mathematics, the AS level was to assist pupils in making the jump between GCSE mathematics and the new Advanced-level modules. It was also suggested that 'students proposing to take A level mathematics [should also] take a GCSE paper in Additional Mathematics' (p. 31). Recent refinements to the original vocabulary and aims offered in Dearing's Report have led to Advanced level courses being termed AS during the first year and A2 during the second year of study. The modular nature of these courses facilitates the award of the AS qualification after one year has been successfully completed. The Advanced GNVQ is not referred to as the 'Applied A level' as originally suggested, but has been renamed as an AVCE (Advanced Certificate in Education).

Using Dearing's equivalent qualifications model, it would be possible for students to select a combination of post-16 qualifications which were of a recognised standard and could be used to gain entry to university. Each GNVQ was deemed equivalent to two A levels, and two AS levels equated to one A level. Dearing's review also advocated a broadening of disciplines encouraging students to take five AS levels (or their equivalent) in the first year of post-GCSE study and then to specialise in up to three subjects during the second year of sixth form education. To maintain a breadth of learning, Dearing recommended pursuing a science or technology-related subject, a modern foreign language, an element from Arts and Humanities and a subject illustrating how the community works (such as business studies, economics, politics, law, sociology). Ideally, this mix of subjects would facilitate the development and assessment of a range of Key Skills such as the three assessed skills of: Application of Number, Communication and Information Technology; and the three non-assessed skills: Improving Own Performance and Learning, Working with Others and Problem-solving.

The new AS and A2 level specifications for mathematics have been rewritten to account for the changes in curricular policy and can be downloaded from the relevant exam body website (e.g. www.ccea.org.uk or www.edexcel.org.uk). From September 2000, all Advanced-level courses (AS and A2) include opportunities for pupils to gain Key Skills qualifications at levels 2–3. Similarly, GCSE courses have been reviewed to incorporate opportunities for pupils to work at Key Skills levels 1–2. The Advanced GNVQ has been renamed as the Advanced Vocational Certificate in Education (AVCE) to minimise the gap between the vocational and academic routes to university and also includes the Key Skills at levels 2–3.

For the less able pupils, the increased flexibility resulting from the revised National Curriculum granted pupils over the age of 14 the opportunity to follow Foundation and Intermediate level GNVQ courses and to take some NVQ units through school which include work-related placements.

Task 3.5 Key Skills at GCSE and Advanced level

Consult the syllabus of the GCSE and/or Advanced level course you are teaching. Identify the section(s) devoted to Key Skills. Are all six Key Skills addressed? Can you identify the occurrences of the three 'core' skills of Communication, Application of Number and Information Technology?

Notes

1   In the Northern Ireland Curriculum, mathematics is composed of 5 ATs, in Key Stages 1 and 2: AT1 – Processes in mathematics; AT2 – Number; AT3 – Measures; AT4 – Shape and Space; and AT5 – Handling Data and 6 ATs in Key Stage 3: AT1 – Processes in mathematics; AT2 – Number; AT3 – Algebra; AT4 – Measures; and AT5 – Shape and Space, AT6 – Handling Data.
2   The Northern Ireland equivalent is the *School Improvement Programme* (commonly referred to as the 'six pack' (DENI, 1998)).
3   In Northern Ireland this is referred to as the *NI Strategy Document for Educational Technology* (DENI, 1996b).

4 The National Strategies for Literacy, Numeracy and Key Stage 3

Introduction

This chapter deals with the three main initiatives impacting on the role of a teacher in primary and post-primary schools today. In an attempt to raise standards in schools, the government advocated a 'return to the basics' approach whereby national targets were set for literacy and numeracy: almost all pupils were to achieve a level 4 in both English and mathematics by Year 6. To assist teachers in meeting these targets, there would be one hour a day devoted to Literacy and an additional 45–60 minutes, depending on the pupils' age, for Numeracy. Literacy and Numeracy Task Forces were drawn up to review the current teaching of 'the basics' and to suggest the changes required to meet the Government's targets. These changes were the National Literacy Strategy (NLS), National Numeracy Strategy (NNS) and the National Strategy for Key Stage 3 to ease the transition to post-primary school.

Learning outcomes

At the end of this chapter you should be able to:

- discuss the Literacy and Numeracy Strategy in the context of your Key Stage;
- define 'numeracy' and 'mathematical literacy';
- explain the framework of NNS and its main strands of content;
- explain the impact of the three national strategies in your planning and teaching of mathematics.

Why were the National Literacy and Numeracy Strategies introduced?

A number of reports highlighted the current weaknesses in literacy and numeracy skills among the adult population. Evidence of low levels of basic skills and the resultant impact this will have on everyday life includes:

- some seven million adults in England – one in five adults – if given the alphabetical index to the Yellow Pages, cannot locate the page reference for plumbers (*A Fresh Start*: report of Sir Claus Moser's Working Group (DfEE, 1999));
- a survey of 37-year-olds found that three-quarters of women and two-thirds of the men taking part could not calculate a 12.5% service charge in a restaurant (Basic Skills Agency, 1997);
- the same survey of 37-year-olds also found that three-quarters of women and one-half of the men taking part were unable to work out the area of pond liner required even when they were given instructions and the algorithm needed for the calculation (Basic Skills Agency, 1997);
- adults with poor basic skills are four times more likely to experience long-term unemployment (City University report (Scottish Executive, 1999)).

Startling headlines in newspapers have also highlighted the major problems being experienced by the public as a result of professionals making basic numerical errors. A study published in the *British Medical Journal* in 1995 found that only one in six doctors could calculate the correct proportion of the dose required according to a child's weight.

The current need for emphasis on the basics is supported by findings from recent research. The Green Paper (DfEE, 2001a) *Schools: Building on Success* reported that 'standards for pupils aged 11–14 are not high enough. Pupils make far too little progress during these years'. Worthington (DES, 1998) also declared 'standards of literacy and numeracy are not as high as they need to be even among young people with good qualifications'. Literacy and numeracy are viewed as vital skills for the twenty-first century. Pupils must learn properly from an early age otherwise they will struggle in later life.

What is 'numeracy'?

Cockcroft's *Mathematics Counts* defines numeracy as follows:

> We would wish the word 'numerate' to imply the possession of two attributes. The first is an 'at-homeness' with numbers and an ability to make use of mathematical skills which enable an individual to cope with the practical demands of everyday life. The second is an ability to have some appreciation and understanding of information which is presented in mathematical terms, for instance graphs, charts or tables or by reference to percentage increase or decrease.
>
> (*Mathematics Counts*, 1982, p. 11)

Anita Straker (1997), director of the National Numeracy Project, defined numeracy as being:

> more than just knowing about numbers and number operations. It includes an ability and inclination to solve numerical problems, including those involving money and measures. It also demands familiarity with ways in which numerical information is gathered by counting and measuring, and is presented in graphs, charts and tables.
>
> (National Numeracy Project, p. 4)

The National Numeracy Strategy defines it as:

> Numeracy at Key Stages 1 and 2 is a proficiency that involves a confidence and competence with numbers and measures. It requires an understanding of the number system, a repertoire of computational skills and an inclination and ability to solve number problems in a variety of contexts. Numeracy also demands practical understanding of the ways in which information is gathered by counting and measuring, and is presented in graphs, diagrams, charts and tables.
>
> (DfEE, 1988d)

All three definitions of numeracy focus on the ability to work comfortably with numbers and to understand a variety of representations of numerical data.

The National Numeracy Strategy

The reports from the Literacy and Numeracy Task Force recommended that:

- all primary schools should teach a daily, dedicated Literacy Hour from September 1998 and a daily mathematics lesson from September 1999;
- a 'Framework for teaching' should be produced in each area, setting out teaching objectives for each year of primary schooling from Reception to Year 6;
- funding for the Strategies should provide additional, high quality training and support for teachers based on nationally developed materials.

(DES, 1998a)

The National Numeracy Strategy (NNS) commenced in schools in England and Wales in September 1999. Each daily maths lesson has three constituent parts: mental maths, main session and plenary. Depending on the age of the pupils, the length of the lesson varied: in Key Stage 1, Years 1 and 2 have 45 minutes per day, Years 3 and 4 receive a 50-minute lesson, while Years 5 and 6 spend 60 minutes developing their numeracy skills.

The NNS 'Framework' maps out the teaching of mathematical topics from Reception to Year 6 in schools in England and Wales. This 'Framework' is prescriptive but was originally designed to act as guidance for teachers who were concerned about the level of support which would be available to them in the early stages of implementation. Teachers are free to adapt the strategy to suit the needs of their pupils.

Over £50 million was invested in the NNS to offer three years of support to teachers during its implementation in schools. Consultants and 'leading mathematics teachers' offered demonstration numeracy lessons and advice on developing a School Numeracy Strategy to over 60 per cent of schools. Additional support was available for schools with special circumstances. INSET days were recommended to address teachers' professional development needs in numeracy and for whole-school training. 'Numeracy packs' were created which contained video materials of practical teaching, a CD-ROM of ICT resources to support the NNS, and staff development materials such as overhead transparencies (OHTs) and booklets. Additional support was available for schools where there were pupils with English as an additional language (EAL). Advice was also offered regarding the use of calculators, namely that they should not be used as a prop for basic arithmetic and an introduction to them is not recommended before the upper years of Key Stage 2 (DfES, 1998a).

Pupils would also experience continuity in their numeracy education within and across schools as teachers would be working towards the same requirements regardless of school location. Through professional development training in this area, the teachers would also have a common vocabulary and understanding of 'good practice' in the mathematics arena and so using support networks such as the NGfL and the Virtual Teachers' Centre would become increasingly more valuable for exchanging experiences, resources and ideas.

The National Numeracy Strategy Framework and materials can be downloaded from the DfES website at www.standards.dfes.gov.uk/primary/numeracy/ and www.standards.dfes.gov.uk/numeracy/publications respectively.

The structure of the numeracy lesson

The first phase, mental maths and oral work, is teacher-led and lasts around 5–10 minutes. Pupils are given the opportunity to practise and rehearse a variety of strategies to assist them in sharpening their non-written skills.

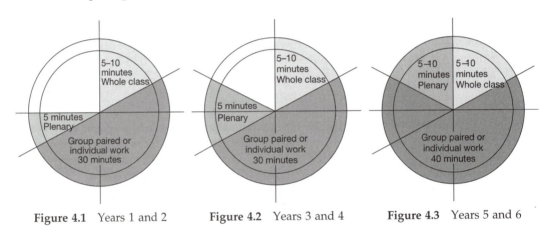

Figure 4.1   Years 1 and 2   **Figure 4.2**   Years 3 and 4   **Figure 4.3**   Years 5 and 6

The following 30–40 minute slot is devoted to group, paired or individual work such as problem-solving tasks (with or without the use of the computer), whole-class activity, practical work, or graded groupwork. The whole class should be working on the same theme but with differentiation by ability built into the individual group's activities. During this time, the teacher can offer focused attention on the work of an individual group so that over the period of a week, each group will receive approximately 30 minutes of uninterrupted teacher attention. During this time, teachers can uncover misconceptions that can be dealt with as a whole class or individualised problems that require one-to-one attention. Increased levels of teacher–pupil interaction within the group situation assist pupils in developing their communication skills in a 'safe' environment by explaining their reasoning when solving problems.

The final 5–10 minutes are devoted to a plenary session in which the groups of pupils feed back to the whole class. This stage is facilitated by the teacher asking questions to each group, who share their work with the rest of the class. Questioning is differentiated by ability with the more able pupils being asked to explain *why* they made certain decisions or to offer reasons why a particular problem-solving strategy worked in that case. The teacher then offers a summary of the key points of the session, making it clear to the pupils what they need to remember for the next day. Any misconceptions are dealt with and tasks that will challenge these misconceptions are incorporated into the next day's work. Homework is set, offering further development of the class activity.

Pupils must learn to work autonomously during the middle phase of the lesson as this time is devoted to the teacher working closely with each group in turn during the week. By improving their skills at communicating, collaborating and listening to others, the pupils will value this time for independent activity.

The NNS Framework for teaching mathematics

Numeracy should not be equated with mathematics (DES, 1998a). Numeracy is viewed as the outcome of being taught mathematics well, so that the skills can be applied in other situations. The Framework encourages teachers to use the strategies and methods recommended to promote numeracy, in their teaching of National Curriculum maths.

The following list outlines the contents of the 'Framework' by Year group(s) and has been adapted from the NNS documentation. The main mathematical topics are also specified with a brief overview of their content domain.

The main mathematical topics covered in the Framework for Reception are:

- counting and recognising numbers:
  - ✓ using songs and rhymes such as Ten Green Bottles, flashcards with digits or pictures;
- solving problems:
  - ✓ recognising patterns, symmetry in tiling, using money;
- measures, shape and space:
  - ✓ mathematical vocabulary such as more, less, longer, shorter, heavier, lighter;
  - ✓ names of solid and flat shapes and position.

Most of this work is covered via 'structured play' in which the teacher or learning support assistant (LSA) works with small groups of pupils asking maths-related questions about their play activities.

Years 1–3 address skills in the areas of:

- numbers and the number system:
  - ✓ counting, estimating, place value and ordering, fractions;
- calculations:
  - ✓ addition and subtraction, doubles, inverse, multiplication and division, HTU calculations;
- solving problems:
  - ✓ decisions, reasoning, real-life situations;

- measures, shape and space:
  - ✓ units, position, direction, movement, time, two-dimensional and three-dimensional shapes and names, symmetry;
- organising and using data:
  - ✓ sorting, classifying, charts and tables.

At this stage the pupils have progressed from structured play to discovery learning and a basic introduction to the written format of maths. Much of the work in phase 2 of the Numeracy Hour is completed using resource-based activities including the use of computers when appropriate. Pupils are encouraged to develop their mental maths strategies further.

For Years 4–6, the mathematics is categorised as:

- numbers and the number system:
  - ✓ rounding, decimals, positive and negative integers, sequences, square numbers, triangular numbers, prime numbers, ratio and proportion, percentages;
- calculations:
  - ✓ principles of commutative, associative, distributive laws, calculator usage;
- solving problems:
  - ✓ real-life contexts, money and measures;
- measures:
  - ✓ units, time, regular polygons, parallel lines, perpendicular lines;
- shape and space:
  - ✓ area, volume, perimeter, symmetry, direction, angles, properties of shapes;
- handling data:
  - ✓ tables, charts, probability.

Over these three years a more formal approach to the learning of maths occurs with increased attention on mathematical reporting and showing their method of calculation. Despite the increased importance of written maths, the pupils still use a wide variety of resources in their learning. Computer 'games' such as simulations and problem-solving activities are frequently introduced and the pupils can reinforce skills learned in class through drill and practice software if necessary. The effective use of calculators is also introduced to this age group.

The NNS advocates an approach to teaching which sets clear learning outcomes and targets, promotes mental maths skills, ensures progress and continuity in learning, uses pupil-centred, active learning strategies and strengthens links within and across local schools.

The use of calculators in the National Numeracy Strategy

The Task Force recognised the value of calculators as a tool in assisting the pupils' understanding of the number system through investigations of number patterns, place value, accuracy and errors, fractions and decimals. However, they did not recommend the use of calculators until the upper end of Key Stage 2 as it was felt that younger pupils had to learn, practise and reinforce their mental maths methods in order that they did not become reliant on a calculator for basic arithmetic. Teachers were encouraged to focus on the 'proper' use of calculators, knowing when to use and how to use the functions, such as memory, effectively. In post-primary schools, it is often assumed that pupils can use their calculators properly, so it is the primary school teacher who must focus on the technical skills of how to complete multi-step calculations when teaching his or her class. Pupils should be able to approximate the answer and use this knowledge to check the number in the calculator's display. Calculators can also be used to challenge pupils' misconceptions such as 'multiplying by 10 means add a zero'. Using a calculator pupils can see that $3.7 \times 10 \neq 30.7$, but instead the digits move one place to the left, making the correct answer 37.

The role of ICT in the National Numeracy Strategy

The DfES publication *Using ICT to Support Mathematics in Primary Schools* suggests that pupils in Key Stages 1 and 2 can use ICT to:

- *explore, describe and explain number patterns,* by using Counter, Multiples, Monty or Minimax software;
- *practise and consolidate their number skills,* using Play Train, Complements, Maths Factory or Function Machine;
- *explore and explain patterns in data,* using sensors for data collection and software to represent the data graphically. Packages such as Handy Graph, Number Box and Pinpoint are recommended;
- *estimate and compare measures of length or distance, angle, time, and so on,* using floor robots such as Roamer or screen 'turtles'. What's my Angle? and Unit the Robot are also encouraged for classroom use;
- *experiment with and discuss properties of patterns in shape and space,* by using software such as Take Part, Strawberry Garden and Versatile;
- *develop their mathematical vocabulary, logical thinking and problem-solving skills, using a computer program to sort shapes or numbers* such as Carroll Diagram, Venn Diagram and Sorting 2D shapes, or simple simulations like Toy Shop.

(DfEE, 2000)

All these activities and associated software are freely available through the DfEE support and guidance materials. The pack addresses the requirements for the NNS and contains a CD of materials for use with classes and includes prepared activities, and photo-copiable resources are also available for pupil use.

ICT will not replace a teacher, but it can be used as a tool to assist the teacher in offering differentiated activities to the class and to motivate reluctant or slow learners. The pupils' learning experience can be enhanced by using some of the techniques mentioned above for whole-class teaching, paired or groupwork; to practise existing skills such as mental maths, for recall of multiplication tables or other number facts in an exciting environment; to present data such as charts or graphs; and being able to zoom in or out on a number line.

The role of parents in the National Numeracy Strategy

Parental involvement in the NNS encourages pupils to take an active interest in their own learning and progress. By seeing their parents are interested in their work in school, pupils also become more involved and keen to learn (DES, 1998a). Parents can develop their children's skills of thinking and reasoning by asking them about the classwork activities and what they have learned in their group. The pupils use and expand the skills they have learned in school by carrying out everyday activities such as shopping, baking, counting money, setting an alarm clock or VCR, or helping with measurements. Practical and useful applications of their knowledge are revealed at home and at school, making learning maths an important and valuable activity. The publication *Money Counts* (FSA, 2000) offers a variety of classroom-based activities set in real-life contexts. *Your Family Counts* (Lawlor and Newland, 2000) provides ideas for parents to support their children's numeracy skills.

Talking about shapes and colours, counting objects and using basic knowledge of symmetry can also be addressed in the context of everyday activities. At the start of each academic year, teachers usually inform the parents of the techniques being taught in class for subtraction and other basic skills so that the parents can help or reinforce these methods at home. 'Homework is most effective when it links to learning in the classroom' (Donaldson, 2002, p. 72). Ideas for activities and resources can be found in the NNS Professional Development materials or through the IMPACT Scheme (University of North London).

The National Literacy Strategy

In response to the government's drive to raise standards, the Literacy Task Force made recommendations on how schools could improve their pupils' attainment in literacy. Over £50 million was invested in 1998–1999 to train and support schools in reaching the national target of 80 per cent of 11-year-olds reaching Level 4. Funding was offered for books, classroom resources and teachers' professional development.

The Literacy Hour (02/98)

The main aim of the Literacy Hour is to promote discursive, interactive, well-paced and confident teaching methods in which high expectations have been set by the teacher and met by the pupils (DES, 1998b). Pupils should be well motivated and actively engaged in their work, whether it is whole-class, group- or individual work. A shift in teaching style away from groupwork and towards whole-class teaching was envisaged using the allocated time-frame. Classroom organisation should allow teachers to spend increased amounts of time working alongside a group of children for a 20-minute slot once a week. This undivided attention will benefit both the slower learners who may get neglected at times and also the more able pupils who are often left to 'cruise'. By tailoring the questioning and answering to the ability of the small group, the teacher can ensure pupils are progressing during this stage in the lesson.

Literacy in the mathematics classroom

In the primary school classroom, a cross-curricular approach can be taken to the Literacy Hour so that pupils may work together on stories with a mathematical focus. A number of mathematical storybooks exist for the Key Stage 1 and 2 pupils, which are based on mathematical shapes and numbers, sorting, counting and grouping objects, odd and even numbers and concepts such as pi and exponential growth. Some typical examples of these books are:

- *The Greedy Triangle* by Marilyn Burns
- *From One to One Hundred* by Teri Sloat
- *More or Less a Mess* by Sheila Keenan
- *Even Steven and Odd Todd* by Kathryn Cristaldi
- *Spaghetti and Meatballs for All* by Marilyn Burns
- *Sir Cumference and the Dragon of Pi* by Cindy Neuschwander
- *Sir Cumference and the First Round Table* by Cindy Neuschwander
- *The King's Chessboard* by David Birch
- *The Fly on the Ceiling* by Julie Glass.

In the upper primary school classroom (Key Stage 2), the more able children may be interested in working on simplified biographies of famous mathematicians, for instance. A timeline of great mathematicians or scientists could be constructed from the individual work of groups. Pupils can develop their research skills by finding and using reference books to obtain relevant information matching a writing frame. Alternatively, the spelling of key mathematical terms and vocabulary can be reinforced during the Literacy Hour using calligrams or drawing and labelling the various two-dimensional and three-dimensional shapes. Prefixes such as tri-, pent-, oct-, and dec- can be discussed in relation to everyday life with examples such as tricycle or tripod, the Pentagon building in the US or the pentathlon in sport, an octopus or an octogenarian and decimal numbers or a decade. These techniques are often repeated in the early years of post-primary education to ensure that all pupils have the same standard of mathematical awareness.

Sometimes, it may be more appropriate to use the word 'language' to explain the elements of literacy occurring in the maths classroom. The mathematical meanings of words should also be discussed so that pupils understand the use of everyday words in the mathematical context as well as the real-life situation. For example, think of the difference between the everyday use and the mathematical meaning of the following words:

- mean
- take away
- acute
- similar
- translate
- regular
- expression.

For example,

The <u>mean</u> old man didn't pay his bus fare.
The boy ate a Chinese <u>take away</u> for his dinner.

The young girl was taken to hospital with an <u>acute</u> pain in her side.
The two girls were wearing <u>similar</u> dresses to the party.
The Frenchman asked his son to <u>translate</u> the menu.
The two friends asked for a <u>regular</u> coke with their pizza.
The <u>expression</u> on the boy's face was delight when he saw his new bicycle.

Perhaps now it is easier to see why some pupils are confused in the maths classroom!

Task 4.1 Maths words

For each of the words below, create a sentence with the everyday (non-mathematical) use of the word and then another sentence explaining the mathematical meaning:

• average	• sum	• difference
• group	• error	• parallel
• reflex	• plus	• kite
• variable	• mode	• simplify/solve
• equals	• factor	

Mathematical literacy refers to the ability to understand the mathematics that occurs in newspaper articles, magazines, sports, advertisements and many other situations in life. In terms of developing the pupils' mathematical literacy, teachers can assist by discussing the following issues as they arise in the syllabus:

- interpreting graphical and tabular representations of data;
- understanding probability in relation to the likelihood of a situation occurring in everyday life such as a lottery win;
- interpreting statistics reported in a newspaper – pie charts, graphs – in the context of sport, economy, our lifestyle, world issues;
- understanding the importance of using a representative sample in statistical reports;
- using 'basic' arithmetic skills such as calculate a percentage discount, VAT, work out change, add on a gratuity in a restaurant;
- reading a timetable, converting from a 24-hour to 12-hour clock;
- understanding a bank statement;
- reading a telephone, electricity or gas bill correctly;
- working out exchange rates;
- using ratio and proportion in cooking or building;
- working confidently with fractions or decimals;
- calculating areas or volumes for painting or decorating walls, or making garden ponds;
- communicating mathematically to a variety of audiences.

Coursework and other oral and written pieces in mathematics also allow pupils to engage in communicating their mathematical ideas and findings to an audience within and outside the classroom. Using ICT it is now possible to 'write' for any audience – scientists in NASA, researchers in universities, businesses and industries who may be interested in new ideas but unable to fund a dedicated research staff.

In many cases the most important form of literacy for pupils is being able to understand and interpret the question in the examinations. Like all aspects of education, the area receiving the most attention in the classroom is the one in which measurements can be made – namely, the assessed parts of the course.

National Strategy for Key Stage 3

Research from Keele University revealed that just over 60 per cent of pupils in the early years of secondary education were making 'reasonable progress', while the remaining 30 per cent of pupils fell into one of three categories:

1 The *disappointed* – 20–30% of pupils were bored.
2 The *disaffected* – 10–15% of pupils were beginning to truant or behave badly on a regular basis.
3 The *disappeared* – 2–5% of pupils had given up school altogether.

(Barber, 1997)

The aim of the Key Stage 3 National Strategy was to address these problems by 'transforming teaching and learning in a way that will engage and attract pupils across the curriculum' (DfES, 2001b).

Based on the work of the NNS and NLS, the National Strategy for Key Stage 3 focuses on five strands: English and mathematics plus literacy and numeracy (from 2001 to 2002) followed by science, ICT and the foundation subjects of history, geography, music, art, RE, PE and D&T (from 2002 to 2003). The Strategy emphasises the need for a short, snappy starter activity as part of the whole-class teaching, followed by a teacher-led demonstration of the work to be completed alone or in pairs/small groups. Next, the pupil-centred activity occurs and finally the lesson ends with a whole-class plenary where the learning is reviewed.

The four main principles of the Strategy are:

* *expectations* – high expectations and challenging targets set by teachers;
* *progression* – developing the work covered in KS2 into KS3 without re-teaching;
* *engagement* – use of activities which motivate pupils and require active participation;
* *transformation* – using professional development and support mechanisms to guide and refine teaching.

(DfES, 2001b)

Task 4.2

By referring to the *Qualifying to Teach* document (TTA, 2001), map each of these principles to the teaching requirements for ITE. For example, your planning, preparation, assessment, monitoring and recording will assist pupils to *progress* in their learning.

Training materials to assist teachers in implementing the Key Stage 3 Strategy are available from the DfES for the following themes: Assessment for Learning, Teaching Repertoire, Structuring Learning, and Knowing and Learning. Case Studies of 'best practice' in schools and mini-packs containing teaching resources such as videos and CDs are also available for each year group on the DfES website (www.standards.dfes.gov.uk/keystage3).

The Mathematics Framework for Key Stage 3

In the context of maths, the purpose of the National Strategy for Key Stage 3 was to:

- promote continuity across the transition from Key Stage 2 to Key Stage 3;
- ensure pupils working below level 4 received an opportunity to 'catch-up';
- provide practical support and guidance to teachers.

(DfES, 2001b)

Like the NNS, the Key Stage 3 Framework consists of yearly teaching programmes linked to the National Curriculum programmes of study. These programmes continue and extend the progression and expectations in pupils' mathematical abilities from primary school. In Year 7, the level 4 work is revised but most of the content is directed at level 5; in Year 8, level 5 work is consolidated and some work at level 6 begins; Year 9 constitutes a revision of level 5 work and continuation of level 6 activities. For the more able students, level 7 and some level 8 objectives may be addressed.

Within the yearly programmes, key objectives central to the pupils' progress are highlighted and planning charts exemplify the grouping of mathematical topics throughout the year. Examples of what the pupils should know and be able to do at the end of each academic year are included to illustrate the depth of content and coverage of material. The final section of the Framework contains a checklist of mathematical vocabulary spanning the content for the three years.

A summary of the distinctive features of each area of maths at Key Stage 3 are included in the programme and teachers are encouraged to use a mixture of paper-based, practical and ICT approaches in each topic. A three-part lesson similar to that of the NNS is advocated with the requirement that each lesson contains direct teaching and interaction with the pupils, and activities or exercises that the pupils will complete in class. The development of thinking skills is highlighted in terms of the application of mathematics in novel contexts or investigations.

The plenary

A plenary is multi-functional. It is usually a means of bringing the class together to round off and summarise the main learning points of the lesson (DfES, 2002a). Often it is used to re-focus the pupils on what they have achieved and to look forward to future work. If pupils are offering their own feedback from a learning activity, then it is also the time when teachers can assess learning, identify misconceptions and plan accordingly. Ofsted raised concerns during the Key Stage 3 pilot that 'teachers tended merely to sum up what happened during the main phase and pupils did not have the opportunity to articulate what they had learned'.

Although the majority of plenaries occur at the end of a lesson, many teachers find it useful to initiate some discussion midway through the lesson to consolidate under-standing and move pupils to the next stage of the learning process. Plenaries can range from two minutes during a sequence of related lessons to twenty minutes at the start or end of a topic. Some ideas for suitable pupil involvement in plenaries is offered in the DfES document *The Plenary*, which is available online from the Standards website (www.standards.dfes.gov.uk/keystage3) (DfES, 2002a).

Low-achieving students in Key Stage 3

For students working at level 3 in mathematics, booster materials are available to assist pupils in 'catching up' with the rest of the class. The *Springboard 7* materials issued in November 2001 (DfES, 2001c) were designed as a two-term teaching programme to com-plement and not replicate the teaching materials created for summer numeracy schools. The purpose of the materials was to allow the low-ability pupils to work alongside their peers who had already achieved level 4 at the end of Key Stage 2, but to 'catch up' on unlearned skills while consolidating new learning with their classmates. The National Strategy's *Springboard 7* pack of teaching materials can be obtained from the DfES website.

High-ability Key Stage 3 students

At the opposite end of the spectrum, the high-ability students need to be stretched and challenged in mathematics classes. The Key Stage 3 Strategy advocates that teaching is 'blended' to incorporate increased pace (acceleration), depth (extension) and breath (enrich-ment) within the middle phase of each lesson. Approximately 5–10 per cent of pupils in every school are 'gifted' or 'talented'. 'Gifted' students have high levels of attainment in academic subjects, while 'talented' students excel in a creative or expressive art or sport. The DfES publication *Teaching Gifted and Talented Pupils* (2002b) includes a section on *Guidance on Teaching Able Mathematicians*, with a focus on developing the pupils' skills in problem-solving, communicating and reasoning. It encourages teachers to establish a class-room ethos that celebrates success for all pupils to reduce the social pressures that result in underachievement in this subgroup of students. It also counsels the use of challenging questions at an appropriate level of difficulty with extension material of an open-ended nature. The emphasis is on quality and not quantity: focusing on one challenging question is deemed more worthwhile than responding to 20 routine questions. The DfES *Framework for Teaching Mathematics: Years 7, 8 and 9* offers suggestions for extension material for the more able students. Further sources of ideas, support and guidance can be found on the following websites:

www.mathsnet.net
www.1000problems.com
www.counton.co.uk

www.cut-the-knot.com
www.worldclassarena.org
www.nrich.maths.org

The transition from Key Stage 2 to Key Stage 3

The main reason for pupils becoming disengaged and disaffected in the early years of post-primary education is the lack of continuity in the learning process between the two schools. Many secondary schools spend six weeks or almost a full term getting to know the pupils' level of attainment in mathematics. During this time pupils become bored and frustrated being exposed to the low-level work that they have already mastered at primary school. Before the introduction of the Key Stage 3 Framework, the pupils also found the style of teaching in secondary schools too dry and didactic compared to the interactivity of the NNS lessons.

Although the Common Transfer Form summarises pupils' attainment in the end of key stage assessments, teachers in post-primary schools often find it difficult to interpret this information in terms of the pupils' strengths and weaknesses in the various areas of mathematics. As a result, transition units have been introduced to complement the existing information available for each pupil. The transition units are intended to ensure that:

- pupils experience a lesson structure they are familiar with and understand;
- there is a consistency in teaching approach that will help pupils to respond to new people in new surroundings;
- pupils are able to build on their early successes and demonstrate what they know, understand and can do in the context of the work they did in Year 6;
- teachers are better informed about pupils' strengths and weaknesses and can use the lessons to confirm their assessments and plan teaching programmes that meet the needs of their pupils;
- there is greater continuity and progression and less repetition of work.

(DfES, 2003a)

The Year 6 transition unit is completed during the summer term and focuses on the pupils' problem-solving and mathematical reasoning skills in the context of Number. This unit is then developed further in the Year 7 transition unit to sustain the same teaching style and also maintain the momentum in the learning process. The key objectives for Key Stage 2 are revised and extended in Year 7 (DfES, 2002d). During this time the teacher can assess the pupils' abilities and become familiar with the collective areas of strengths and weaknesses within the class. Using this information, future lessons can be planned to address the needs of the students without restricting their progress or losing any of the pupils' enthusiasm for the subject.

Year-on-year transition units are also available for use within Key Stage 3. The key topics addressed are the links between fractions, decimals and percentages, and thinking proportionally (DfES, 2003b; 2003c). Further exemplification and details of the transition units can be found on the DfES website.

Part II

The 'bigger picture' in teaching mathematics

5 Being an effective mathematics teacher

Introduction

What is an effective maths teacher? Why are some teachers more effective than others? What does 'effective' mean in terms of teaching and learning? Can you be an effective teacher all of the time and for all pupils? Or is your effectiveness more transparent to subgroups within the class? This chapter is composed of three main themes: considering the qualities of an effective teacher, exploring heuristics available to guide teaching, and establishing a positive learning environment.

Learning outcomes

At the end of this chapter you should be able to:

- discuss the characteristics of an effective teacher;
- relate Stones' heuristic for teaching maths as a body of knowledge and a mode of enquiry to the structure of the NNS;
- discuss the key components in establishing a positive learning environment;
- highlight the typical resources used in teaching mathematics.

What makes an effective teacher of mathematics?

There are two basic requirements for teachers: 'to have a thorough knowledge of the subject matter and classroom experience' (Stones, 1994, p. 3). The former ensures teachers have an up-to-date knowledge of the material they will be delivering and the latter ensures they can deliver it. If teaching is solely the skill of transmission, then the teacher needs the material to transmit and an effective means of transmission. Expressed in this form, the 'teacher' could easily be a computer ... so what does a human offer that makes teachers 'real people'?

Stones (1994) describes the pedagogy of teaching as follows: teachers are enquirers; they attempt to solve pedagogical problems by investigating the conceptual structure of the topic they intend to teach and then use this knowledge to determine the most appropriate means of teaching for understanding. They also use teaching strategies designed to reveal pupils' misconceptions so that they understand what the pupils are thinking and can address the pupils' intuitive models through challenging problems and questioning. Part of learning requires the development of cognitive linkages or 'schema' (Rummelhart, 1980; Wittrock, 1981) in which prior knowledge is updated and refined with internalisation of new skills and concepts (Brown and Campione, 1986). Using analogies helps pupils to relate new knowledge to existing knowledge, so assisting pupils in remembering vast quantities of information or new rules for solving tasks. Relating new ideas to current practice assists pupils' ability to recall material quickly and easily.

The simplest pedagogical skill to master is that of *exposition* or *telling*. But learning is not a one-way street composed only of teacher talk. The pupils need to be engaged in the process – actively involved in the lesson and able to apply its outcomes to the real world. 'Quality teaching should aim for quality learning' (Stones, 1994, p. 17).

Stones (1994) also stresses the role of effective influences on a pupil's learning experience. Positive effects such as enjoyment, feelings of success and fostering a pupil's self-esteem all contribute to positive reinforcement of the content covered in the lesson. Negative effects lead to rejection of the subject matter, or low emotional feelings, so the content of the lesson is forgotten by the pupil. It should be noted that reinforcement and feedback are two separate entities. Reinforcement is 'an event that increases the probability that an activity will be repeated, without necessarily being logically connected to it' (Stones, 1994, p. 19), while feedback is the difference between where the pupil is in the learning continuum and where the teacher had intended the pupil to be. Clearly, feedback is of particular importance in the teaching and learning process.

Research completed by Askew *et al.* (1997) in UK schools found that effective maths teachers shared the same belief or set of values – the *connectionist orientation*. These teachers eschewed the transmitting of subject knowledge in favour of exploring the connections in maths with the children through discovery. The teachers themselves were aware of these connections, particularly in the primary curriculum, thereby indicating solid subject knowledge, so they felt that effective teaching was composed of the following four objectives:

- making connections between the pupils' prior knowledge and new concepts or skills;
- connecting the pupils' informal intuitive knowledge with formal mathematics;
- connecting the various representations of maths: concrete activities, mathematical language and symbol systems;
- connecting areas of maths such as addition and subtraction (inverses), linking fractions, decimals, percentages and proportion as different ways of writing the same entity.

For further reading, consult Askew *et al.* (1997) and Thompson (1999).

Effective lesson planning

Effectiveness in terms of a lesson can be summarised as:

- a clearly thought out plan for the lesson;
- well-structured delivery and pace;

- a variety of activities to achieve the intended learning outcomes or key objectives;
- informative review and reflection.

Stones (1994) advocates three phases in a lesson: the preactive, the interactive and the evaluative phase. In the *preactive phase* the teacher identifies the prior knowledge needed for the topic, plans the order of presentation of the material, gathers the necessary resources for the lesson such as calculators, worksheets and rulers, and creates overhead transparencies or interactive whiteboard resources, and so on.

The *interactive phase* can be thought of as the 'actual teaching' phase. This is when the teacher is in the classroom initially introducing the aims of the lesson before moving on to a mind-capture to engage the pupils and hold their attention while he or she asks questions, discusses a new skill or concept and assesses and reviews the pupils' understanding of the key learning outcomes. The teacher sets the pupils to task and then monitors their progress informally as he or she circulates around the room. Time is set aside for the teacher to work alongside small groups or individual pupils, and both formal and informal assessment of the pupils' work may occur at various stages during this phase. The lesson is concluded by recapping on and discussing the learning outcomes of the lesson with the pupils in the plenary.

The *evaluative phase* completes the teaching process. At this stage, the teacher reflects on the lesson in terms of the intended coverage of the content, the perceived extent to which the pupils' understood the work as determined by their responses to questions and the work completed alone, the timing and pace of the lesson, the active involvement of the pupils and their behaviour. The language used in the evaluative phase should mirror that used in the lesson plan.

Task 5.1

Think of three different mathematics topics across the Key Stage(s) you intend to teach. Using bullet points, list the possible content of the first in the series of lessons in each topic. How will you capture the pupils' attention? Share and discuss your ideas with a friend or tutor.

A pedagogical analysis

A lesson plan always has aims and learning outcomes. The aims of the lesson are 'the general and less explicitly defined statements of intent in teaching' (Stones, 1994, p. 36). The more specific and explicated intentions of the lesson are called the key objectives or learning outcomes. There are usually two categories of learning outcomes: affective and cognitive. The affective learning outcomes are normally expressed in terms of the teacher's aspirations for the lesson, while the cognitive learning outcomes relate to what the pupils should be able to do at the end of the lesson. Learning outcomes must be measurable, so they should be expressed using the appropriate vocabulary.

Task 5.2

Consider the following verbs and categorise them into two groups – the ones which can be used to create measurable learning outcomes and the ones which cannot:

List, locate, define, create, know, explain, understand, state, write down, categorise, plan, think of, find, remember, identify, group, consider, bring, use, show, relate.

Stones (1994) avers that there are three types of cognitive skills in learning: Remembering, Identifying and Doing. Each of these skills has a different level of specificity (1 = very general; 3=very specific). See Table 5.1 for an example.

Table 5.1

Level of specificity	Remembering	Identifying	Doing
1			Use 3-figure bearings to solve a problem
2		Distinguish between exemplars and non-exemplars of 3-figure bearings	
3	Remember the criterial attributes of 3-figure bearings		

Reading this table from the bottom left-hand corner upwards and along the diagonal, the Remembering skill is a prerequisite for the Identifying skill, which in turn is a prerequisite for the Doing skill. Remembering is the low-level skill of regurgitating the teacher's definitions or a rule for solving a problem (such as Pythagoras' Theorem). The Doing skill is the high-level skill of applying the new knowledge in a novel context (working out the length of a ladder resting against a wall). The aim of any lesson should be the 'Doing' skill. The breaking down of a concept in this way is called a *pedagogical analysis* of the concept. This matrix of skills is the optimal route for a teacher to take in order to attain the intended goal of teaching. Effective teachers complete a pedagogical analysis for every topic they teach. As you become more experienced, this skill of breaking a concept into its pedagogical parts becomes natural and almost unconscious.

What are exemplars/non-exemplars and criterial attributes?

The word 'exemplar' is used to describe an example that can be shown to pupils to illustrate abstractions. Exemplars also illustrate the criterial attributes of the skill or concept being taught. Criterial attributes refer to the core elements of the concept or skill. Non-exemplars have the converse meaning – namely, examples not possessing the criterial attributes of the concept or skill. For a more detailed explanation, consult Stones (1994).

The criterial attributes for three-figure bearings are:

- there must be three figures or digits;
- the angle is measured from the north;
- the angle is measured in a clockwise direction.

So the following three diagrams are exemplars:

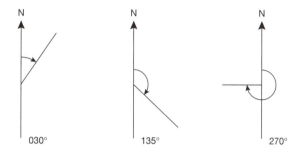

while these diagrams are non-exemplars:

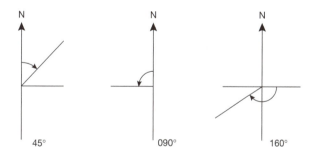

Effective teachers use exemplars and non-exemplars during whole-class teaching to determine the pupils' level of understanding of the topic. They also build in opportunities to test for misconceptions using this technique.

Task 5.3 Exemplars and non-exemplars

In the above six diagrams can you explain why the first three are exemplars and the second three are non-exemplars? How would you integrate this into your teaching? Create a set of exemplars and non-exemplars for a 12-/24-hour clock or different types of angles – supplementary, complementary, vertically opposite, acute, obtuse and reflex.

Stones' heuristic for teaching subject knowledge and the NNS/Key Stage 3 Strategy

Consider the recommended three phases in the NNS and Key Stage 3 Strategy for mathematics: the mental maths, the main part and the plenary. How does Stones' heuristic support this lesson structure?

First, think of the types of questions you will ask in the mental maths section. You are capturing the pupils' attention with a realistic problem (albeit modified to ease the mental calculations) and you are requiring the pupils to remember and re-use the strategies they have already discovered. For example, if the calculation is adding two 2-digit numbers such as 34 and 58, then the pupils are remembering to add 30+50 and also 4+8 to get 80+12=92. Alternatively, they may prefer to add 58+30 = 88 and then add on 4. Regardless of the method the pupils use, they must still *remember* the place value of each of the digits and ensure their addition is accurate. As part of the teacher–pupil interactions, a discussion of the types of approaches being used will ensue and from this, the pupils will be able to *identify* quick and effective methods compared to the slower, more tedious processes. They will also be able to *identify* incorrect methods where the place value of the digits has been ignored.

The main part of the lesson allows the pupils to practise their *doing* skill. Working in small groups or pairs, the pupils can use the strategies rehearsed in the first phase of the lesson to assist them with the calculations in the given tasks. They will be applying their skills and understanding of mathematics in the new or novel context. Through peer discussion and collaboration, the pupils will be able to detect alternative approaches to the task through remembering and identifying similar examples covered in the earlier part of the lesson.

The final stage – the plenary – will be similar to the last section of the mental maths phase where the pupils will be sharing and identifying strategies and methodologies for solving the task. This discussion will encourage the pupils to *remember* the technique they used in completing the calculation as they explain it to other members of the class. They will be *identifying* reasons why their approach was effective or accurate, and finally the pupils will be *re-doing* the calculation in a step-by-step manner with the teacher or at the board themselves.

The three-stage heuristic advocated by Stones fits well within the recommendations of the NNS and Key Stage 3 Strategy due to the need for high levels of teacher–pupil interaction in lessons and the importance of addressing the key objectives for the lesson. Where misconceptions occur in a class, the Stones' heuristic offers an ideal framework for challenging the misconception through the use of exemplars and non-exemplars and a class debate.

Planning problem-solving

Stones (1994, p. 166) avers 'traditional approaches to teaching are unlikely to teach the abstractions and bodies of principles essential to true learning'. He also advocates the use of problem-solving to teach for understanding. There are two types of 'problems' that teachers can assign to their pupils: open and closed. Closed problems have a single solution, so assessment is either correct or incorrect. These problems have a 'best way to solve' methodology and are tackled using algorithms. For instance, consider the closed problem:

> A group of 130 Year 4 children are going on a school outing to a zoo. How many coaches are required to transport the children if each coach has seats for a maximum of 35 children?

In this case, the 'best way to solve' approach is dividing the number of children (130) by the number of seats (35) and then adding one coach if there is a remainder. The algorithm required in the calculation is 'long division' or the 'chunking' method if preferred.

Open problems, on the other hand, have no 'optimal' solution and heuristics or guides have to be used in place of algorithms. For example, consider the case where

> A golf ball lands 4 metres from a bunker and 3 metres from the hole. How far apart are the bunker and the hole?

Clearly, the direction in which the measurements are being made will influence the answer!

Effective teachers are aware that it is only through exposure to problems of this latter form that pupils can begin to establish ways of thinking about the processes involved in problem-solving. A variety of experiences is essential when attempting to develop the pupils' repertoire of techniques when dealing with abstractions of this nature. An essential aspect of successful problem-solving is being able to *identify* the problem. What are the key issues? What are the variables? What do we know and what do we need to know to obtain an answer?

An approach called 'means–end analysis' (Newell and Simon, 1972) is often used to assist pupils in focusing on what they are doing, where their ideas are going and keeping 'on track'. Means–end analysis requires the pupil to look at the difference between his or her current state of knowledge about the problem and the state of knowledge required for finding the solution to the problem. By breaking the problem into smaller, more manageable units, the current knowledge increases as mini-problems are solved, so the difference between the pupil's current position and where he/she wants to be becomes lessened over time.

Effective teachers often use language in the form of verbal cueing to assist and encourage the pupils in the right direction without domineering the problem-solving process. Using positive feedback as often as possible, these teachers use the following heuristic to assist the pupils' thought processes during problem-solving:

- identify the problem – pupils learn how to tackle problems of this nature;
- call on the relevant concepts and principles from existing knowledge – teacher asks 'Have you seen something like this before?' or 'What did we do the last time we had an equation like this?' (Transfer skills from previous experiences);
- analyse the task – teacher input: 'Have you found the solution?' 'What do you think we need to do with this value now?';
- prompting – assist the pupils in developing the thought processes used in problem-solving;
- facilitate experiences of success so that independent activity is promoted.

Polya (1945) also offers helpful advice on encouraging pupils' problem-solving approaches. He uses a four-stage process: identify the problem, devise a plan, carry out the plan and look back – a similar approach to that outlined above.

Teaching skills embedded in the heuristics

In both heuristics, the internalisation of the new concepts is a key learning outcome of the teaching process. For a pupil to reach the stage of 'Doing', he or she must have mastered the 'Remembering' and the 'Identifying' stages. Similarly, to be an effective problem-solver, the pupils must be able to carry out the 'Doing' stage in a previously unseen context. So how does an effective teacher ensure that pupils have reached this stage?

The following list highlights the five steps inherent in all lessons where new concepts or principles are being uncovered either through direct teaching or discovery via problem-solving:

- Questioning
- Show and Tell
- Guiding and Cueing
- Feedback
- Practice.

In relation to the NNS, the questioning occurs in Stages 1 and 3 – to engage the pupils in mental maths and also to review the learning in the final plenary. If particular mental strategies have been discussed, there will be some Show and Tell from the pupils and perhaps a little Guiding and Cueing from the teacher. The second phase of the lesson – the groupwork – addresses the Practice step with some Feedback from other members of the group. While the teacher is working alongside a group, there may be more Show and Tell from the pupils, Guiding and Cueing from the teacher, plus Feedback from both the pupils and the teacher. Finally, the Plenary stage will focus predominantly on the Feedback with some Show and Tell as appropriate. Clearly, the structure and requirements of the NNS and KS3 Strategy fit well with the Stones' heuristics for both subject knowledge and problem-solving.

Establishing a positive learning environment

Effective teachers are aware of the importance of establishing a positive and open learning environment in their classroom. Regardless of the age and ability of the pupils, these teachers ensure success in maths is achieved and celebrated by all students to foster self-esteem. Pupils need to experience three states of mind to assist their learning: attentiveness, receptiveness and a feeling of appropriateness (Kyriacou, 1997). Attentiveness is the state of being 'on task'. It is the act of listening to the teacher and other pupils, responding to questions, paying attention to the criterial attributes, thinking about the processes involved in the calculation, being 'engaged' in the classwork activity. The appearance of the class-room and the teacher's role in the learning process plays an important part in ensuring attentiveness.

Receptiveness is the willingness to learn. Not all pupils will be receptive to a mathematics lesson, often because of previous feelings of failure or because they do not see the relevance of the topic being studied – e.g. quadratic equations! It is the teacher's role to encourage pupils' receptiveness to learn, which may mean they have to adopt a different approach to teaching such as using real-life examples to illustrate the role of mathematics outside the classroom.

Appropriateness refers to the appropriateness of the task or activity being set, the teaching methods being used, and the depth of coverage of the content material in relation to the age and ability of the pupils. In general, appropriateness is the 'goodness of fit' between the pupils' ability and the work being set. Effective teachers automatically build opportunities for pupils to experience these 'states of mind' during their lesson.

Organising the maths classroom

In most primary school classrooms, the teachers have their room divided into sections with wall displays illustrating the concepts or work covered in each subject. Similarly, in the mathematics department of secondary schools, the walls are also used to display pupils' work in a variety of topics and from a variety of age groups. Using colourful displays not only enhances the appearance of the room, but it also indicates that the teacher values his or her pupils' achievements. Quite often, a mixture of abilities will be displayed so that the less able child can see that his or her work is as important to the teacher as that of the most able student in the class. Laminated posters and professionally produced materials are also important to attract the pupils' attention and engage them in the topic. As with all wall displays, it is important to update them regularly. There is nothing more offputting than seeing your work from Year 8 still on display when you are in Year 13! Effective teachers take pride in the appearance of their classroom and, as a result, the pupils also take pride in their work.

The role of the teacher throughout the academic year

The classroom climate changes throughout the year and effective teachers also adapt their role to accommodate changing circumstances and requirements. With new classes, the teachers and pupils spend some time 'getting to know' each other and determining the 'limits' in relation to behaviour, attendance, submitting homework assignments on time, and so on. Usually, the teacher will be more strict than usual during the first term, assuming the role of the leader and organiser of the mathematical activities. However, once authority and respect have been established, a little more flexibility appears in the teaching approaches and the interaction between the teacher and the pupils increases. By this time, the teacher is a facilitator of the educational process and a motivator of pupils. There is more sharing of the control and a wider range of teaching strategies is introduced. Gradually, effective teachers will introduce more open-ended project work, site visits, investigations, modelling or simulation work that uses and extends the pupils' mathematical knowledge and thinking skills. In this environment, the pupils are given more autonomy and the teacher assumes the role of a guide, offering assistance through leading questions and giving advice. When used sparingly, a short change in the classroom climate will be sufficient to re-educate the pupils on the expected standard of behaviour.

Effective teachers ensure their classes are easily managed and controlled throughout the school day. The classroom climate and pupils' dispositions are usually more positive early in the school day, and many effective teachers use this time to introduce and develop more thought-provoking and challenging mathematical activities. After lunchtime, pupils tend to be restless or tired, which means that a more structured and controlled teaching style is more effective for afternoon classes.

Previous experiences of maths

Failure in mathematics in the early years of schooling can lead to a negative attitude towards anything numerical in later life. How many times have you heard an older person saying 'Oh, but I was never good at maths in school!' or 'I always hated maths!'? Society seems to be prepared to accept people's deficiencies in the mathematics arena, but how many people admit that they are illiterate? Young people today have so many role models who were failures in maths at school and yet have succeeded in life that it makes the maths teacher's job particularly difficult when trying to convince pupils that mathematics is an important life skill in the real world. Nevertheless, effective teachers find ways of engaging the most reluctant of learners, particularly in mathematics. It is important to avoid reinforcing the same feelings of failure from one year to the next, so effective teachers try to find new and creative ways of reinforcing and extending the pupils' basic numeracy skills without resorting to the same textbooks used in the junior classes. By changing the context of the calculation, the same numerical skills can be addressed only using examples that relate to the pupils' age, interests and social life. For example, in primary school teachers often use questions such as 'Jane has £3 and she spends £1.75 on sweets. How much change does she get?' A similar question could be offered to a low-ability Year 8 pupil in the form: 'Jane has £30 and she buys a CD costing £11.75. How much change does she get?' Or in Year 11, 'Jane has £30 and put £11.75 of petrol into her car. How much change does she get?'

Re-teaching the same mathematical skills in the same way as they were taught previously is unlikely to produce a different result – namely, understanding. Effective teachers use their professional and subject knowledge to devise alternative approaches to the topics when assisting pupils in overcoming their feelings of failure or their negative attitude towards mathematics as a subject. ICT often plays an important role in offering a new approach to learning.

Task 5.4

Investigate the software available for basic numeracy skills or the packages used in the Key Stage below the one you intend to teach.

Dealing with underachievement in maths

Effective teachers never demoralise their pupils by passing a negative comment on a pupil's contribution in class, or by marking a number of questions in the homework wrong without suggesting the pupil sees the teacher for additional help on the topic. They are aware that pupils who feel they are not valued, stop trying and develop a lack of interest in the subject.

Effective teachers refuse to believe that pupils in the lower streams or the bottom group in the primary classroom are 'failures'. They stop the downward spiral of pupils lacking confidence in their own ability, becoming de-motivated and being inattentive in class by offering pupils equally interesting and challenging work like their peers in the higher streams. Using repetitive and unchallenging material in class and for homework only reinforces pupils' perceptions of having low-level mathematical skills. All pupils are entitled to develop their mathematical 'understanding', so a carefully selected problem-solving activity should be integrated into the classwork to allow the pupils to apply their knowledge in a relevant situation. The standards in maths expected by the teacher should be challenging but realistic – within the pupils' zone of proximal development (Vygotsky, 1962). Pupils will recognise that the work is within their extended grasp and so will always be motivated. This type of planning is typical of effective teachers when dealing with pupils who are underachieving in maths. By instilling self-belief into the pupils' minds, the self-fulfilling prophecy (Rosenthal and Jacobson, 1968) increases the chances that those pupils will believe they have the ability to succeed and consequently, they *will* succeed mathematically.

Task 5.5

Make a list of the activities you could use to engage reluctant learners. What are the issues that are important to their age group outside school and how can they be addressed in the maths classroom?

Gender issues in maths

Much of the research in the 1970s and 1980s focused on the underachievement of girls in mathematics, with a particular emphasis on the impact of stereotypical perceptions embedded in society. Traditionally, the sciences, including mathematics, were seen as a male preserve in the middle classes – boys were trained to run their father's company or become businessmen, while a girl's role was to care for others and look after a family. Consequently, the sciences and maths were viewed as male subjects, while English, humanities and the social sciences were deemed suited to girls' needs. Although these beliefs are not encouraged in schools, these perceptions are deeply embedded in our society and research (Licht and Dweck, 1984; Theobald, 1987; Walkerdine, 1989) indicates that their impact on pupils' attitudes and performance in the core subjects still exists today. Effective teachers are aware of these issues and are careful to avoid reinforcing them through the use of gender-biased language in the classroom or over-emphasising the contributions of the boys in class discussions.

Effective teachers also know that historically females were considered to lack the capacity to think rationally and to reason (Walkerdine, 1989), so the sciences and maths became designated as masculine subjects and girls were not encouraged to progress in this area. Those girls who did excel in maths were viewed to be hard-working, conscientious and dedicated, while boys who excelled in maths were considered to have 'flair' and a 'natural talent' for the subject. Even the most mathematically able girls were made to 'feel they lacked something even if they were successful' and therefore 'their achievements were downgraded' (Walkerdine, 1989). Similarly, in the past teachers accounted for girls' errors as resulting from insufficient mathematical ability, but they attributed boys' poor performance in maths as a lack of effort or low levels of motivation. Lack of maturity in boys was also perceived by teachers to mask his true potential in maths (Walkerdine, 1989). It is not surprising, therefore, that research by Licht and Dweck (1984) revealed that relative to boys, girls tended to have less confidence in their ability to succeed which affected their self-esteem. In terms of classroom interaction, effective teachers know how to encourage girls to participate in the maths lesson and promote their self-esteem while, at the same time, containing the boys' enthusiasm to contribute.

Girls are also known to experience 'learned helplessness' where they attribute failure in maths to lack of ability. In contrast, boys attribute their failure to learning difficulties or lack of effort in maths, thus maintaining their self-esteem. Walkerdine (1989) has revealed that sometimes teachers unwittingly reinforce the girls' feelings of learned helplessness and inhibit their performance due to the choice of teaching pedagogies. The teacher's personal style is also reported as having been a significant factor in pupils' identification with, or rejection of, aspects of schooling, including maths. To be an effective mathematics teacher, it is important to consider the range of cognitive styles of learning being used in the classroom to ensure that both girls and boys receive equal opportunities to develop and progress in the mathematics classroom. Effective teachers pay close attention to their attitude towards pupils during classroom discussions and when offering praise and encouragement in the form of oral or written feedback. Walkerdine (1989) declares that statements made by teachers about their pupils can influence learning, making the predictions become true. So, as an effective teacher, are you acknowledging the girls who are showing flair in mathematics? And are the hard-working boys being recognised for their effort? Are your comments consistent with your intentions to encourage pupil success in maths, regardless of gender?

The macho image of mathematics also raises some problems for mathematically able girls in the same way as the more feminine image of English causes concerns for boys who excel in the subject. Kelly (1987) and Thomas (1990) found that curriculum subjects which become designated as masculine can conflict with girls' developing sense of femininity and hence, influence their participation and motivation in the subject. This is particularly important in the post-primary classroom where young people are developing their sense of identity. Walkerdine (1989) refers to this as the 'double bind' – in her research, girls explained this as follows: 'you're supposed to do well in maths but it's quite dangerous, you may be seen as less feminine. It's not good as a girl to excel at things that aren't girls' subjects'.

Task 5.6

During your teaching placements, keep a diary of the level of participation of the girls in your class in oral work, groupwork or collaborative projects and written work. Do you agree with Walkerdine's research findings? Explain with evidence.
As a teacher, how can you change the attitude of girls to maths? What impact does this have on the boys in the class?

What types of resources are available for teaching mathematics?

Effective teachers use a range of resources for teaching such as ICT to demonstrate a concept or skill using a laptop and data projector, or they encourage pupils to work in groups on the class computers developing their understanding of a new concept.

For the computer to be used as a teaching tool, a data projector and screen is needed to facilitate whole-class observation. Most schools would use the whiteboard or a screen with the data projector. However, the recent introduction of Smart Boards allows a higher degree of interactivity to occur with the software. A Smart Board works like a touch screen when application software is used and has a 'Notebook' facility when used with the pens. Any handwritten notes or examples completed on the Smart Board using the pens can be converted to text in Word or Notepad and stored as a text file for recall at a later date. Some interactive whiteboards, such as the Promethean board, have built-in subject-specific features which increase the level of creativity and flexibility in the lesson delivery when used with the pupils.

Modern and effective teachers also make use of new technologies such as digital cameras and scanners for illustrating occurrences of mathematics in everyday life. By using scanned images from books or using the internet and downloading a photograph of a bridge, for instance, the equation of the curve can be estimated as a quadratic. Similarly, photographs of everyday objects and shapes can be investigated for symmetry. Shears and stretches can be illustrated easily in this medium, as can enlargements and translations.

Sensors and motion detectors can also be used for modelling real-life situations. By capturing data for circular motion, oscillations and time and distance, a number of mathematical models can be created to demonstrate instances of mathematics in society. A number of internet sites also offer opportunities to investigate the Golden Ratio or link between mathematics and art.

Using the ExamPro software, teachers have access to a large database of all GCSE past paper maths questions in electronic format. The software assists the teacher in creating topic-based test papers comprising old exam paper questions by allowing searches and selections based on the area of interest. These can then be printed out and used for school examinations or homework assignments. QCA TestBase offers a similar facility with Key Stage 2 and 3 tests. Both CDs are produced by Doublestruck in association with QCA (QCA, 2002a, 2002b). Further information can be obtained by e-mailing info@testbase.co.uk.

Conclusion

Effective teachers make teaching look easy, but underneath their relaxed and confident façade, these teachers have a solid understanding of mathematical concepts and their interconnectedness. They are aware of the importance of setting targets for their pupils, planning interesting and engaging activities to enhance and extend pupils' mathematical knowledge and skills, challenging misconceptions and using ICT appropriately to go beyond the classroom. In addition to their pedagogical skills in encouraging learning, these teachers are also aware of the importance of establishing a positive and open learning environment where everyone's contribution is valued and the pupils' self-esteem is fostered through celebrating success.

6 Classroom management and working with pupils

Introduction

How do you manage a class? What makes the pupils listen to the teacher? How do you deal with the many and varied questions from pupils? Where do you get the time to work with pupils needing extra attention? This chapter introduces you to the complex issues surrounding working with pupils and how to manage a class. In terms of maintaining good discipline in the classroom, the advice is similar to that given by the dentist – 'prevention is better than cure'. This chapter aims to offer insights into how to establish yourself as a teacher and therefore reduce the opportunities of misbehaviour in your classroom. As with all aspects of teaching, this is advice but, depending on the circumstances and situations, it may or may not work for you. Nonetheless, this chapter is a good starting point for you to establish your own style and approach which suits your personality and temperament.

Learning outcomes

At the end of this chapter you should be able to:

* appreciate the importance of the teacher–pupil relationship;
* choose the most appropriate teaching strategy for your classes;
* ensure the key issues of good classroom management are built into your lesson plan;
* use the least- to most-intrusive strategies to control the class.

The teacher–pupil relationship

Teaching and learning are two activities that are highly charged emotionally. Pupils' concerns about their mathematical ability, insecurities and inhibitions result in learners being concerned about 'losing face' or becoming embarrassed in front of their friends if they answer a maths question incorrectly or if they don't understand a process or cannot use an algorithm that their friends have mastered quickly. You, as a teacher, can also be under great emotional stress if you are experiencing difficulty controlling a rebellious group of students who are reluctant learners of maths. Therefore, the teacher–pupil relationship is the key factor to reducing and often removing these high levels of anxiety. By ensuring that pupils accept your authority and there is mutual respect between yourself and all the pupils, a potentially highly volatile situation becomes a calm working environment.

The teacher's authority

Maths teachers are responsible for organising the pupils' mathematical learning, including the management and sequencing of the learning activities. To assist this process, you must also manage pupils' behaviour.

Four main factors have been identified as being crucial for establishing and maintaining authority (Kyriacou, 1997):

- status;
- teaching competence;
- classroom control;
- discipline strategies.

Teachers who appear relaxed and self-assured when delivering a maths lesson are viewed by pupils with respect (Robertson, 1996). Pupils can sense and often see the teacher's enjoyment of maths in facial expressions, tone of voice and gestures. These teachers often move freely around the classroom, circulating among the pupils as they work in groups, asking questions to motivate pupils where necessary, engaging in a brief and controlled conversation to a student who may have represented the school in a sports or musical activity. This freedom to exercise the rights of status is evident to the pupils and, by expecting respect from a class, the teacher is usually rewarded with that respect. Teachers who frequently need to deal with discipline problems lack the respect of their pupils.

Teaching competence is an obvious factor in determining authority. Pupils deserve a sound education and, if a teacher cannot deliver a good maths lesson, pupils often feel denied the opportunity to learn mathematical skills and that the teacher does not care about their future employability. Consequently, pupils do not care for or respect the feelings of the teacher, which leads to discipline problems. Maths teachers who avoid these dilemmas are those who possess a strong subject knowledge and can evoke an infectious and shared enthusiasm and interest in all aspects of mathematics (Kyriacou, 1997). These teachers also have the ability to create and maintain effective learning experiences within the maths classroom by relating the subject to everyday life and highlighting the interconnections between topics. They give encouraging feedback, both orally and in writing, in good time so that the pupils have the opportunity to improve their mathematical performance based on the teacher's comments.

Pupils also make their decisions regarding the teacher's authority based on the perceived skills used to control the class. Teachers who have routines for ensuring an orderly entrance into and exit from the classroom and who start and finish lessons on time, command more respect and authority than those who have poor time-keeping skills.

By virtue of the subject, mathematics is perceived as highly organised, logical and sequential – factors typical of a traditional lesson. During the normal classroom activity, authority is depicted through the teacher's control of noise levels, pupils' movement around the room, particularly during investigative maths. Maths teachers assert their authority when gaining the pupils' attention, for issuing instructions, vigilance and through maintaining respect for other pupils. The latter skill is often apparent in teacher–pupil interactions during class discussions when the teacher ensures all mathematical ideas and suggestions (right or wrong) are treated with respect. By challenging pupils who laugh at their peers and by reprimanding them for improper behaviour, the teacher can be seen asserting his or her authority. The same applies for safety within the classroom when pupils are using a compass, ruler, scissors or other equipment that may harm or damage other people or property. By establishing clear classroom rules and through applying and reinforcing them consistently, pupils should be aware of the teacher's expectations regarding behaviour in the maths classroom.

Rapport and respect

The second important element in a good teacher–pupil relationship is the rapport between the two parties and the need for mutual respect. When pupils are asked what makes a good maths teacher, they identify instances of what a good maths teacher *does*, rather than offer a list of qualities. For example, pupils describe situations where teachers have been firm but fair, consistent in their treatment of pupils without showing favouritism and not being overly strict in particular circumstances. They discuss how the maths teacher 'teaches well', saying how he or she explains things clearly, has interesting lessons, does exciting work, offers help, is friendly and patient, has time outside class for questions. Overall, the pupils say they 'like' the maths teacher – he or she has clearly established a rapport with their pupils through understanding their concerns or by making maths alive and relevant (Kyriacou, 1997).

The maths classroom offers more opportunities for the mutual respect that works hand-in-hand with rapport. Maths teachers respect the pupils as individuals by remembering their names and using them frequently when addressing pupils in class. They respect pupils as mathematicians by adopting an appropriate range of teaching strategies to encourage, engage and motivate the pupils to excel mathematically. Good maths teachers design tasks or problem-solving activities that are within the extended grasp of pupils, in order to allow them to feel a sense of success when they have reached a solution to the problem. By being allowed to be active learners rather than passive recipients of information, the pupils also respect the teacher for giving them autonomy in learning maths. The provision of individual worksheets or structured problem-solving tasks for the more- and less-able mathematicians in the class also demonstrates the teacher's respect for learners' needs. These pupils also appreciate and respect their teacher for his or her extra work in tailoring the task to meet their educational needs. Finally, the teacher's concern for the pupils' mathematical development within and across a series of lessons also highlights the teacher's respect for pupils' educational progress. By ensuring progression and continuity between lessons, pupils can see that their teacher cares about their learning and so respect for the teacher grows.

Teaching strategies

Whole-class teaching

Most lessons begin with whole-class teaching where the teacher highlights the aims for the lesson and then teaches the new concepts or skills. This type of teacher-centred activity is called exposition. The teacher is the focal point giving information, showing algorithms and demonstrating mathematical skills and techniques. The pedagogical approach is explaining and then questioning the pupils. Pupils are required to listen, think and respond verbally to questions relating to the low-level skills of remembering and identifying as identified by Stones (1994). Effective questioning uses a mixture of low-level and high-level questions interspersed with statements provoking discussion (Askew and Wiliam, 1995).

Teachers need to ensure that the material used in whole-class teaching will gain and sustain the pupils' attention for the duration of the mathematical explanation. Context plays an important role, since pupils can be easily engaged if the maths has links to their own lives. The clarity of the explanation depends on its structure and length, and the language used by the teacher. Criterial attributes of the new skill should be clearly stated and exemplars and non-exemplars used to check pupils' level of understanding of the topic.

Exposition can be challenging for any teacher due to the diverse range of abilities within the class. Didactic teaching of this nature should be checked for its appropriateness to all pupils in the class, from the lowest to the highest ability.

Drill and practice tasks

Note-taking and textbook exercises fall into the category of passive learning. For the purposes of exam revision, pupils should have a notebook containing definitions of mathematical terminology, diagrams such as the properties of two-dimensional and three-dimensional shapes, key equations or algorithms, and worked examples.

Pupils need time to practise and internalise the new mathematical skills, so the completion of textbook exercises is a vital part of the teaching and learning process. However, it is not enough to ensure that pupils have time to practise the skills; pupils also need regular feedback from the teacher on their progress. By checking answers in class, the teacher and pupils can identify and correct any misunderstandings before these are reinforced through continued practise.

Classroom activities of this format are teacher-directed with little or no pupil control. The pupils are given the opportunity to practise and reinforce the skills and concepts already taught so that they are internalised for use in other contexts.

Individualised programmes of work

Worksheets, workbooks and computer-assisted learning packages are the most common forms of individualised programmes of work in maths. This approach allows the pupils to work at their own pace and level. It may be considered as differentiation by ability taken to the extreme. In terms of recording pupils' progress, computer-based materials such as Integrated Learning Systems (ILS) will offer built-in progress reporting facilities for the teachers to view at their own discretion, while progress through a workbook or completed worksheets can be checked manually. Paper-based activities will require dedicated teacher time for marking and progress to be recorded manually. Any areas of concern can be noted and further one-to-one teaching offered as necessary. For the more able students, individualised work may be of an investigational or open-ended nature to stretch the pupils' mathematical thinking.

Experiential learning

Pupils often learn more by doing than by hearing, so experiential learning offers the pupils an opportunity to get some hands-on experience of mathematics in action. Both cognitive and affective experiences will occur, since all the senses are involved in this type of learning. Typical examples of experiential learning include watching a video or simulation of a mathematical process such as tessellations, Fibonacci numbers, Golden Ratio; using role plays or site visits to exemplify mathematics in society, for social arithmetic such as banking, interest rates, mortgages, hire purchase and repayments on a new car or planning journeys requiring timetables; listening to other people's viewpoints and understanding an alternative perspective, such as guest speakers discussing job prospects, and work experience.

Small groupwork

Social and communication skills are developed through the medium of groupwork. Pupils learn to collaborate, discuss, reflect, explain their mathematical ideas, listen to others and respect their viewpoints, appreciate the mathematical skills of their peers and experience recognition of their own mathematical ability. In general, pupils' thinking skills are developed through communication within the group context (Leikin and Zaslavsky, 1997), which has the added advantage of encouraging higher order thinking (Becker and Selter, 1996). Problem-solving tasks are most appropriate for groupwork activities as there are multiple opportunities to experiment with different techniques. Ideal group composition is high- and middle-attaining pupils together or middle- and low-attainers with equal numbers of boys and girls (Askew and Wiliam, 1995). Effective groupwork requires goals or targets (to motivate pupils) and the use of individual accountability (to prevent 'free riders') (Reynolds and Muijs, 1999).

Investigational work

This pedagogical approach emphasises skills such as problem-solving, discovery learning, autonomy, self-regulation, co-operation and collaboration, discussion and reasoning, plus many other higher-order thinking skills. Work of this nature should promote deeper understanding of the mathematical processes in problem-solving (Baker, 1993). Investigational work is often introduced as an element of groupwork in primary school. However, as the pupils progress through their schooling, investigations become an individualised activity in preparation for GCSE coursework. Further information on GCSE coursework is provided in Chapter 12.

Task 6.1

Relative to the requirements of the NNS, KS3 Strategy or Key Stage you will be teaching, plan activities where you can use the above techniques in your teaching. Justify your decisions to a friend or colleague.

Discipline and behaviour management

It is a well-known fact that prevention is better than cure. An abundance of advertisements on television tell us to look after our bodies; healthy eating is actively promoted in schools, as is the importance of regular and sustained exercise. The same fact applies to teaching. In terms of discipline, prevention *is* better than cure. Effective maths teachers are identified by the well-organised classroom with minimal misbehaviour resulting from the low level (almost unnoticeable) use of discipline strategies in their classes (Brophy and Good, 1986; Secada, 1992). They rarely have to shout and never publicly ridicule a pupil.

Through the careful planning, preparation and monitoring of learning experiences, pupils' attention and motivation are sustained in a lesson. Good and Brophy (1991) offer a clear description of an effective teacher in action:

> Effective teachers were well prepared and thus able to teach smoothly flowing lessons that provided students with a continuous 'signal' to attend to. They seldom had to interrupt the flow in order to consult the lesson plan to see what to do next or to obtain a resource that should have been prepared earlier, and they seldom confused the students with false starts or backtracking to present information that should have been introduced earlier. They ignored minor, fleeting inattention but dealt with sustained inattention before it escalated into disruption, using methods that were not themselves disruptive. Thus they moved near inattentive students, used eye contact when possible, directed a question to them, or cued their attention with a brief comment. They realised that when teachers deliver extended reprimands or otherwise overreact to minor inattention, they lose the momentum of the lesson and break the signal continuity that focuses students' attention. Typically, problems multiply and escalate in intensity when students are left without such a focus.
>
> (p. 196)

Six main issues arise from this description which require further clarification:

- flowing lessons;
- continuous signal;
- advance preparation of resources;
- sequence of lesson;

- tactical ignore;
- least-intrusive to most-intrusive methods for classroom control.

What is a flowing lesson?

All lessons in post-primary schools, and in some primary schools, have three phases: pre-active, interactive and evaluative. Within the interactive phase (the classroom-based stage), there is the introduction to the lesson, the presentation of new material or the recapping on existing knowledge from a previous lesson, the application or student-directed activity, the assessment and the conclusion. Clearly, there are five shifts in focus from the teacher-led introduction to the shared class discussion to student-directed activity to teacher-led marking and the predominantly teacher-directed conclusion. It is the transition from one activity to the next that may disrupt the flow of the lesson. Effective teachers make these five transitions appear seamless to the students who move directly from one focus to the next without any slippage in their attention or concentration. Lessons of this nature are called 'flowing'. There are no gaps or pauses while the teacher checks the next step in his or her lesson plan or notes. All the resources required in the lesson are at the teacher's fingertips, and worksheets, books or other resources are distributed while the pupils are engaged in a mathematical activity. At no stage are the pupils left with nothing to do.

How to maintain a continuous signal

A continuous signal is maintained through the appropriateness of the teaching strategy and by ensuring that the pupils remain attentive. The former is decided at the planning and preparation stage when the teacher completes the pedagogical analysis of the content, determining the learning outcomes for the lesson and applying Stones' skills of remembering, identifying and doing to the structure and sequence of content domain. The latter – ensuring that the pupils remain 'on task' – is addressed through a variety of informal and formal assessments.

By questioning the pupils in the early part of the maths lesson, the teacher will capture the pupils' attention from the outset. A lively or imaginative introduction will sustain the pupils' attention as he or she wishes to hear how this introduction links to the mathematics they will be doing in class. Extensive periods of teacher exposition quickly lead to boredom, so teachers should intersperse their explanations with a few oral and/or written questions to ensure the main points in the teaching have been identified – such as the criterial attributes. Through questioning the students the whole class becomes involved in the lesson once more and the change in activity refreshes the students' concentration.

The use of exemplars and non-exemplars as part of the questioning process also allows the maths teacher to evaluate the progress of the lesson at an interim stage and to judge whether additional reinforcement of concepts is required. The movement from teacher-centred explanations to pupil-centred mathematical activity in the application stage assists in maintaining continuity in the signal. By circulating around the room, the teacher will be able to monitor the pupils' progress in the task and will be able to decide on an appropriate time to stop the class and ask for feedback or share answers to a written exercise. Again, this change in activity will offer a break from the written work, but the marking process will ensure that the pupils remain attentive. A mixture of self-assessment and peer-assessment can be used as appropriate.

Teachers can deal with lapses in pupils' attention by directing questions at those pupils who appear to be disengaged in the work. A quiet reminder to listen more carefully may be sufficient to regain the pupil's attention. Similarly, if off-task behaviour occurs during the exposition phase, it is often more effective to move beside the pupil(s) and continue teaching than to disrupt the flow of the lesson by reprimanding the pupil(s).

The importance of advance preparation

Sound planning and preparation is a prerequisite for maintaining the flow of any lesson and establishing a continuous signal. In determining the sequence of the lesson, teachers will make assumptions on the pupils' existing knowledge, such as assuming that they know how to read a protractor if the topic is three-figure bearings. In most cases, this skill will be addressed by the teacher as part of a demonstration using the overhead projector. Once the angle has been found, the bearing can then be written using three figures. In this way, the prerequisite knowledge is reinforced before the main aspects of learning begin. If this practical approach to three-figure bearings is to be used in the lesson, the teacher's advance preparation checklist will be:

- an overhead projector (OHP) available in the room;
- prepared overhead transparencies (OHTs) showing a variety of acute, obtuse and reflex angles so that the pupils can see the teacher measuring each in turn;
- a class set of protractors;
- a worksheet for the pupils to practise their skills in measurement and recording as three figures;
- an answer sheet for marking in class.

Ideally, the teacher should have the OHT sitting ready on the OHP when the pupils arrive in the classroom. The protractor should also be beside the OHT. If possible, the criterial attributes should be written on the board in advance, but kept hidden from the pupils until they have been identified during the class discussion. In the transition between the presentation phase (demonstration using OHP) and the application phase (pupil-centred activity), the teacher will need to distribute the worksheets. By having the criterial attributes already written on the board, the teacher can ask the pupils to copy them into their maths notebook before starting the worksheet. This will focus the pupils' attention, while also providing time for the teacher to move around the room with the worksheets and protractors. A similar approach can be taken at the end of the class when the pupils are copying down the homework, the teacher can collect in the protractors. By anticipating areas where there are potential problems such as the distribution and collection of equipment, the teacher can have a strategy already prepared for addressing them.

The sequence of a lesson

If a pupil is confused, then the continuous teaching signal is lost, thereby opening the door for misbehaviour by members of the class. A clearly thought out and well-planned lesson will not lead to confusion among the pupils. Confusion in maths classes occurs when the teacher assumes a higher level of prerequisite knowledge than actually exists, when explanations are unclear, muddled or introduce unfamiliar mathematical terminology, when the instructions for the pupil-directed activity are unclear or when the teacher rushes the final part of the lesson due to misjudging the time.

To avoid confusion and the disruption it brings to a classroom, teachers should always check the assumed prerequisite knowledge in the introduction to the lesson. Teachers should be willing to adapt their lesson plan to re-teach or revise the prerequisite knowledge if necessary. This may result in the intended learning outcomes for the lesson not being met. However, there is no point in attempting to build on mathematical knowledge that doesn't exist. New terminology in maths should be introduced gradually and with examples. Teachers should encourage the use of the new vocabulary during classroom discussions. However, constant correction of the pupils for not using the new terminology may discourage them from contributing in future oral work. The sequence of steps required to complete a calculation should be illustrated using a number of worked examples before setting the pupils to work alone. Often, it is valuable to spend some time working through these examples as a class, with the pupils suggesting the next step.

By avoiding the need to backtrack or leave pupils dangling in the middle of an explanation while you look for your OHT, opportunities for misbehaviour or lack of attention are reduced. A disorganised teacher gives the impression that he or she doesn't know what they are doing, particularly when maths is perceived to be a logical and structured subject. If there are discontinuities in the flow of the lesson, pupils will infer that the teacher doesn't care about their learning as little time was spent preparing for their lesson. Pupils may then challenge the teacher's authority by being disrespectful, leading to the teacher having to 'deal with' the pupil in terms of correcting the misbehaviour. Other pupils may react by adopting a similarly scatterbrained approach as their teacher when submitting maths homework. All these factors add to the volume of classroom management activities that need to be carried out by the teacher within the lesson, leaving increasingly less time for the actual learning process and increasing the number of opportunities for disruption by pupils.

In the next section, a series of brief case studies will be used to highlight a number of classroom management strategies that may be adopted to deal with the situations. The context of the problems has been kept to a minimum to allow you to discuss the situations further by adding other factors into the scenario.

The various tactics used to deal with the misbehaviour advocate the notion of least- to most-intrusive strategies and are based on the work of Bill Rogers (Australia) and Brophy and Good (USA).

Case Study 1

Class: Year 9 boys   Duration: 70 minutes   Topic: Constructions

Scenario: At various stages throughout the lesson, individual boys dropped their protractor/ruler/compass. It was clear that these incidents were isolated and not intended to disrupt the lesson.

How do you react?

The use of the 'tactical ignore'

Not all pupil misdemeanours require attention and actions. In some cases, it is more profitable for a teacher to tactically ignore an action and maintain the pace and flow of the lesson. For minimal disruption, such as a dropped pencil/ruler/mathematical resource, the tactical ignore is a more appropriate choice of strategy than to lose the teaching 'signal' to the majority of the class by verbally dealing with the individual's clumsiness. If pupils are attentive and focused on the teacher's exposition, they may not even hear the pencil or ruler dropping, so, from the pupils' perspective, no disruption occurred. Accidental disturbances such as these should be dealt with at the lowest possible level. Where a tactical ignore is appropriate, then use it, otherwise a brief glance in the pupil's direction to say 'just leave it there for the moment' may be sufficient to deal with the situation.

The 'tactical ignore' should not be used if it is obvious that the misdemeanour was intentional – for instance, if one group of pupils engages in persistently dropping objects to disturb others in the class or to make their friends laugh. 'Laddish' or immature behaviour should not go unnoticed, as pupils will deem this acceptable behaviour if it is not challenged and corrected by the teacher. Similarly, muttering insults at the teacher after being reprimanded for forgetting a homework, say, should also be corrected, particularly if it was said loud enough to be heard by other members of the class.

The continuum from least- to most-intrusive strategies for classroom control

In most situations, least-intrusive strategies can be used to correct minor problems before they become full-blown discipline issues. By being vigilant and alert, most teachers can anticipate a problem and 'nip it in the bud' before any damage is done. Least-intrusive strategies are recommended and are evident in experienced and effective teacher's classrooms. Bill Rogers illustrates these tactics in his set of four videos in the *Managing Behaviour Series* (1997). The following overview is adapted from this series of teaching materials and his books on classroom management.

To discipline effectively while minimising damage to the pupil's self-esteem, teachers should:

- choose the correct language;
- attend to content and pitch;
- select the best strategy;
- progress from least- to most-intrusive strategies to maximise the options remaining should the misbehaviour persist.

Case Study 2

Class: Year 8 girls   Duration: 40 mins   Topic: Handling data – pie charts

Scenario: Three girls arrived slightly late to class, rushed in and let the door slam behind them. Teacher shouted 'Don't slam the door!'

Lesson focused on an explanation of how to represent data as a pie chart and was uneventful. Teacher set the class the task of drawing a pie chart for a given data set, declaring 'Don't cheat by copying your friend.' She then asked the class 'Who needs a protractor? Don't yell out.'

How could the teacher have used positive language in her lesson?

Positive and negative language

Instructions and commands should be expressed in a positive tone. For example:

'Close the door quietly' is preferable to 'Don't slam the door'.

'Try doing these questions on your own' should be used instead of 'Don't cheat by copying'.

'Raise your hand if you need a protractor' can be used in place of 'Don't yell out'.

Case Study 3

Class: GCSE class   Duration: 40 minutes   Topic: probability

Scenario: Student teacher with a high-ability GCSE class. It was his first week of teaching so he looked nervous and made poor eye contact with the class. There were no visual aids or resources to assist the explanation. Pupils were noisy and started asking awkward questions to try to confuse the student teacher.

Where did he go wrong?

Congruence of tone and gesture

Small behaviours can convey messages as powerfully as the words we speak; for instance, the teacher's posture and stiffness can indicate feelings of discomfort in his role showing concerns about authority and uncertainty about controlling the class. Indecision in the teacher's voice or tone can send signals that contradict the spoken words and may indicate a lack of subject knowledge.

Conversely, attention can be obtained through standing upright at the front of the room in an authoritative stance but in silence. The expectation of silence from the pupils and the expectancy of compliance is usually achieved. Similarly, eye contact, facial expressions and gestures can be sufficient to correct minor misdemeanours. For additional effect, name-dropping to alert their attention may be necessary.

Case Study 4

Class: GCSE class   Duration: 60 minutes   Topic: investigations

Scenario: Low-ability GCSE class working in groups of 4 on a maths investigation. A pupil in one group was more involved in another group's discussion than his own task. There were obvious signs of disengagement in the activity and interest in other people's work. The rest of the group were working well together.

How do you get the pupil back on task without causing a scene?

Privately understood signals

Teachers are individuals, so each person will have their own levels of expectations regarding pupils' behaviour and noise levels in their classes. Different teachers also have different ways of dealing with pupils. Quite often, teachers will use privately understood signals to communicate non-verbally with pupils. For instance, pupils have the habit of turning round to speak to their friends sitting in the row behind. Teachers will often correct this behaviour by saying the pupil's name and then drawing a circle in the air to indicate 'turn round'. Pupils are very quick to pick up on these privately understood signals. Some teachers also use the phrase 'all legs on the floor please' to stop pupils from swinging on the back two legs of their chair. Pupils who are daydreaming or watching their classmates working are often brought back on-task by the teacher standing in front of their desk and tapping twice on the table. The pupils' attention is diverted by the noise and seeing the teacher's finger pointing at the maths notebook is sufficient indication that they should return to work.

Case Study 5

Class: Year 4   Duration: 30 minutes   Topic: direction – compass points

Scenario: Teacher is dealing with a group of five students who have been off sick for a week missing a substantial part of the topic. The rest of class are working in small groups on a paper-based treasure hunt. One group of pupils located in the opposite corner of the room are off-task and persistently chatting about a birthday party.

How do you deal with the group's behaviour?

Pause, . . . direction

Quite often teachers are dealing with another pupil or group of pupils when they notice inattention in another part of the room. It is not feasible to go and stand beside the disruptive student(s), so some verbal encouragement and direction are used.

For example,

'John (pause), John (pause) have you finished the treasure hunt?'

'Gail (pause), Gail (pause) are you designing your own treasure hunt yet?'

The pauses are a necessary part of commanding the pupil's attention. Once you have his attention, you can direct him back to work again.

Case Study 6

Class: Year 7   Duration: 40 minutes   Topic: Area and volume

Scenario: Pupils have a worksheet showing a number of three-dimensional shapes. It is the plenary session and the teacher is questioning the pupils on their strategies for working out the volume of these shapes. One student is colouring in each shape and not contributing to the discussion.

What do you do?

Distraction and diversion

To maintain a pupil's self-esteem, it is often necessary to distract or divert his or her attention in a positive manner without a verbal rebuke, as indicated above by the last privately understood signal. By standing beside a pupil who is doodling and doesn't appear to be listening to the teacher's instructions, the invasion of space distracts his or her attention away from doodling and forces them to listen to what the teacher is saying. Questioning pupils who appear to be 'off-task' also regains their attention and concentration. However, statements such as 'Amy, what did I just say?' should be avoided.

Case Study 7

Class: Year 2   Duration: 30 minutes   Topic: Counting money

Scenario: Pupils working in groups of four on a task involving the use of plastic coins. One of the pupils in the nearest group to you refuses to share the coins with the rest of her group and the other pupils are resorting to snatching the coins out of her hand.

How do you deal with the situation before someone gets injured?

Distraction and diversion

If tensions rise very quickly and unexpectedly in the classroom between two students, it is worth asking one of the troublemakers to bring their classwork book to you to check their progress. This way, you are withdrawing the student from a volatile situation and allowing him or her to calm down. Once you have marked/discussed some of the work, you can quietly ask about the 'heated debate with student X' and calm the situation. Similar treatment with the other student should ensure no further disagreements. If necessary, one of the students can be moved to another seat in the classroom.

Case Study 8

Class: Year 8   Duration: 40 minutes   Topic: Scale drawings

Scenario: It is the plenary phase and the teacher is explaining the homework. Two disengaged students are talking at the back of the room. When reprimanded, the students speak back to the teacher.

What should the teacher say?

Partial agreement

Pupils who answer back when they are asked to stop talking in the maths class frequently challenge the teacher for the last word, saying 'Why pick on me? I was talking about the homework!' Such situations can be defused by focusing on the primary behaviour – talking – and not the secondary action of speaking back to the teacher. Partial agreement in the form of 'I accept that you may have been discussing the homework, but I would like you to pay attention to what I am about to say' prevents further arguing.

Case Study 9

Class: Year 5   Duration: 30 minutes   Topic: Co-ordinates

Scenario: A pupil wants to use the maths CD-ROM to play a co-ordinates game. However, the teacher feels it is important that he consolidates his knowledge first by completing the paper-based activity of plotting given points in the first quadrant.

How can she delay his movement to the computer?

When ... then directions

Again, this is the use of positive language to reduce teacher–pupil conflicts.

'You *can't* use the maths CD-ROM *because* you haven't finished all the questions yet' should be rephrased as '*When* you've finished the questions *then* you can use the maths CD-ROM'. Using this approach places the emphasis on the pupil completing the required amount of the work before he or she can go to the computer.

Case Study 10

Class: Year 9   Duration: 60 minutes   Topic: Straight line graphs

Scenario: Pupils are exploring graphs of the form $y = mx + c$ using graphics calculators. Two pupils are chatting continuously about their boyfriends.

How do you deal with the situation?

Choice direction

This is similar to the above case of 'when . . . then' directions but is used in the context of separating pupils who are chatting continuously. '*Either* you and Maria stop talking *or* you move to the desk at the front of the room.' Again, the outcome of the reprimand depends on the pupil's subsequent actions. The pupil has the choice to stop talking and remain in her seat or to continue talking and risk being moved to another desk away from Maria. It is the language of choice.

Case Study 11

Class: Year 8   Duration: 40 minutes   Topic: Ratio and proportion

Scenario: Desks are arranged in groups of six and pupils are working on the main part of the lesson, writing down examples of equivalent fractions and percentages to the given ratios. Pupils are supposed to be working alone initially, and then discussing their lists in pairs. There are a number of instances of misbehaviour during the early part of this phase and the teacher is heard saying: 'Harry, why haven't you got your notebook out?', 'Orla, why are you talking?' and 'Mark and Lydia, why are you not working?'.

How could the teacher have re-phrased these questions to prevent a flow of irrelevant excuses from the pupils?

Question and feedback

Unlike classroom instruction, open questions should be avoided when dealing with behaviour management. Focus on what the pupils *should* be doing instead of asking them what they are actually doing . . .

'Harry, could you get your books out please.'

'Orla, you should be writing down examples for each ratio quietly.'

'Mark and Lydia, you should be working alone at the moment.'

Case Study 12

Class: Year 7   Duration: 35 minutes   First lesson in new school

Scenario: NQT teacher establishing himself in a new school and new job. Year 7 pupils are also new to the school, so he is encouraging them to create a series of classroom rules.

Why is ownership of the rules important to pupils?

What are the main rules you are hoping to obtain?

Why do you need classroom rules?

Rule reminders

During the establishment phase when you meet a new class, pupils should be introduced to school and classroom rules. These all derive from the child's three fundamental rights:

- the right to feel safe;
- the right to learn;
- the right to be treated with respect.

Rule reminders can be used to impose order in the classroom:

'What is our rule about working noise during an investigation?'

'You know our rule about asking questions.'

Case Study 13

Class: Year 9   Duration: 40 minutes   Topic: Area and volume

Scenario: High-ability class. Pupil arriving late to school every morning. He enters the classroom during the plenary discussion on working out the volume of a can of beans. Teacher expresses her concern at him being late again, saying 'Martin, you've missed the maths lesson again. This is unacceptable.'

What does she say next?

Take-up or face-saving time

Following a reprimand, pupils need time to do the things the teacher has asked them and teachers should create circumstances to allow the pupils to comply without losing face. For example:

'Martin, take your coat off and put your bag under the table . . . As I was saying, the volume of a cylinder is found by multiplying the area of the base by the height of the cylinder. How do we work out the area of the base?'

The teacher continues her lesson, secure in the belief that Martin will comply with the teacher's requests. Glaring at Martin while waiting for him to remove his coat and slide his bag under the table will only make the experience a humiliating one. Such approaches are highly intrusive and often lead to the pupil speaking back.

Case Study 14

Class: Year 5   Duration: 40 minutes   Topic: Measuring angles

Scenario: NQT demonstrating to her class how to use a protractor properly when measuring angles. Pupils are set to task, measuring angles on a worksheet and comparing answers. One pupil becomes frustrated when he cannot manipulate the protractor effectively and starts shouting across the room. As the NQT approaches the pupil to help him, he throws the protractor at her.

What should she do?

Cool-off time

In cases of serious misbehaviour in the classroom, it is important to give pupils 'cool-off' time before you engage with them to sort out the problem. 'Cool-off' time allows a teacher to move a pupil away from the circumstances that are causing him to react aggressively and 'deferring' the consequences until he is in a more receptive frame of mind. Once the pupil has calmed down and can deal with the situation intelligently, the teacher can talk to the pupil. Never engage with the disengaged!

Structure for dealing with disruptive pupils

The 'four Ws':

- What I did.
- Why I did it.
- What rule I broke.
- What I can do to fix it.

Using the four Ws, teachers can encourage pupils to reflect on and offer reasons to explain why they are being reprimanded. By understanding why they are being punished, pupils are more likely to accept the punishment (extra homework, lines, detention) and not challenge the teacher.

Final advice

The key to good classroom management and discipline is 'certainty not severity' and also the need for 'with-itness'. When implementing any of the discipline strategies, it is important to be as consistent as possible. Favouritism is noticed and is disliked by pupils. Match the sanction to the crime – there is no point in sending one student to detention for forgetting a homework, if another student only gets lines for fighting in the classroom.

If extra work is set as a sanction, always follow up and check that it has been completed. Ask to see the work and if the student cannot produce it, then add an additional exercise or maths task to the work to be completed. Consult with more experienced teachers, the form teacher or year head if a particular pupil is causing you difficulties in class. Finally, be familiar with the school's policy on discipline so that you know the order of events, rules and implications regarding the awarding of sanctions.

'With-itness' refers to teachers who are said to be 'on the ball' – alert, vigilant and can see trouble brewing. A 'with-it' teacher can nip problems in the bud before any serious disruption occurs. They check the classrooms in advance if these rooms are used as break and lunch rooms; they rarely sit down, instead spending the lesson circulating among the pupils, monitoring their work, yet remaining vigilant and aware of the behaviour of the rest of the class, even when assisting a pupil on a one-to-one basis. Pupils who misbehave look at 'with-it' teachers while misbehaving, so the use of eye contact is doubly effective for 'with-it' teachers.

Task 6.2

During one of your placements, keep a diary of instances of misbehaviour in your maths classes. Are there any patterns? Alongside the event, list the type of strategy you used to address the issue. Which ones worked effectively for you and why?

7 Misconceptions in maths

Introduction

In this chapter the reader is introduced to the common misconceptions experienced by pupils in secondary schools. Since many of the areas relate to the primary curriculum, this chapter is also important for the primary school mathematics teacher. By raising a primary school teacher's awareness of the common misconceptions, perhaps these naive ideas and untaught 'rules' can be eliminated before they become deeply rooted in a child's mathematical skills base. So what are the common misconceptions in elementary maths? How are these manifested by the teacher? How can we 'break the chain' and remove these misconceptions permanently?

Learning outcomes

At the end of the chapter you should be able to:

- discuss some common misconceptions in each of the ATs;
- challenge the naive, intuitive models from a pupil's childhood;
- identify misconceptions in given examples;
- understand the implications of this chapter from a teaching perspective.

Background

In Chapter 2 the theories of learning by Bruner and Gardner were discussed and an appreciation was established that young children arrive at school with some basic knowledge of the number system. To make sense of the world around them, children create their own set of rules that work for their experiences and situations. However, the assumptions children make are often inaccurate and the skills they use have no theoretical basis (and may be incorrect). Even after they reach school, pupils are often reluctant to use the new techniques taught by the teacher in place of these simplistic approaches. Why should they give up something that has been working well for them? In most cases, children retain their old approach and add parts of the teacher's technique to supplement the cases when their 'personal' method fails. Consequently, new and contrived methods of calculation become embedded over time. Bruner (1996) avers

> Deep seated naive theories can only be dislodged when the teacher attempts to appreciate the child's view of things so that he or she can use convincing counter-examples to persuade the pupil to abandon the naive theory and adopt the informed approach.

(p. 49)

It is only by understanding how the child thinks about problems that teachers can then do something to change these thoughts. A research study was carried out on Children's Skills in Mathematics and Science (CSMS) (Hart, 1995) which revealed a number of interesting, surprising and often quite shocking results on the misconceptions still held by secondary school pupils on the 'basics'. This chapter draws heavily on the findings of the CSMS study and the work of Hart (1995). For ease of referencing, a selection of the findings will be grouped by AT to highlight the typical mathematical misconceptions of pupils. Readers are recommended to consult Hart (1995) for further details.

Number

The number system

The language of the number system itself does not promote reasoned thinking. The numbers between 11 and 19 show little connection to their roots – namely, ten-one to ten-nine. Similarly, new words are introduced for the multiples of ten: twenty, thirty, forty. Do these really indicate their true connections with two-tens, three-tens, four-tens, and so on? Would it be clear to a child that 'twenty' is two-tens? When we move into the larger numbers, does the label fifteen thousand one hundred and fifty two clearly describe the structure of the digits in 15,152?

By looking at the Chinese number system, it is obvious why their children excel in international tests such as the Third International Mathematics and Science Study (TIMSS). The number system is highly ordered, the language 'explains' the construction of the number, so addition and subtraction become much simpler (see Table 7.1).

Table 7.1 The Chinese numbering system

1	yi	11	shi yi	21	er shi yi
2	er	12	shi er	22	er shi er
3	san	13	shi san	23	er shi san
4	si	14	shi si	24	er shi si
5	wu	15	shi wu	25	er shi wu
6	liu	16	shi liu	26	er shi liu
7	qi	17	shi qi	27	er shi qi
8	ba	18	shi ba	28	er shi ba
9	jiu	19	shi jiu	29	er shi jiu
10	shi	20	er shi	30	san shi

Task 7.1

Identify the mathematical patterns in the Chinese number system as listed above. Using these patterns, predict how the Chinese will represent the following numbers: 31, 38, 40, 80, 62, 75.

Clearly, the use of the English language for mathematics does not develop an intuitive understanding of the structure of numbers. Perhaps this is the cause of some of the misconceptions that follow.

The CSMS study revealed that only 61 per cent of 12–13-year-olds, 62 per cent of 14-year-olds and 66 per cent of 15-year-olds answered the following question correctly:

$$\begin{array}{r} \text{Subtract} \quad 2312 \\ -\ 547 \\ \hline \\ \hline \end{array}$$

If a pupil had responded with 2235, what would this tell you about their method of calculation? Let us consider the order in which subtraction is normally taught in schools, namely questions with

1 no borrowing;
2 borrowing from tens column;
3 borrowing from hundreds column;
4 borrowing from either tens or hundreds column or both (mixture of 2 and 3 above);
5 mixed questions (with and without borrowing).

By doing calculations such as:

$$\begin{array}{ccccc} 5 & 18 & 78 & 159 & 896 \\ -\ 2 & -\ 13 & -\ 34 & -\ 42 & -\ 651 \\ \hline \end{array}$$

the pupils 'acquire' the rule 'big number minus small number', so when they see questions such as

$$\begin{array}{cccc} 32 & 45 & 123 & 453 \\ -\ 19 & -\ 27 & -\ 68 & -\ 394 \\ \hline \end{array}$$

answers such as 27, 22, 65 and 141 result – that is, the pupils take the smaller number away from the larger number, regardless of its place value. The need to 'borrow ten' is unnecessary in their eyes! They have already established a rule from the earlier examples that gives them an answer (even if it is incorrect). Bruer (1997) offers two additional 'rules' that some children may also adopt – namely, 'borrow from zero' and 'borrow across zero' (pp. 94–95).

Although the incline of difficulty would appear to be an appropriate approach to learning the skill of subtraction, it has actually allowed the children to practise and reinforce the wrong 'rule'. Perhaps by using a mixture of large and small digits in the numbers from the beginning, pupils would appreciate that the position of the digit has a meaning and then the need to borrow ten would be accepted, as there would be no opportunity to create their own alternative rule.

In terms of multiplication, most children prefer the concept of 'repeated addition'. This is fine for the whole numbers, but it becomes a little awkward when fractions and decimals are introduced. What does ¾ × ½ mean? Due to the use of whole numbers when introducing multiplication, pupils naturally conclude 'multiplication makes bigger', which has implications for work involving fractions.

Consider the problem involving fractions in the context of an area shown in the figure below:

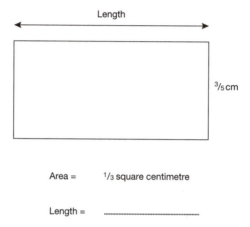

Length

$^3/_5$ cm

Area = $^1/_3$ square centimetre

Length = ...

The pupils were told that the Area = 1/3 square centimetre. Only 7 per cent of the 14-year-olds and 5.6 per cent of 15-year-olds correctly answered this question; the majority of pupils did not attempt it, saying '3/5 is bigger than the area, it cannot be done' (Hart, 1995). Clearly, this problem challenges the pupils' idea that multiplication makes bigger.

Finally, the old favourite – 'to multiply by ten, add a zero': this idea dominates the pupils' thinking when manipulating decimals. If asked to work out '5.4 × 10', most pupils will write 5.40. Sometimes pupils will recognise that 5 × 10 is 50, so that answers such as 50.40 may also occur.

Misconceptions also arise when pupils are asked to identify which number is bigger – 0.75 or 0.8. Clearly, 75 is bigger than 8, so pupils identify the first number. Again, a lack of understanding of place value leads to these problems.

Fractions

Addition of fractions also results in errors. Pupils are keen to use the strategies suited to whole numbers, so the rule 'add tops and add bottoms' is frequently used, making

$$\frac{3}{8} + \frac{2}{8} = \frac{5}{16}$$

for 8.5 per cent of 12-year-olds, 19.7 per cent of 13-year-olds, 14.3 per cent of 14-year-olds and 16.7 per cent of 15-year-olds (Hart, 1995); and

$$\frac{1}{3} + \frac{1}{4} = \frac{2}{7}$$

for 18.3 per cent of 12-year-olds, 29.1 per cent of 13-year-olds, 21.8 per cent of 14-year-olds and 19.9 per cent of 15-year-olds (Hart, 1995).

Task 7.2

What strategies could you use to challenge this misconception?

Algebra

Pupils tend to think that different letters have different meanings, so if $x = 3$, then y cannot equal 3, nor can any other letter. If more than one variable has the same value, then the pupils become confused. In general, less able pupils will try to ignore a letter in an equation or see it as a shorthand for an object – e.g. 3 apples and 2 bananas cost 86 pence is often written as $3a + 2b = 86$. The majority of pupils can deal with variables if the letter can be evaluated numerically from the outset. Fewer pupils can cope with arithmetic operations being applied to the variable, such as $3t + 2 + 4t = 7t + 2$. In the CSMS study, only 36 per cent of pupils could correctly add 4 to $3n$ to get $3n + 4$ and only 17 per cent of pupils could multiply $n + 5$ by 4 correctly. Having a particular variable represent more than one number is also viewed as confusing by approximately 75 per cent of the cohort. So is it realistic to look for generalisations in investigational work if pupils have little conceptual understanding of what a variable really is?

Measures

Length

Length is one of the first measurements a pupil meets, even before he or she reaches school. Children compare the heights of toys, the lengths of pencils or crayons, the sizes of books, and so on. However, pupils tend to focus on the position of the endpoints and often neglect to check that both starting points are aligned (Hart, 1995). In the following figure, Hart (1995) found that 86.4 per cent of 12-year-olds thought line B was longer, leaving 13.6 per cent of that age group thinking that both lines were the same length or line A was longer.

Even when endpoints of lines were aligned (shown below), there was still confusion over the actual length of the line: 19.5 per cent of 12-year-olds thought Lines E and F were the same length. Clearly, pupils were 'counting squares' to come to this conclusion:

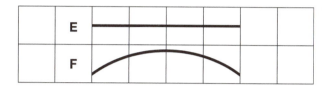

Another interesting outcome occurred where the starting position and endpoints of the lines were aligned but Line C was not horizontal, as shown in the figure below.

In this case, the following results were obtained.

Answer	12-year-olds	13-year-olds	14-year-olds
Line C is longer	42%	45%	52%
C and D are the same length	48%	48%	45%

If almost half the pupils cannot identify the diagonal line as being longer than the horizontal line in the diagram above, then how will these pupils understand the concept of hypotenuse in right-angled triangles?

Area and perimeter

Perimeter and area are often taught in parallel or consecutively in textbooks, which leads to confusion. Many pupils think area and perimeter are related, so if the area doesn't change, then the perimeter hasn't changed either. Therefore, they consider a rectangle measuring 12 cm × 5 cm with an area of 60 cm² as having the same perimeter as a rectangle measuring 20 cm × 3 cm.

Volume

Since volume is usually taught after area to make the link 'Volume = area × height', most textbooks encourage students to count the number of cubes in the base layer and then multiply by the number of layers. If teachers are going to use the formula approach effectively, they must challenge the usefulness of this counting method. Shapes such as triangular prisms offer a good starting point.

Right-angled triangles

Imagine you are drawing a right-angled triangle on the board. Does it look more like (a) or (b) below?

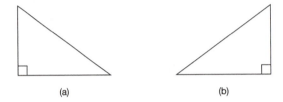

(a)   (b)

Most teachers draw a right-angled triangle like (a). Most textbooks also have right-angled triangles similar to that in (a). However this 'right-pointing' orientation can lead to misconceptions too. Some pupils think the name 'right-angled triangle' refers to the direction of the point, so they refer to triangle (b) as a left-angled triangle. If pupils are oblivious to the link between the name and the 90° angle, then what sense will they make of the definition that the hypotenuse is the side opposite the 90° angle?

Shape and space

Two types of transformation will be discussed in this section: reflections and rotations. In each case, only single transformations are considered. In the CSMS study (Hart, 1995), reflections in vertical or horizontal lines were clearly understood by pupils, with 84 per cent of the group responding correctly. However, when slanted mirror lines were used, only 23 per cent of pupils could draw the correct image.

The object being reflected also added to the pupils' problems as single points were more often correctly answered than flags with three key points for reflection. The presence or absence of a grid had minimal effect on pupils at the two extremes of the ability continuum. For those pupils who had internalised the idea of distance and direction, the presence or absence of a grid made no difference to their results, while the pupils who were struggling with the concepts made the same mistakes with and without the grid.

Pupils tended to ignore the slope of the object when both the object and the mirror line were slanted. Approximately one-quarter of the pupils drew images that were parallel to the object. However, over 90 per cent of pupils could correctly reflect single points in a slanted mirror line. Clearly, the analytical approach whereby each individual point was reflected and all the points joined at the end had not been mastered by the pupils.

Pupils also lacked familiarity with the terminology when trying to explain their reasons for the chosen position of a mirror line. Words such as perpendicular, right-angled or 90° were rarely stated and distances were only mentioned by 21 per cent of the pupils.

What does this tell us about our role as teachers? Do we encourage pupils to explain their thinking and reasoning sufficiently or are we more interested in the number of pupils getting the right answer?

Task 7.3

Consult Hart (1995). Chapter 10. 'Reflections and Rotations' and create a worksheet of examples to test the common misconceptions in this topic. Evaluate its effectiveness with a class.

Handling data

Hart (1995) also discovered that pupils experienced difficulties in applying their knowledge about plotting points when presented with a non-rectangular axis. Even with an example, less than one-third of 14-year-olds and only 38 per cent of 15-year-olds could correctly plot the given points. Over 90 per cent of pupils demonstrated their competence in block graphs and elementary representation of data. However, their understanding of continuity in straight-line graphs was 6 per cent for 13–14-year-olds and 20 per cent for 15-year-olds. Pupils also experienced problems when they had to choose suitable axes to plot a mixture of positive and negative points. A number of pupils did not include zero on their axes.

Equations of straight lines, gradients and the intersection of two lines were all addressed in terms of their key role in mathematics. Less than 20 per cent of pupils could correctly identify the graphs of functions such as $x = 2$, $y = 2$, $y = 2x$ and $x + y = 2$. The connection between gradient and parallel lines was not understood, with many pupils declaring that parallel lines must be vertical or horizontal, or who used visual inspection to determine if the lines 'look' parallel instead of calculating the gradient. Due to the previous problem of not recognising infinitely many points on a continuous straight line, pupils found the concept of solving simultaneous equations by finding the intersection point beyond their understanding. However, the same pupils could correctly complete the process involved in using this technique, but clearly they had no understanding of the underlying concepts. It was simply mastery of a taught technique.

The spatial responses associated with the distance–time graphs indicated the difficulties and misconceptions being experienced by pupils when faced with this form of data. Pupils could not conceptualise the abstract notion of 'distance from the origin' and thought the peaks and troughs represented going up and down hills.

Implications for teaching

The CSMS study revealed a high proportion (almost half) of secondary school pupils had difficulty dealing with abstract concepts, so solving questions of this nature were virtually impossible. Most students, however, had mastered the low-level basic concepts of mathematical literacy. However all teachers should recognise that there are likely to be one or two students who:

- cannot use a ruler accurately as they do not line up the endpoint with the zero mark;
- are less confident than most about working with fractions, even for basic addition and subtraction;
- misunderstand the mathematical meanings of words such as 'share', 'similar' and 'straight', as they think share means divide equally, similar objects means objects that are alike without accounting for shapes being in direct proportion to each other, and straight means vertical or horizontal but not slanted.

Due to previous experiences of confusion in past mathematics lessons, some children will be only too happy to have any answer and are not concerned if it doesn't make sense. They will be willing to 'mix and match' their naive and intuitive models with snippets of what they remember about the teacher's methods until they obtain an answer. Only the higher ability students understand and learn from written feedback on their performance in homework assignments or tests. For other students, it is just a case of the teacher telling them how he or she would have calculated the answer, with no real understanding why the alternative method is right. Teachers should ask pupils to explain how they worked out the answer and verbalise the reasons behind their choice of actions. By making the *teacher understand the pupil*, he or she will be in a better position to understand why the mistakes are being made and how to address the misconceptions more effectively. By talking about their thinking processes, pupils also learn.

Visual representations of data, such as distance–time graphs, are often hard to conceptualise. Using sensors, this data can be captured automatically and displayed on a computer screen almost instantaneously so it would be possible for pupils to 'act out' the graphs in their textbooks to help them understand the occurrences of plateaux, peaks and troughs.

The research has shown that it cannot be assumed that children will 'understand things when they get older'. Understanding only improves slightly over time and for skills (such as mental arithmetic) which are not practised regularly and developed, performance is likely to decrease over time. Ideally, the curriculum should be 'spiral', with topics being re-visited in increasing levels of depth and sophistication over time. However, the reality of the situation in schools means that the curriculum is actually two-dimensional, with the same material being re-taught time and again. New approaches, strategies and introductions to topics need to be given so that pupils can have a fresh start and perhaps understand the concepts when explained in the new context. Identifying the gaps in a pupil's knowledge base and then plugging them with a little teaching holds little possibility for understanding and successful transfer of knowledge and skills to another context.

Bruer (1997) also offers an insight into the misconceptions and use of intuitive theories when high-school physics graduates are faced with simple mechanics problems. By setting questions that are not commonly seen in textbooks or in computer-based learning (CBL) materials, it is possible to assess the students' level of understanding rather than the application of 'rote-learned' rules. Computer programs and micro-worlds are discussed in a range of mathematical contexts from Numeracy at primary level to more advanced level mechanics problems involving Newton's Laws.

Lochhead and Mestre (1988) also revealed that basic algebraic misconceptions existed in university students. When told that there were 6 times as many students as professors and that there are 10 professors, the students found it easy to calculate that there were 60 students. However, by removing the actual number of professors and forcing the students to work in the abstract, the majority of students wrote the equation $6S = P$, where S is the number of students and P is the number of professors. Using this equation, if there were 10 professors, there would be $\frac{5}{3}$ students! Clearly, the students reverted to basic intuitive models of thinking rather than putting their algebraic knowledge to use.

Statistics students experienced similar problems in transferring the statistical principles learned in the lecture theatre to real-life situations (Tversky and Kahneman, 1981). The students were told that in a large sample of professionals, 70 per cent were engineers and the remainder were lawyers. The students were then asked to consider the profile of one of these professionals and to attempt to identify his or her profession. Despite the probability of an engineer being more than twice that of a lawyer, students abandoned the laws of probability when presented with information such as 'the subject likes to debate'. The subject was identified as a lawyer, despite the much greater statistical likelihood that he or she was an engineer.

In another scenario, Linda was described as 30 years old, bright, outspoken and involved in social issues such as disarmament. Students were asked to choose whether she was a bank teller or a bank teller who was an active feminist. More than 80 per cent of the students thought Linda was a bank teller who was also a member of the feminist movement. These statistics students disregarded their statistical education and reverted to intuitive thinking: 'Abandoning or bracketing any formal knowledge they have of statistics, probability, or logical analysis, they respond instead on the basis of dominant images, prevalent stereotypes, or favoured ways of framing a problem' (Gardner, 1991, p. 70).

For more information on the other misconceptions experienced by pupils and young adults and for ideas to challenging these misconceptions, consult Hart (1995) and Bruer (1997).

8 The role of ICT in the mathematics classroom

Introduction

This chapter presents an overview of the role of ICT in relation to mathematics teaching and learning. The TTA requirements of 04/98 and 10/01 for ICT in Initial Teacher Training are outlined as a starting point for focusing on the discussion of the logistics of using ICT in the classroom. Ideas for the types and ranges of ICT suitable for use in the maths classroom are described in this chapter. However, more detail of their actual application is offered in Chapter 9. The chapter concludes by highlighting the use of the internet for teaching and also for creating resources.

Learning outcomes

At the end of this chapter you should be able to:

- describe a variety of ICT resources suitable for use in the maths classroom;
- discuss factors which influence your decision on the type of ICT being used;
- use the internet effectively to enhance your teaching and for professional development.

Forms of educational technology

Computers in education is not a new phenomenon. Since the 1960s, the use of software for teaching and learning has been encouraged by a number of researchers, with particular emphasis in mathematics on the use of Logo and the SMILE series of software designed for the BBC Bs and Apple Macs. Time and the availability of technological expertise have progressed rapidly, leaving much of the 'old' software obsolete on these new machines. However, it is worth reflecting on the experiences and pitfalls in the early days to ensure that the same mistakes are not repeated. Like any new innovation, some people embrace it with joy, while others choose to ignore its existence. However, the use of ICT in teaching and learning mathematics is a requirement of the National Curriculum, the NNS and the Key Stage 3 Strategy, and it is therefore imperative that you know when and how to integrate ICT into your maths lessons at every level.

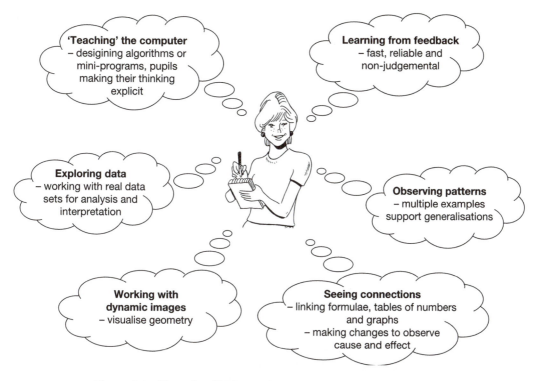

Figure 8.1 The role of ICT in enhancing the learning of mathematics

The NFER publication *Mathematics and ICT: A Pupil's Entitlement* (1995) offers a good overview of the six major ways in which ICT can enhance the pupils' experience of mathematics.

Requirements of the DfEE circular of April 1998 (04/98)

Since 1999 all existing teachers and librarians have been offered opportunities to receive Approved Training in ICT using money available from the New Opportunities Fund (NOF). The principal aim of the training was to 'equip teachers with the necessary knowledge, skills and understanding to make sound decisions about when, when not, and how to use ICT effectively in teaching particular subjects' (TTA, 1999, p. 1). Differences between subject specialisms, key stages and special needs schools were taken into account when designing the 'Expected Outcomes' and training materials. A CD-ROM containing Needs Identification materials was circulated in advance of the training program being available, to offer teachers opportunities to gain an insight into the level of personal ICT competence required for effective teaching in their subject area prior to signing up for a course. Each CD-ROM included exemplified lessons taught using various amounts of ICT combined with a wide variety of resources and software. The use of information and communications technologies such as video conferencing, a video camera, digital camera, interactive whiteboard, touch-sensitive screens, CAD/CAM software, and many more was illustrated in addition to the use of the stand-alone or networked computers.

The Expected Outcomes were categorised into themes, and exemplars of how teachers could meet these outcomes were described fully. Video clips of teachers in action in the classroom alongside their lesson plan containing the teaching and learning objectives were available to the user. At the end of each video clip, the teacher reflected on and evaluated the effectiveness of his or her lesson in meeting the key objectives. For both the novice and the more experienced teacher, a number of thought-provoking and valuable ideas are offered through this resource. Copies are available from the Teacher Training Agency Publications Unit (telephone 0845 606 0323 or e-mail: *publications@ttalit.co.uk*).

The key features of the NOF ICT training initiative, as outlined in the TTA documentation (1999), were to:

- assist teachers with their training in ICT skills and to incorporate the use of ICT in their subject;
- ensure that the majority of training occurs within the school to encourage the use of ICT in the classroom;
- support and develop the teachers' use of the National Grid for Learning as a source of professional development and assistance during the training process;
- precede the training by the identification and prioritisation of individual teacher's need in ICT against the Targeted Outcomes.

(p. 1)

In designing the requirements for teachers in terms of integrating ICT into the normal classroom routine and how to use ICT to assist them in their administrative duties, the TTA have offered a prescriptive list of linkages between the generic statements and the exemplary ideas of how to implement these requirements. The Expected Outcomes were summarised into the following five points:

- knowledge and understanding of the contribution that different aspects of ICT can make to teaching particular subjects;
- effective planning, including the use of ICT for lesson preparation and the choice and organisation of ICT resources;
- the use of ICT in whole-class teaching;
- assessment of pupils' learning of the subject when ICT has been used;
- the use of ICT to keep up-to-date, share best practice and reduce bureaucracy.

(TTA, 1999, p. 1)

Like all aspects of teaching, the ICT training fell into four categories:

- planning;
- teaching;
- assessing and evaluating;
- the personal and professional use of ICT.

Teachers were required to produce a portfolio of evidence, illustrating how they could integrate ICT into their subject teaching. The Learning Schools Programme (LSP) supplied a number of activities to guide the teachers through the four-stage process. Many schools set targets for staff completion of the NOF ICT training to motivate the departments and demonstrate the support from the Senior Management Team in the school.

Task 8.1

While on teaching placement, try to gain access to the NOF resources for mathematics and/or a teacher's NOF portfolio to see examples of the use of ICT in your chosen Key Stage.

Deciding to use ICT

Whether ICT is to be used by all pupils individually, in groups or by the teacher for a whole-class demonstration, three key principles apply. By asking the following questions, a teacher can distinguish between occasions when the use of ICT is suitable and unsuitable for the purpose:

1   Does the use of ICT support good practice in teaching the subject?
2   Is the use of ICT directly related to the teaching and learning objectives present in the lesson plan/scheme of work?
3   By using ICT, will you or your pupils achieve something that could not otherwise be achieved? Or will using ICT allow you to teach or the pupils to learn something more effectively or efficiently than could otherwise be achieved?

(TTA, 1999)

If the answers to *all three questions* are 'Yes', then using ICT will make a significant contribution to the teaching and learning process for that lesson/scheme of work. It is important to remember to apply these three questions on every occasion in which you are tempted to use ICT. Remember, teachers do not use ICT for the sake of it or because it is 'fashionable'; ICT is a valuable resource and should be used to achieve objectives beyond those normally considered by the teacher (DfES, 2003).

All the above ICT requirements are subsumed in the new TTA document *Qualifying to Teach*.

The logistics of using ICT in mathematics

In addition to determining the suitability of using ICT in meeting the objectives of the lesson, it is also important to address the practical considerations resulting from its use. For example, if the lesson depends on each pupil having access to a computer simultaneously, then the computer suite may need to be booked. However, if the pupils are only working on the computer for 5 or 10 minutes at isolated times during the lesson, it may be possible to organise subgroups of pupils to work together during these periods, taking turns on a single computer so that you can remain in the mathematics classroom and access the terminals in that room. Alternatively, if the ICT element of the lesson can be delivered just as effectively as a teacher-led demonstration followed by a discussion or group-work using pen-and-paper methods, then the pupils do not need access to computers at all. In this case, the teacher must ensure that the demonstration is visible from all areas of the classroom and in all lighting conditions, including strong sunlight. Clearly, the planning stage of a lesson may range from booking rooms, borrowing an extra computer or two from other classrooms, to setting up projection equipment for a demonstration. If you require all the pupils to use the computers for an extensive period of time during the lesson and the computer suite has been booked, it is wise to inform the IT technician of the day and time at which you will be attending and also the software you intend to use so that he or she can ensure the package is installed and working in advance of your arrival. Prior to the lesson, spend a break-time or lunch-time to check that your worksheet or set of instructions matches the version of the software you will be using with the class. Also, make sure you obtain a list of the user-names for your class before you go to the computer suite.

Another important element for the mathematics teacher to consider is the 'value' of using a graphics calculator instead of a computer package to achieve the desired teaching objectives. It is often the case that computer suites are designed to maximise the number of available terminals with minimal consideration given to desk space for recording and note-taking during the practical activity. Consequently, if the lesson involves limited use of educational technology, and a graphics calculator could be used to meet the objectives as easily as a computer, then teachers would be strongly urged to use the hand-held machine rather than the computers. By remaining in the maths classroom, teachers will have access to the full range of mathematical resources rather than the limited stock they bring with them to the computer room.

In terms of graphing software, a graphics calculator is a good match to current computer-based packages for tabulating, plotting, drawing and zooming in on functions. It can solve simultaneous equations using both the algebraic and graphical methods, and it can be easily adapted to investigate functions of the form $f(x) = mx + c, f(x) = ax^2$, $f(x) = x^2 + a, f(x) = (x + a)^2$, and so on. Matrix algebra and transformation geometry are also easily computed on the current models of graphics calculators, offering an alternative to geometry packages.

Exemplification of the possible uses of ICT in the secondary mathematics classroom as offered by TTA (1999, p. 9) are included in Table 8.1, on p. 105. They are grouped in terms of their value as a contribution to pupils' learning in mathematics and as a vehicle for supporting secondary mathematics teachers.

Expected outcomes from ICT training in mathematics

All students completing Initial Teacher Training (ITT) are required to demonstrate their ICT competence as defined by the TTA document *Qualifying to Teach*. The following criteria relate to ICT:

2.5   They know how to use ICT effectively, both to teach their subject and to support their wider professional role.

2.8   They have passed the Qualified Teacher Status skills tests in numeracy, literacy and ICT.

3.3.10   They use ICT effectively in their teaching.

(TTA, 2001)

To obtain Qualified Teacher Status (QTS) you must ensure that you have demonstrated your capacity to teach effectively using ICT in a variety of instances – different age groups, ability levels and in a variety of contexts using a range of resources.

Standard 2.5

This standard focuses on two aspects of ICT competence relating to 'knowledge': 'how best to use ICT to teach the subject(s) they are trained to teach' and the trainees' 'own ICT skills ... to complete pupils' records of progress, prepare resources for pupils and keep to a minimum their administrative tasks' (TTA, 2004, p. 23).

The majority of the evidence of achieving this standard will be obtained during the school-based teaching experience. Trainee teachers will be able to explain how they selected and used suitable software with their classes based on the range and availability of resources and access to computers. Their lesson plans will highlight the intended purpose of ICT in achieving the learning outcomes for the lesson and there should be evidence of planning for differentiation by ability in the worksheets and extension material prepared for the pupils. Lesson evaluations will reflect on the trainee's perception of the effectiveness of ICT for enhancing the pupils' learning in each lesson.

The lesson plan file is also a source of evidence of downloading resources from websites such as the National Grid for Learning (NGfL) or Teacher Resource Exchange (TRE), and adapting them to match the age and ability of the pupils. Use of peripheral devices such as digital cameras will be evident from the resources and visual aids used by the trainee or the integration of peripherals such as data-logging into the main part of the lesson for pupil use as indicated in the lesson plans. Some students may also use the spreadsheet as an electronic register of attendance for each lesson if the school does not already have an attendance monitoring process in operation.

Throughout the school placements, trainee teachers should be able to find or create opportunities to use data projectors and interactive whiteboards with at least some of their classes. Using a mixture of whole-class teaching and individual or groupwork, trainees should demonstrate their ability to use graphics calculators or subject-specific software. For communicating with their peers, tutors or other advisers, the use of e-mail, discussion groups and bulletin boards should be recorded as evidence for the assessor in the lesson plan file.

Standard 3.3.10

This standard overlaps with 2.5, but focuses on how trainee teachers use ICT in their teaching. In this case, the focus is on 'using ICT with discrimination, knowing where and how it can be used to have the greatest effect on pupils' learning' (TTA, 2004, p. 52).

Again, the majority of the evidence will stem from the contents of the trainee teacher's lesson-plan folder. The types of evidence required for this standard include:

- actual use of software with classes;
- print-outs demonstrating searching and adapting of materials from the NGfL or the TRE for use with a class;

- providing pupils with opportunities to use ICT for investigative or self-directed work;
- appropriate use of ICT terminology in verbal and written communications with pupils;
- use of a range of teaching strategies alongside ICT usage;
- awareness of copyright, privacy, reliability and confidentiality issues associated with the internet;
- evidence of confidence and independence when using ICT;
- ability to apply existing ICT skills to new packages.

Standard 2.8

This standard ensures that trainee teachers can demonstrate their personal competence when using ICT: 'they have passed the Qualified Teacher Status tests for numeracy, literacy and ICT' (TTA, 2004, p. 26).

These tests are computerised and should be taken in the final year of training. Trainees have an unlimited number of attempts to pass the tests, but they must pass all three to be awarded QTS. All tests are contextualised in the day-to-day work of a teacher. Downloadable support materials and interactive practice tests are available from the TTA website (www.tta.gov.uk/training/skillstests/). The outcome of the tests is 'pass' or 'fail'. In the former case, the print-out of the result should be retained as evidence of passing the test(s) and will be needed by the training provider. In the event of an unsuccessful outcome, trainees receive a print-out of the result and an indication of the areas of development and of how far the performance was from the benchmark. The ICT test is composed of tasks assessing the trainee's ability to use word-processing, spreadsheets, databases, Powerpoint, e-mail and the internet.

Table 8.1 offers a detailed description of the types and range of activities suitable for the maths classroom as described in 04/98 (the predecessor to 10/01). The interested reader is encouraged to consult this document for exemplars of good practice in schools or visit www.tta.gov.uk/teaching/ict/exemplification.htm for a revised version of this information.

Task 8.2

Create a table, listing your areas of personal ICT competence in terms of strengths and weaknesses. Using the TTA document *The Use of ICT in Subject Teaching: Identification of Training Needs for Secondary Mathematics* (Publication no. 10/3–99), create an action plan for developing both your personal ICT competence and competence in teaching using ICT. Plan to integrate ICT regularly into your teaching while on school placement.

Table 8.1   Areas for, and examples of, the incorporation of ICT in secondary mathematics lessons

ICT has the potential to make a significant *contribution to pupils' learning in mathematics* by helping them to:

Skill	Exemplar
Practise and consolidate number skills	By using software to revise or practise skills and to give rapid assessment feedback.
Develop skills of mathematical modelling through the exploration, interpretation and explanation of data	By choosing appropriate graphical representations for displaying information from a data-set. By experimenting with forms of equations in trying to produce graphs which are good fits for data-plots. By using a motion sensor to produce distance-time graphs corresponding to pupils' own movements.
Experiment with, make hypothesis from, and discuss or explain relationships and behaviour in shape and space and their links with algebra	By using software to: • automate geometric constructions; • carry out specified geometric transformations; • perform operations on co-ordinates, or draw loci.
Develop logical thinking and modify strategies and assumptions through immediate feedback	By planning a procedure as a sequence of instructions in a programming language, or a sequence of geometrical constructions in geometry software or a set of manipulations in a spreadsheet.
Make connections within and across areas of mathematics	To relate a symbolic function, a set of values computed from it, and a graph generated by it to a mathematical or physical situation, such as the pressure and volume of a gas, which it models.
Work with realistic, and large, sets of data	In using box and whisker diagrams to compare the spreads of different data-sets. To carry out experiments using large random samples generated through simulation.
Explore, describe and explain patterns and relationships in sequences and tables of numbers	By entering a formula in algebraic notation to generate values in an attempt to match a given set of numbers.
Learn, and memorise, by manipulating graphic images	The way the graph of a function such as $y = x^2$ is transformed by the addition of, or multiplication by, a constant.

ICT also has the potential to offer valuable support to the *teacher of secondary mathematics* by:

Helping them to prepare teaching materials	Downloading materials for classroom use from the internet, such as mathematics problems for pupils to solve with accompanying teachers' notes, software for computers and graphics calculators, reviews of published resources.
Providing a flexible and time saving resource that can be used in different ways and at different times without repetition of the teacher's input	By enlarging fonts, adding diagrams or illustrations, adapting parameters used in problems.
Providing a means by which subject and pedagogic knowledge can be improved and kept up-to-date	Accessing the Virtual Teacher Centre in the NGfL to obtain practical advice, to exchange ideas with peers and 'experts' outside school.
Aiding record keeping and reporting	Storing and regularly updating formative records which can form the basis of a subsequent report.

Source: TTA, 1999, p. 9.

Enhancing the teaching of mathematics using ICT

Learning from feedback

A wide variety of educational software for mathematics education is promoted in catalogues, magazines, shop windows and high-street stores. The majority of these packages are designed to assist pupils in the mechanical calculations of maths or 'drill and practice'. The main benefit of this type of software is the speed and reliability of the feedback, plus the use of innovative and exciting ways to assist the primary school child (or younger) with number work, such as counting, adding and subtracting, through the use of a CD-ROM. At the opposite end of the scale, GCSE revision courses are also available with promises of 'pass your GCSE maths or your money back', 'a fast-track route to success', and so on.

With the availability of such a plethora of educational computing resources, it is important for teachers to choose carefully, evaluate and critically review all aspects of the software and to be clear how, when and where the software can be integrated into the current scheme of work. Attention needs to be given to the methods of calculation advocated or exemplified by the software – does it complement and endorse the teacher-approved methods, or does it illustrate an alternative means of calculation – say, subtraction, which may confuse the young mathematician still coming to grips with the new technique? Much of the drill and practice work in number assists the development of mental arithmetic skills without the tedium of repetition and with the benefit of immediate feedback on results. Software of this type is appropriate for meeting short-term goals, but does not develop higher order thinking skills nor does it encourage an increased depth in mathematical understanding.

Similarly, a number of packages exist that address other numeracy skills such as working with money, fractions, percentages, shapes and measurement (see Chapter 4). Again, the context is colourful, fun and often uses a virtual character to set the problems for the child. In the majority of cases, minimal use of the keyboard is needed – simple mouse clicks are used to select a response or a single number entry is required before moving on to the next stage. To differentiate between the different levels of ability within a class, the software usually operates across a number of 'levels' of work, encouraging progression in terms of the difficulty of the calculations. This facility is particularly important as it allows the most and least able pupils to use the same package, therefore promoting the self-esteem of the less able group and often motivating all pupils to try harder by competing against their peers in reaching the highest level.

Seeing connections

Computer simulations place mathematics in a real-life context. They encourage the development of higher-order thinking skills such as reasoning, strategic planning, deduction, forward thinking and decision-making. Software of this type has the additional advantage of enhancing a pupil's social and emotional development. In some simulations, such as SimCity, the pupils' decisions impact on the people in the virtual city – their work, home and economy. Through making ill-informed judgements, a pupil can turn a thriving commercial centre into a ghost town – a visual exemplification of 'cause and effect' for the pupils. Even the impact of the weather, landscape, geographical and geological location of the city can alter the decision-making process. As a means of incorporating cross-curricular themes, such as economic awareness, citizenship and personal development, simulations offer exposure to a variety of social and emotional experiences. Overall, they can be thought of as a practice-run of the future and, if built up over time (as the pupils mature), they can be a valuable experience for life outside the classroom.

Other simulations (or adventure games for younger pupils) focus more specifically on mathematical clues and decisions. For example, Carmen Sandiego Maths Detective offers a motivating environment for problem-solving, requiring younger pupils to solve a range of word problems and simple algebraic equations and calculations, and develop their geometry skills, while Desert Quest and Maths Mission offer opportunities to 'use and apply mathematics' in interesting contexts.

Observing patterns in modelling

Mathematical modelling removes the uncertainty of what will happen next that is typical of simulation software. In mathematical modelling the pupils have control of subsequent stages in the problem. By modelling a situation or 'event', the pupils manipulate the variables, changing each of them in turn to determine the impact of each one on the overall problem. This is in complete contrast to the processes in simulations where the pupils can only view the impact of the resultant combination of changes, not each of them separately. Through modelling, a pupil can design, implement and analyse an 'event'; learn through experimentation and exploration, and review the results. Pupils have increased power in terms of controlling the pace and timing of this type of learning. It offers opportunities for students to answer their own questions and concerns as they work through the situation. Cognitive processes such as metacognition – thinking about one's own thinking – occur naturally and the pupils develop an inquiring mind through exposure to a range of suitable stimuli.

The most common form of modelling that occurs in mathematics is that of 'What would happen if . . .?' scenarios. These are usually approached through spreadsheets that set up the dependent conditions (as mathematical equations) and ask the pupils to change each of the variables in turn.

Exploring data

Another modelling situation that overlaps with the Control strand of ICT is one requiring the use of sensors. Using sensors, pupils can model real-life situations on a smaller scale. For example, using light sensors, pupils can record the time it takes a moving object (a toy car) to travel between two fixed points (the light sensors) on a surface (a table). By recording the motion of a moving object in this way, it is possible to produce distance–time graphs or velocity–time graphs by choosing the appropriate options in the data-logging software. By encouraging pupils to model real-life situations, such as an undulating road or motion on an inclined plane investigated by tilting the table, the pupils can relate the visual situation to the electronic representation. The effects of friction can be simulated by altering the smoothness of the table through the use of various materials (such as a plastic tablecloth or paper tablecloth used at children's parties, a cotton or fine textured tablecloth, coarsely woven hessian, and so on).

In a similar way, the light sensors can be arranged to measure distances in the vertical plane. To model the effects of gravity and challenge pupils' misconceptions regarding the acceleration of the free fall of objects of equal mass, the light sensors can record the time when the objects pass each sensor and then graph the motion of the object. By comparing the graphs, the gradient of the velocity-time graph can be shown to be the same for both objects, thereby illustrating 'gravity' as a constant acceleration of 9.8 ms^{-2}. By using multiple sensors and ensuring that the sensors at either end of the measurement are sufficiently far apart, it is also possible to demonstrate that the two objects reach a terminal velocity. Discussions of air resistance and other factors influencing the real-data can be explored.

'Teaching' the computer

Another form of modelling is that of controlling a sequence of events or programming. A typical example is the use of a floor turtle ('Roamer') in primary schools. By entering a sequence of commands such as forward 50, right 90, forward 30, left 90, back 20, the pupils can direct the turtle to a range of different locations. Using a floor mat showing the streets in a village, it is possible to create a story for the children where the Roamer goes to the Post Office to buy stamps and post a letter, then visits the shops before taking the purchases to an old person in another part of the village. From there, it can be directed to the bus stop for the journey home. By teaching the computer, the pupils are learning how to formalise their thinking, sequence their actions and articulate ideas clearly and accurately (Papert, 1980).

Taking this idea into the upper classes in a primary school, the Roamer can be replaced by Logo, a turtle that can be programmed to move in the same way, except on the computer screen instead of the floor. Using sequences of *forward* and *backward* commands, the turtle can be made to move anywhere on the screen. The direction of motion can be controlled by the *right turn* and *left turn* commands that allow the angle of turning to be specified by the user. Even with these four commands, pupils can develop an understanding of inverses through taking a particular set of commands and discovering the instructions needed to allow the turtle to retrace its steps. The software allows the pupils to observe the feedback and alter or refine it if necessary.

Much research has been carried out on the role of Logo in enhancing pupils' understanding of angle and distance (Clements, 1985, 1986; Clements *et al.*, 1986; Battista and Clements, 1986). Even higher-level computing concepts such as the use of procedures, parameters and recursion can be introduced to pupils at a relatively early age. The idea of variable can be demonstrated quite clearly using Logo procedures, and it assists pupils in conceptualising the role of variables in algebra.

As the pupils' mathematical skills develop, Logo becomes less effective in demonstrating new topics. The command language is quite limited and GCSE topics do not sit easily with this software. Consequently, a package called Zeno is recommended for use with pupils in the upper end of secondary school.

The Zeno command language (syntax) overlaps with that of Logo with the usual *forward*, *backward*, *left turn* and *right turn* commands being replaced by *fd*, *bk*, *lt* and *rt* respectively. Like Logo, the *fd* and *bk* commands also require a distance, while the two commands

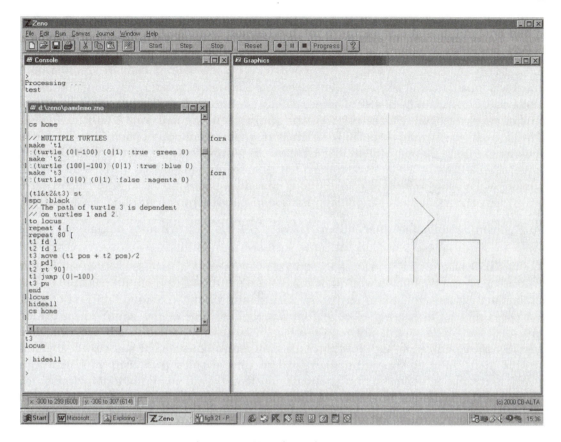

Figure 8.2 Visualising loci in Zeno

facilitating turning are followed by an angle through which the turtle will rotate. In addition to covering the same basic programming skills as Logo, Zeno allows pupils to create an infinite number of turtles. Each turtle has its own properties and can be made to move independently of the others, or it can be programmed to be dependent on the position of a number of other turtles. The position and direction of motion can be redefined easily using list processing. Investigations into the locus of an object moving according to the motion of two other objects can be simulated using three turtles in the Zeno environment. By viewing the process and interacting with the dependent turtle, pupils gain an insight into the concept of locus and can visualise other loci, even if the pupils have no access to the computer (see Figure 8.2).

Working with dynamic images

Zeno also uses a simple convention to specify a matrix, thereby facilitating investigations into the transformational properties of matrices. The Zeno language contains additional primitives (commands) for carrying out transformational geometry such as reflections, rotations, enlargements and translations.

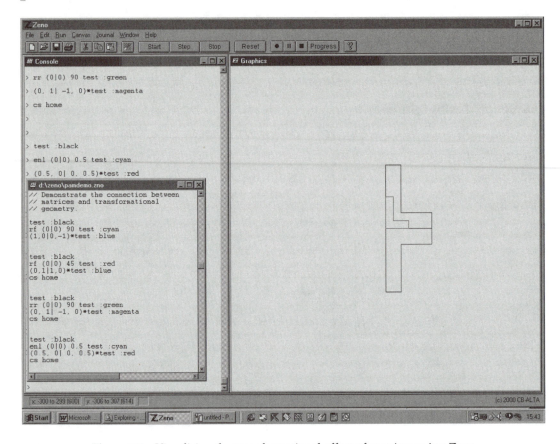

Figure 8.3   Visualising the transformational effect of matrices using Zeno

All these transformations can be applied to any predefined shape (normally written as a procedure). Using these primitives, confirmation of the matrix transformations can be established (see Figure 8.3).

Zeno also facilitates the use of complex numbers (in addition to real numbers, as discussed). Using the notation (a|b) any complex number of the form $a + bi$ can be represented and manipulated algebraically. By applying i^n to a shape for various values of n, the pupils can discover that $i^2 = -1$, $i^3 = -i$, $i^4 = 1$ and so on. The task can be extended to investigate $1+i$ leading into an investigation of $a+bi$ revealing the modulus and argument of the complex number in terms of its transformational effect. Zeno is particularly useful in demonstrating the interconnections between matrices, transformational geometry and complex numbers – a connection often missed by even the most able mathematicians in school. Examples of the use of Zeno in lessons are included in Chapter 9.

Other dynamic packages include Cabri-Géomètre and Geometer's Sketchpad which are excellent resources for developing geometrical proof and constructions. By being able to manipulate diagrams dynamically on screen, pupils are more likely to generate their own conjectures and test them. Dynamic geometry also assists pupils' development of mental imagery as the software demonstrates the results of transformations or mathematical constructions, encouraging pupils to reason and interpret a geometrical proof. These packages can also be used to challenge pupils' misconceptions.

Observing patterns in numbers

Pattern recognition and rule spotting is a more natural way of encouraging primary school pupils to use an algebraic formula to represent their ideas. Using graphics calculators, numbers can be generated to form a sequence, offering a stimulus for pupils to see patterns and discover rules to re-create the set of numbers. The usual sequence of events – drawing up a table of results, hypothesising and testing the 'pattern' and then generalising the rule to the nth case – can be carried out very effectively using a calculator or a spreadsheet, depending on the complexity of the pattern and level of generalisation required. For instance, the pattern of numbers stemming from the 11 times tables can be easily spotted and represented algebraically, as can the patterns occurring in the 99 times tables for single- and multi-digit numbers.

On the other hand, the use of a spreadsheet may be more apt for sequences such as the odd and even numbers where it would be important for pupils to 'translate' their thought processes into an equation. As before, the equation can be tested easily in the spreadsheet and immediate feedback is offered on-screen. By considering a group of related sequences such as the triangular numbers, square numbers, pentagonal numbers, hexagonal numbers and so on, pupils can establish a formula to generate each of these sequences and then extend these results to a higher level of generalisation for the nth-ogonal numbers. An investigation of this nature is clearly more suited to a spreadsheet than to a graphics calculator. Spreadsheets are also more applicable when pupils wish to work backwards in solving a problem rather than using the conventional beginning to end methods. There are certain occasions when working backwards is a noticeably more effective and efficient means of obtaining the answer to a problem, as illustrated in Chapter 9.

Going beyond the norm

Spreadsheets also play an important role in solving simultaneous equations. Using the matrix method, pupils can establish the routine for solving simultaneous equations with two variables. However, it is clear that this process also works with the 3×3, 4×4, 5×5, ... cases too. Therefore, by introducing the built-in function for finding the inverse of any square matrix, pupils can solve simultaneous equations in 3, 4, 5 or more variables with ease. This technique allows pupils to address real-life problems with many dependent variables. By writing the problem in terms of n equations with n variables, pupils can convert the problem to its matrix format before solving it on the computer. Obviously, this is only one example of the power of the computer in achieving objectives far beyond the scope of a normal classroom, but as you become more experienced in teaching, you will develop an insight into other cases.

ICT for organisation

A final resource for mathematics teachers is the internet. A number of websites offer advice, help, ideas and even ready-made lesson plans for the mathematics teacher.

However, it is worth remembering that what works well for one teacher in one classroom does not necessarily suit the needs and style of teaching of another teacher. Nonetheless, it is worth spending some time browsing through these sites, if only for a few ideas of 'mind captures' and novel introductions for your own use. Another useful feature of these lesson plans is the ready-to-use nature of the worksheets or the opportunity to adapt a worksheet to match the needs of your class (in terms of level of language, font size etc.) and the context in which the topic is being taught.

Numerous sites are also available that offer freeware packages to teachers – again, check the appropriateness and relevance of the software before using it with a class. One of the main attractions of the world wide web for mathematics teachers, however, is the huge number and wide variety of interactive sites addressing all aspects of the National Curriculum. These range from the standard drill and practice number skills sites to interactive problem-solving and puzzles, and Flash animations showing a mathematical process. For instance, www.smilemathematics.co.uk/ offers a full range of National Curriculum materials for mathematics where pupils can practise their mental arithmetic skills. Other pupils may wish to focus on assessing their knowledge in Attainment Target Measures and Shape and Space using investigations such as:

- Angle Bisectors in a Quadrilateral at www.cut-the-knot.com/Curriculum/Geometry/CyQuadri.html;
- Pythagoras' Theorem at www.cut-the-knot.com/pythagoras/index.html or www.cut-the-knot.com/pythagoras/pythTriple.html.

Probability may be approached in the context of a simulation of Buffon's Needle at www.cut-the-knot.com/Curriculum/Probability/Buffon.html or using the Random Clock Hands simulation at www.cut-the-knot.com/Curriculum/Probability/Indy.html.

Data handling and statistics sites are located at:

- Census At School: www.CensusAtSchool.ntu.ac.uk/.
- Predictions for world populations in the future: www.sunsite.unc.edu/lunarbin/worldpop/.
- Database of track and field records: www.sci.fi/~mapyy/tilastot.html.
- United States census data as a teacher's resource: www.census.gov/dmd/www/teachers.html.

These websites can be used as a starting point for simple data representation at primary school level (use a subset of the data if necessary) or for working out means, standard deviations and correlations in post-primary maths classrooms.

A range of basic calculus and algebra tasks may be found at Calculus@Internet. Higher-order thinking skills and problem-solving are evident in sites such as The Maths Forum at http://forum.swarthmore.edu/mathmagic/.

More diverse aspects of mathematics can be revealed through fractals, geometry and art such as the Fractal Microscope at http://archive.ncsa.uluc.edu/Edu/Fractal, or the maths aspects of http://artsedge.kennedy-center.org/teaching_materials/curricula/.

For the older students interested in doing some research into famous mathematicians, the website www-history.mcs.st-and.ac.uk/history/ opens the door to biographies on all the famous mathematicians, with separate sections on famous female mathematicians and the most popular biographies.

There are numerous interactive mathematical games and puzzles at www.cut-the-knot.com/Curriculum/index.html and www.funbrain.com or www.primarymaths.co.uk.

Associations such as the Centre for Innovation in Maths Teaching (www.ex.ac.uk/cimt/), the Association of Teachers of Mathematics website (www.atm.org.uk) and the Institute of Mathematics and its Applications (www.ima.org.uk/) all offer an excellent range of resources, teacher materials, newsletters and articles. Primary specific support and online resources for use by pupils can be found at the GridClub (www.gridclub.com) or MyMaths (www.mymaths.co.uk).

Inter-pupil collaboration in an online Maths Club can be encouraged through NRICH (http://nrich.maths.org.uk) based in Cambridge, with separate sites for primary school (PRIME maths) and able (PLUS+) pupils.

For worksheet generators, EdHelper is recommended at www.edhelper.com/ or www.mathbuilder.com/. Some teachers still prefer a good textbook as their fireside reading, so Chartwell-Yorke offer a good selection of ICT resource materials for the maths classroom (www.chartwell-yorke.co.uk).

For additional ideas on how to integrate ICT into your lessons, consult the DfES website for publications such as *Using ICT to support Mathematics in Primary Schools* and *Integrating ICT into Mathematics at Key Stage 3* or use the DfES support materials for the NNS and mini-packs for ICT. Another excellent text is *Teaching Mathematics with ICT* by Oldknow and Taylor (2000).

Task 8.3

During your teaching placements, keep a diary of your use of ICT when teaching. The following headings may be helpful.

Topic	Type of ICT	Teaching style	Benefit of using ICT/ disadvantages	Recommend for future work?
Name of topic or PoS	Internet, CD-ROM, spreadsheet, graphics calculator	Individual, pairs, groupwork, teacher-led, pupil-centred	Going beyond the norm, pupil access, resources	Reasons

Part III

In the maths classroom

9 Using maths resources

Introduction

This chapter addresses a number of different types of lessons and approaches to teaching. They are chosen to exemplify a range of resources and options that you may or may not wish to try in the classroom. The aim of this chapter is to encourage you to experiment with novel ideas when teaching mathematics and to illustrate some of the opportunities for creativity in the maths classroom. As you become more experienced as a teacher, you will adjust and refine these ideas to suit the needs and abilities of your pupils.

Learning outcomes

By the end of this chapter you should have a number of ideas on how to use the following resources in the maths classroom:

- textbooks and pens on whiteboards;
- visual aids;
- generic ICT packages;
- subject-specific software;
- graphics calculators.

Overview

In Parts I and II of this book, the reasons for lesson planning were discussed and the advantages of advance preparation in the light of classroom management, control and achieving content coverage were also emphasised. The importance of being prepared and having all the relevant subject knowledge at your fingertips assists you in maintaining the flow of the lesson and therefore sustaining the pupils' attention. Teachers who are disorganised and have to dash around gathering together all their resources and equipment at the last minute are not valued or respected by pupils. Lack of preparation implies lack of interest in the welfare of your class. Pupils also notice the teacher who has taken the time and effort to put together an effective and stimulating learning experience. Clearly, you will exhaust yourself if you 'put on a performance' for every lesson when you are teaching full-time. However, during ITE you are teaching a restricted timetable, so you should have surplus time and energy to expend on developing such lessons.

Lesson plans

The structure of a lesson plan has already been discussed. However, the following template (Figure 9.1, pp. 120–121) highlights each of the stages and emphasises the need to plan and think through the skills and steps required in the learning process. In keeping with the NNS and Key Stage 3 strategy, each lesson should have three stages: mental maths, main part and a plenary. Chapter 5 made the links between each of these stages and the Stones' heuristic of identifying, remembering and doing (Stones, 1994). In most cases, the introduction to the lesson followed by the presentation phase assist pupils in *identifying* the criterial attributes of the skill or concept being taught. The *remembering* phase is assessed through the use of exemplars and non-exemplars that challenge the pupils to recognise the application of the criterial attributes in an unseen example. The *doing* comes in the application phase when the pupils are asked to complete a particular exercise, worksheet or activity that requires them to practise using the skill or concept just learned. Within the template, you will notice the presence of sections such as resources, prerequisite (or assumed) knowledge, language, numeracy, ICT and differentiation.

Teaching resources

In terms of resources, maths teachers frequently use:

- textbooks, worksheets, coloured pens for the whiteboard or chalk on a blackboard;
- rulers, protractors, compasses, set squares;
- calculators – graphics calculators or calculators connected to the OHP;
- overhead transparencies – of charts, graphs, notes, maps, exemplars and non-exemplars;
- visual aids – nets, blocks, rods, straws, paper shapes for symmetry, three-dimensional solids such as boxes (Toblerone, Smarties tubes, cuboid and cubic boxes from chocolates, pyramids), polystyrene solids cut into fractions, scale models, mirrors;
- digital cameras;
- laptop with generic software such as spreadsheets, databases, presentation, word-processing or computer art packages;
- subject-specific software – NNS packages, CD-ROMs, LOGO or Zeno, Omnigraph, Derive, Cabri-Géomètre or Geometer's Sketchpad and SPSS;
- interactive internet sites;
- sensors and data loggers;
- Integrated Learning Systems.

Language

The literacy or language elements of teaching have already been stressed through reference to the National Literacy Strategy in particular, the importance of learning how to pronounce and spell mathematical vocabulary. In each lesson, teachers reinforce the new terminology in the context in which it should be used and also offer opportunities for the pupils to explain and use these new words too – either in whole-class teaching, group-work or paired work. Both young and old learners should have the chance to practise using new words. Most of these opportunities arise in the Introduction and Presentation phases, and also in the Conclusion when teachers are recapping on the learning outcomes achieved in the lesson.

Numeracy is usually thought of as mental arithmetic in the maths classroom since all classroom work is numerical. By practising and reinforcing pupils' mental maths skills regularly, teachers are assisting in developing pupils' listening skills and their ability to visualise the maths. Depending on the age and ability of the pupils, this mental maths could range from number bonds or times tables, to knowledge of the Pythagorean triples in a context, or simple geometric identities. In most cases, the mental maths activities are revising and reinforcing concepts or subject knowledge covered in the previous lesson and prerequisites of the current lesson.

This chapter emphasises the role of ICT as an integral part of mathematics teaching and learning. A range of resources has already been mentioned, but the list is by no means exhaustive.

Differentiation

Differentiation occurs by ability in the normal classroom. Many teachers have a restricted view of differentiation and only deal with the less able students when preparing mater-ials and considering the usefulness of resources. In keeping with the ethos of the NNS and Key Stage 3 Strategy, gifted pupils need to be given challenging materials to extend their existing range of skills and encourage the use of higher-order thinking and reasoning. Repeated use of 'more of the same' as a means of keeping these pupils working is of little advantage to the more able student – they just become quicker and quicker at the maths being covered in the exercise or task. Alternatively, they resort to misbehaviour through boredom with the mundane nature of the tasks being set.

Ideas for teaching

The remainder of this chapter will consider a variety of maths topics which are taught as part of the National Curriculum. Each topic is categorised by the type of teaching resources used – these categories are used for descriptive purposes only and should not be consid-ered as the 'best' or 'the only way' of teaching this aspect of maths. The following sections will be considered:

- traditional 'chalk and talk' – using textbooks, worksheet resources and a board;
- using visual aids and OHTs;
- using ICT – a laptop, data projector and whiteboard or Smartboard.

The final section is by far the largest since it represents the move towards using ICT as a teaching resource in the classroom in the same way as the overhead projector was the educational technology of the 1970s and 1980s. This final section will be split according to

TOPIC		CLASS		DATE	
POS		TIME		ABILITY	

RESOURCES

PREREQUISITE KNOWLEDGE

LITERACY

NUMERACY

AIM

LEARNING OUTCOMES

INTRODUCTION

PRESENTATION

Figure 9.1 Lesson plan template

EXEMPLARS/NON-EXEMPLARS

APPLICATION

ASSESSMENT

HOMEWORK

CONCLUSION

EVALUATION

the types of ICT or software being described for use by teachers and pupils. In some cases, ICT is being used as a demonstration medium to illustrate key concepts and to introduce or summarise the key learning outcomes. In other cases, ICT is being used as an integral part of the learning process, or as a means of facilitating the students going beyond the maths to investigate examples the pupils could not do using paper-based methods.

Traditional 'chalk and talk' methods

This approach to teaching has been well established through the generations. It is the delivery of a lesson by the teacher with very little interaction with pupils. The teacher talks 'at' the pupils rather than 'with' them and once the methodology has been demonstrated on the board, the pupils are expected to complete many exercises from the textbook to practise and reinforce the new skill. To increase the effectiveness of this approach in the modern classroom, teachers use the board as 'a shared page in a whole-class jotter'. The teacher asks the pupils guiding questions about what they think the next step should be and then completes it on the board, leaving the pupils to focus on the thinking process behind the calculation rather than on the mechanics of the calculation itself. The work is completed as a collaboration between each pupil in the class and their teacher. The feelings of success are shared when the correct answer is reached and the pupils feel a sense of ownership of the mathematical processes that encourages them to adopt these techniques in their own work too.

The majority of lessons you will observe, and those delivered by experienced teachers will use high proportions of the interactive version of this approach as children need to be taught how to represent their thinking process and method of calculation neatly and in a logical sequence on the page. Typical examples of topics taught predominantly in this fashion are basic numeracy skills such as addition, subtraction, multiplication and division, conversions between units, positive and negative integers, logarithms, indices, differentiation and integration. Mathematical skills and algorithms that have a specific, ordered sequence of events and are context-independent are best delivered in this way. These skills can then be applied in a variety of other contexts presented to the pupils in innovative and creative ways. The teachers can also isolate examples of the same type in the textbook from those requiring additional explanations or a rearrangement of the formula. Thus, an incline of difficulty exists in many textbook exercises that needs to be identified by the teacher so that only those examples matching the teaching and learning outcomes addressed in the lesson are set during the application phase of the lesson.

Task 9.1 Working on the board

- Look carefully at the different presentational styles of the experienced teachers.
- Is there a common pattern in how they use the board?
- Do they position a key formula in a dominant area of the board and ensure it always remains visible, regardless of where they are writing?
- Do the teachers group similar ideas together on one side of the board? Are they ordered in any way?
- Where are the key words for the topic displayed?

Use of visual aids

Visual aids impact significantly on the pupils' learning. They may be used for a variety of reasons:

- to capture the pupils' attention at the start of a lesson;
- to engage the pupils in an activity;
- to remind or reinforce rules or results;
- to assist the teacher's explanation of a concept which can be illustrated visually;
- to motivate the pupils;
- to assist the pupils in visualising a mathematical process.

If not overused, visual aids can produce a very stimulating and exciting environment in the maths classroom. In the majority of cases, visual aids are used to offer concrete examples of a process before asking the pupils to move to the abstract notion of working from memory or a textbook. Young children require extensive use of visual aids such as counters, building blocks or unifix cubes, particularly when learning the basic operations of addition, subtraction, multiplication and division. By being able to physically add to or remove objects from a list or group of objects, the pupils can act out the process of addition or subtraction. Similarly, five piles of three objects allow the pupils to visualise the mathematical operation 3×5. By counting the total number of objects the pupils will be able to establish $3 \times 5 = 15$. The reverse action can be demonstrated when illustrating the physical process of dividing a group of 15 objects into groups of 3 objects.

Fractions are another case where moving objects into groups may be beneficial to the younger pupils. For instance, supposing we knew there were 20 people outside an ice-cream shop and half the people in the queue were going to buy cones and the other half would choose tubs. Then we can split the queue in half and count the number of people in each subgroup – 10. As a maths story, this could be written as $\frac{1}{2}$ of $20 = 10$. Visual aids may also assist the pupils in understanding the form of a fraction. If a pizza was split into 6 identical sections, then a whole pizza is written as $\frac{6}{6}$ whereas each sector of the pizza is $\frac{1}{6}$, i.e. one piece out of a possible six pieces.

Symmetry in the form of both line symmetry and rotational symmetry also benefits from the use of visual aids. Whether the shape is a letter, number, picture of an object or a piece of cardboard folded in half and then cut randomly, the idea of line symmetry can be demonstrated through folding the shape exactly in half. Pupils will be able to see whether parts of the shape jut out from underneath or above a side, or whether the shape's edges are aligned and completely smooth. The fold along which the shape is bent indicates the 'line' of symmetry. Using a variety of shapes and objects, the teacher can move from whole-class teaching to groupwork or paired activity, thereby allowing the pupils to practise the process of folding and checking the shapes. Regular polygons and a collection of two-dimensional shapes can also be investigated using this visual method. Mirrors or mirrored cardboard also make an effective way of investigating the presence of line symmetry, particularly of letters, or as a tool in assisting pupils in drawing the 'reflection' of a given half of a shape. Using the same shapes, rotational symmetry can be approached using similar teaching strategies. Pupils can compare and contrast the types of shapes that possess both line and rotational symmetry with those possessing only one form of symmetry. The two-dimensional shapes can be physically rotated on the pupils' tables to see how many times the object fits into its outline. The symmetry of these shapes can be added to the other properties of the shape already learned.

The link between area and volume can also be illustrated visually by holding up a number of two-dimensional shapes and relating these to the cross-sectional area of a selection of three-dimensional shapes. Cubes and cuboids are fairly common shapes for boxes of chocolates and these will make good visual aids to assist your explanation of volume. Smarties tubes and the triangular shape of Toblerone offer easy access to the cylindrical and triangular prism solids, while the shape of cones and square-based pyramids are self-explanatory and already known to most pupils. However, the origins of the formula for their volumes is less easy to explain using the 'cross-sectional area × height' approach of above.

The nets of three-dimensional solids can be investigated through carefully dismantling the above boxes by cutting down the selected sides of the shapes. By working in groups and through the use of carefully planned worksheets, a number of different nets for each solid can be created. This will assist the pupils in visualising the existence of more than one net for each carton. The label from a tin may be used to illustrate part of the net of the cylinder, and relationships between diameter and circumference can be easily labelled. By creating their own nets for shapes with specific dimensions, the pupils will develop their understanding of the relationship between the faces of the shape and the parameters of length, width and height. The nets of closed and open 'boxes' can also be addressed using this technique.

By cutting shapes into equal parts, the pupils can be shown the concept of fractions. The dynamic nature of physical resources allows the teacher and pupils to remove parts of the shape and discuss 'what fraction of the shape' they have in their hand or on the table. The role of the numerator and denominator can be defined clearly using phrases such as 'how many parts out of the whole shape' to represent the idea of x parts out of the available y parts of the shape or $\frac{x}{y}$.

The use of overhead transparencies showing maps of the local area allows a practical illustration of the purpose and use of bearings and measurements to be demonstrated easily and efficiently in any part of a lesson. Clear plastic rulers and protractors can be set on the OHTs so that the pupils can see the process, care and accuracy needed to measure angles and distances. The teacher can ask the pupils to direct an aircraft from town A to town B or send the class on an imaginary mystery tour using only bearings and distances. Once the pupils have mastered the skills needed to use protractors and rulers with accuracy you can ask them to design their own 'sky tours' or to act as a pilot boat navigating a large container ship through a lough of varying depths and dispersed with islands.

Graphs, bar charts, pie charts and scattergrams with missing labels and/or titles allow pupils to hypothesise on the data gathered and to identify key features of the graphs which assist them in reaching their conclusions. Line graphs or barcharts with peaks at 9 a.m. and 3 p.m. may indicate that the data relates to something connected to school, such as the number of people in the street outside the school, the number of cars parked near the school or moving past a particular junction near the school, the number of buses stopping at the bus stop closest to the school, and so on. The pupils may suggest reasons for collecting this data – identifying the need for a crossing patrol, traffic lights or widening of the road. Alternatively, the peaks may coincide with the start of shifts at a local factory or hospital, especially if additional peaks occur at 9 p.m. and 3 a.m. for night-shift workers. By using graphs with information missing, the pupils learn to use the patterns to think about the meaning of the data – to create hypotheses, test them and reflect on alternative explanations. This approach also stresses the importance of labelling statistical representations of data correctly and accurately to avoid misinterpretation.

Probability is often a difficult concept for many pupils to understand. The use of dice, coloured counters or cubes, playing cards and other visual resources will help pupils to experiment and uncover the 'rules' governing probability. Once the basic ideas of probability have been grasped, many teachers use well-known television programmes to show how probability can be applied in real-life situations. Using a restricted set of playing cards, the television show 'Play Your Cards Right' can be used as a role play with the whole class. The teacher can have the cards arranged so that they alternate between high and low, making the probability of guessing 'higher than the previous card' or 'lower than the previous card' relatively easy. The order of the cards is then recorded before a second 'game' is played. This time, the teacher has arranged for the cards to be 'difficult' – lying near the middle of the range or having combinations of cards with low probabilities. Again, the sequence of cards is recorded. Based on their experiences, the whole class can then discuss why one sequence was easier to predict than the other. The teacher can also assist the whole class in working out the probabilities of a 'higher' or 'lower' card at each step, based on their knowledge of the cards already revealed.

There are many other applications of mathematics that can be used in a 'controlled' way to illustrate core mathematical skills and concepts. The numerical activities in the Channel 4 programme 'Countdown' can be adapted for use in the maths classroom as a mental maths activity at the start or end of each lesson.

Task 9.2 Identifying the mathematics in TV game shows

Try to list other TV game shows which use mathematical activities as a core part or a small element of the show. What is the mathematical concept underpinning each activity? Can you use this activity to teach a skill or concept? Can you adapt the activity for use in a 'controlled' way in the classroom? Will the activity highlight a common pupil misconception?

Task 9.3 Identifying the mathematics in sport

All sports events have winners and losers, so measurements must be made to determine the winner. Apart from place value – arranging distances and times in numerical order – what other mathematics are used in sports and how could you use these to engage pupils in the relevant topic? (Consider darts and snooker, for example.)

Using ICT as a tool for teaching

This section considers the use of ICT in a number of topics and also its use as an integral part of the lesson, as a learning experience in its own right and for demonstration purposes. In some cases, the use of ICT promotes mathematics as a body of knowledge, while in other instances the focus is on its use for problem-solving or going beyond the maths normally completed on paper.

To assist the reader, the following sections are grouped according to software. A limited number of examples are offered in each case and the reader is encouraged to consider other uses of the packages, based on the initial ideas provided here. In all cases, it is assumed that a laptop connected to a data projector and whiteboard or Smart Board is available for each lesson.

Using MS Word in the maths lesson

The most common use of Word is the creation and reporting of results from an activity – basic word-processing of information with perhaps the use of tables to record the results. However, Word also possesses a Drawing tool. Initially, this can be used to produce shapes such as regular polygons and label their names and properties.

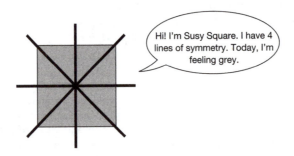

As part of the discussion on transformational geometry (reflections, rotations, enlargements and translations) or on tessellations, a shape drawn in Word can be used as an illustration of each of these aspects of mathematics. For example, consider the following kite shapes – created from right-angled triangles in *Autoshapes ... Basic Shapes* and the *Rotate* or *Flip* options in *Draw*. What types of questions could you ask the pupils about the creation of the shapes? What questions could you ask the pupils related to line symmetry?

Creating the shape:

Autoshape   Flip horizontal   Flip vertical

Once the shape has been created, you should go to *Draw* and *Group* the four triangles so that any subsequent movement of the shape will result in all four triangles moving together.

The kites:

How could you use the Fill Colour to illustrate line symmetry?

Taking each shape in turn, experiment with the *Rotate* facility in *Draw* and think how it could be used to illustrate rotational symmetry of these kites. Using a copy of each shape with the colour changed, it is possible to set each shape on top of the original to check if it is a true match.

In terms of tessellations, it is easy to copy and paste numerous shapes across the page and then use the *Rotate* or *Flip* option to invert them and fill the gaps. Using the *Group* option, the whole pattern can be made into a single entity and then repeated down the page using copy and paste as shown below.

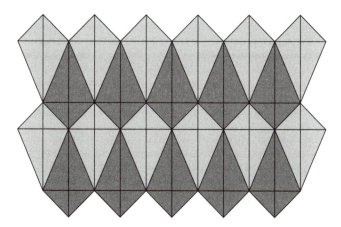

The main ideas in transformational geometry have been introduced at various stages in completing the above activity. Initially, the creation of the shape demonstrated the use of reflection (vertically and horizontally) and enlargements (changing the shape of the lower triangles). The ability to rotate shapes was seen during the investigation of rotational symmetry, while translations were an integral part of the creation of the tiling pattern. By introducing each step gradually and using the appropriate terminology, pupils can experience the geometrical transformations and be encouraged to use the vocabulary as they talk about their work.

The use of ICT makes the investigation of tessellating shapes quicker as it allows more time for pupils to explore a range of different shapes and to decide which ones tessellate and which do not. For example, the pupils can discover which of the regular polygons can tessellate or which pairs of regular polygons tessellate.

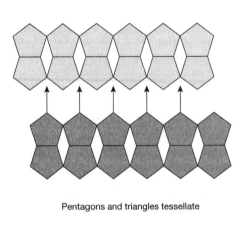

Pentagons and triangles tessellate

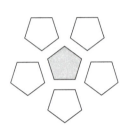

Pentagons alone do not

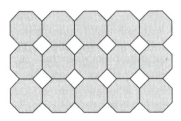

Octagons and squares tessellate

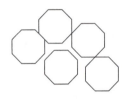

Octagons alone do not

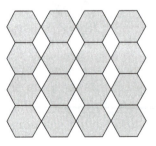

Hexagon and rhombus tessellate

Hexagons alone also tessellate

In the primary school, pupils often use software such as Versatile or Numbers, Words and Pictures. The latter software contains a number of packages, one of which is called Painter. Painter can also be used to create tessellations, except with a higher level of simplicity. By activating the *Symmetry* and *Tiling* options, pupils can draw one half of a shape and see the reflection being drawn simultaneously on the opposite half of the screen. The

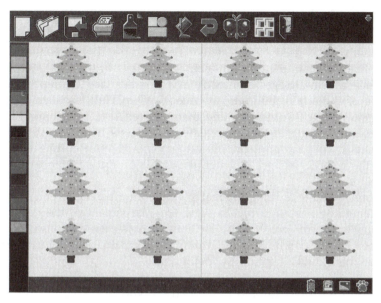

Figure 9.2   An example of a tessellated design

pupils can then use the Colour and Fill options to improve their picture before clicking on the Tiling button. On the first mouse-click, the pupil's image is replicated 4 times; the next click shows 16 images and so on until the pupils have produced wallpaper or wrapping paper with their personal design (see Figure 9.2).

Using Powerpoint for a maths quiz

Based on the Word activity in Figure 9.1, teachers can create a maths quiz using powerpoint to 'test' the pupils' ability to recognise shapes when the properties are listed. Initially, the answers are covered. However, a mouse click can be used to remove the image, revealing the correct answer (see Figure 9.3).

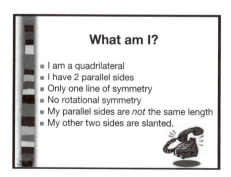
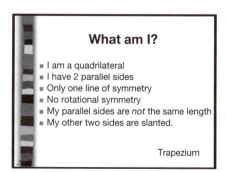

Figure 9.3   Partial revelation in a Powerpoint quiz

Using a digital camera for demonstrations

A digital camera can be used to investigate symmetry and the geometric properties of shapes in real life. For example, the symmetry of bridges in the local area – foot bridges, road bridges and railway bridges, symmetry in a person's face, the repetition of shapes in the appearance of the school building, symmetry when fruit is cut in half, tessellations on wooden floors or brick driveways, and many more. Also, by zooming in on the head of a sunflower and looking at the arrangements of seeds in the centre, or counting the number of florets in a spiral on a cauliflower or pine cone, or cutting an apple horizontally through the middle instead of lengthwise will produce instances of the Fibonacci numbers in real life.

It is not always possible to bring the real example into the classroom, so a picture taken by a digital camera allows all pupils to view an enlargement of the item under investigation and, using a data projector, it also facilitates whole-class demonstrations and discussions. This type of work can be integrated into the normal classroom activity and may be used to capture the pupils' attention by looking at:

- the presence of the Golden Ratio in the natural world;
- the use of rectangles with Fibonacci dimensions in art and architecture;
- the equation of curves that best fit the shape of the bridges;
- the equation of motion of an object being thrown across a playground or sports field;
- line symmetry in people's faces and how looks change if you reflect different sides of a person's face;
- the occurrences of reflections, rotations, translations and enlargements in the structure and architecture of the school building or famous buildings around the world;
- types of symmetry in different fruit – using pictures of different cross-sections;
- identifying the two-dimensional shapes in wooden floors, brick driveways and patios.

In many cases, the use of pictures from a digital camera can be used to engage the interest of the pupils of any age and the novel context can be used to teach the necessary mathematical skills. The pupils can then work on similar real-life tasks, but in a different context to reinforce the concepts.

Using spreadsheets for problem-solving

Spreadsheets for primary schools

Another package from Black Cat software is Number Box 2. This offers a spreadsheet facility with a number of colour-coded levels of sophistication. Depending on the age group and ability level within the primary classroom, different settings can be selected for different levels of functionality. For example, pupils can define the type of data in a cell to be words, numbers, decimals, dates or time; in the graph options, pupils can select between bar charts and pie charts, two-dimensional or three-dimensional representations of the data, and pupils can rotate the direction in which the chart is displayed. The style of both the spreadsheet and graphs can also be changed when the font and font size options are available to the pupils. For the high-ability pupil, simple maths functions and the facility to enter your own formula are also present. It is clear that the functionality of this spreadsheet package can be increased over time to make the step into Excel or MS Works more accessible for the pupils. Quicksheets containing data sets are pre-loaded to illustrate the various uses of the spreadsheets at each predefined level. These also act as a good starting point for the less experienced user.

Using Number Box 2, pupils can analyse and interpret existing data or enter their own data. Graphs can be drawn and the data can be sorted if appropriate. Calculations can be completed by the more able students using Autosum or by entering their own formulae.

Number patterns

All aspects of problem-solving require the production of a general formula that summarises the results. By investigating patterns of numbers, pupils are more likely to recognise a sequence of numbers if it occurs again in the course of their mathematical work. Using spreadsheets, it is possible to generate sequences of numbers and to discover their general formula. The most common number patterns are the natural numbers (n), the even ($2n$) and odd numbers ($2n-1$), followed by the multiples and then square numbers (n^2, where n is the cell reference for the sequence of natural numbers). Building on these simple examples, pupils can be encouraged to create formulae for the triangular, pentagonal, hexagonal, ... numbers and the Fibonacci series.

Problem-solving

Once the pupils can enter formulae accurately into a spreadsheet, they can progress to 'What would happen if ...?' scenarios where a situation is simulated and then one (or more) of the conditions changes. For example, in the next task the pupils set up a spreadsheet that stores information on sales of items of a school uniform. The pupils can investigate how the total cost changes as they purchase different combination of items and also what happens if the cost price increases by X per cent.

The worksheet shown in Figure 9.4 can be adapted to suit different age groups by investigating the cost of running a tuck shop, organising a disco, hiring a sports hall, and more business-orientated activities for post-primary school pupils such as school fêtes and fund-raising activities spanning a financial year.

Spreadsheets can also be used to encourage pupils to investigate monetary systems such as investments and mortgages. Using the example shown in Figure 9.5, pupils can make an initial decision on which option they would prefer before using the spreadsheet to do the long-term calculations. Similar studies on the difference between simple and compound interest can be illustrated via a spreadsheet.

Problems that match the types of coursework currently used at GCSE level can also be completed using spreadsheets. A typical pair of examples of this would be the Sheep Pen, looking for the maximum area which can be enclosed with the minimum amount of fencing, and the Strawberry Box, where the maximum volume is required from the minimum area of cardboard or other box material (CCEA, 2002). Variations on each theme can be added, such as the presence of a wall for Sheep Pen or an open box (no lid) for the Strawberry Box problem. Line graphs can be drawn in the spreadsheet package of the key dimension against the area or volume enclosed. From the graph, the pupils can also zoom in on a smaller range of values and use the spreadsheet to evaluate the answer to

Mr Smart's School Uniforms

Mr Smart runs a shop specialising in schoolwear.

In order to have some prices at his fingertips when customers make enquiries, he has set up a spreadsheet to do some of the calculating for him.

Create a new spreadsheet containing the following items of clothing:

Item	Unit cost
Shirt	8.99
T-shirt (PE)	3.99
Skirt	15.49
Trousers	21.00
Shorts (PE)	4.99
Socks (PE)	1.49

Mr Smart needs two additional columns for **Number ordered** and **Cost**. Work out the total cost for the following orders:

a) 2 shirts, 3 T-shirts, 1 skirt, 1 pair of trousers, 2 pairs of shorts and 4 pairs of socks.
b) 5 shirts, 2 T-shirts, 3 skirts, 2 pairs of trousers and 6 pairs of socks.

You have £75 to spend on your school uniform. You must buy at least one shirt, one
T-shirt, one pair of trousers, one pair of shorts and one pair of socks. Use the
spreadsheet to work out all the different ways you could spend your £75.

Mr Smart has increased his prices by 8% for the new school year. Predict your answers to parts (a) and (b). Use your spreadsheet to check your calculations.

Figure 9.4 Using spreadsheets: 'What if . . . ?' scenarios

A Windfall

Jenny has a rich uncle who is a mathematician. He wrote this letter to Jenny earlier this year:

> Mathemati Cottage
> Money Bank
> Addishire
>
> Dear Jenny
>   Now that I am getting on in years (I'm 70 today), I want to give you some of my money. I shall give you a sum each year, starting now. You can choose which of the following schemes you would like me to use:
>
> a) £100 now, £90 next year, £80 the year after and so on;
> b) £10 now, £20 next year, £30 the year after and so on;
> c) £10 now, 1½ times as much the next year, 1½ times as much again the year after that, and so on;
> d) £1 now, £2 next year, £4 the year after, £8 the next year, and so on.
>
> Of course, these schemes can only operate while I am alive. I look forward to hearing which scheme you choose and why!
>
>   With best wishes,
>
>
>   Uncle Paddy.

Jenny has asked for your advice — which scheme should she choose?

Figure 9.5   Using spreadsheets: modelling growth

Sheep Pen

Farmer Brown wishes to construct sheep pens to prevent his sheep from escaping into neighbouring fields. He has 1200m of wire and four posts. What is the maximum area he can enclose?

If Farmer Brown constructs his sheep pen against the side wall of his barn, what is the maximum area he can enclose?

Suppose Farmer Brown decides to create the sheep pen inside his barn and uses two side walls. What is the maximum area he can now enclose?

If Farmer Brown can use as many posts as he needs, what is the optimum shape of the enclosure?

Figure 9.7   Using spreadsheets: problem-solving using formulae

---

Max Box

An open box can be made from a sheet of A4 paper by cutting out four square corners.

A4 paper is 297mm by 210mm. For a particular corner size, work out the box's length, width and height.

1. You decide to make a box with corner size 20mm. Find:
   - the length of the box;
   - the width of the box;
   - the height of the box;
   - the volume of the box.

2. Use your spreadsheet to investigate boxes of different sizes made from an A4 sheet. What is the largest volume you can achieve?

3. Investigate the max volume which can be created from other paper sizes.

Figure 9.6   Using spreadsheets: simple formulae – area and volume

Forest Fire

The forester's base is 20m from a river.
He spots a fire 100m upstream and 45m away from the river bank.
First he runs in a straight line to the river to fill his bucket, then straight
to the fire. How far along the river should he run to fill the bucket?

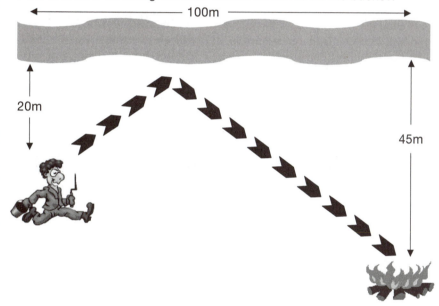

Set up a spreadsheet to help you solve his problem.

What happens if ...

a) the fire is 150m upstream?
b) the forester is 30m from the river bank?
c) the fire is 80m from the river?

Figure 9.8   Using spreadsheets: problem-solving using the sqrt function

BOATS AND AMBULANCES

You are the captain of a ship and one of your passengers has been injured. Your ship is 30 miles from a point that is 60 miles down shore from a hospital as shown in the diagram below. You must order an ambulance to meet your ship at any point along a road that runs parallel to the shoreline. You would like to meet the ambulance at a point that will get your passenger to the hospital in the shortest possible time.

If your boat travels at a speed of 20 mph and the ambulance will average 50 mph, find the distance X at which you should meet the ambulance.

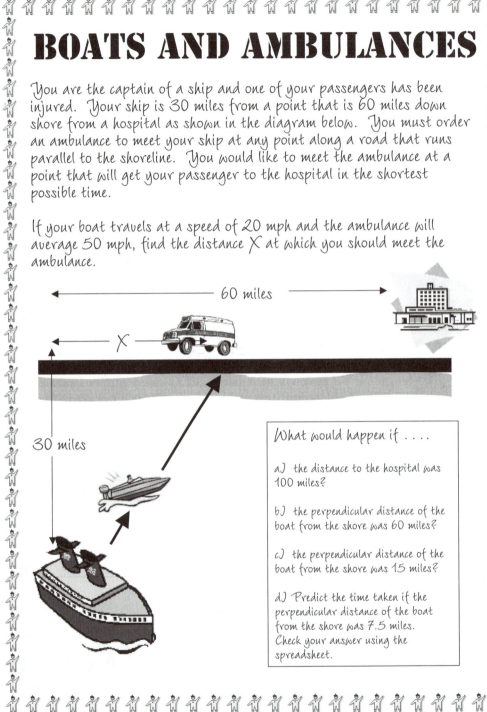

60 miles

X

30 miles

What would happen if . . . .

a) the distance to the hospital was 100 miles?

b) the perpendicular distance of the boat from the shore was 60 miles?

c) the perpendicular distance of the boat from the shore was 15 miles?

d) Predict the time taken if the perpendicular distance of the boat from the shore was 7.5 miles. Check your answer using the spreadsheet.

Figure 9.9 Using spreadsheets: problem-solving using the sqrt and if functions

two decimal places. Discussions related to the accuracy of the manufacturing process will explain the reasoning behind the chosen value for the solution to the problem.

To introduce the use of mathematical functions such as square root (*sqrt*), the Forest Fire task provides a context in which right-angled triangles are used to calculate two key distances. Clearly, the Forest Ranger wishes to reach the fire in the quickest possible time and, assuming that he runs at a constant speed, this problem is asking the students to find the minimum distance.

A similar problem called Boats and Ambulances can also be used as an extension to the above problem, as right-angled triangles are used again. However, two different speeds influence the decision made regarding the point of coming ashore. It is important to remember that the ambulance has to travel from the hospital to the point on the shore before taking the casualty back to hospital, so the landing point depends on both the speed of the rescue boat and the speed of the ambulance. By changing these speeds, the pupils can also investigate how the position on shore changes to minimise the time taken to get to hospital.

Charts

One of the easier features to use in the spreadsheet package is the Chart Wizard. For the younger pupils, the production of pie charts and bar charts can be achieved in a matter of minutes, allowing pupils to experiment with the ways of presenting data to maximise effect and impact. Teachers should offer exemplars and non-exemplars of good and bad practice in the use of charts as pupils are often overawed by the range of options available to them and lose focus on the real purpose of the chart.

Charts showing improvement are usually columnar as this emphasises growth in an upwards direction while growth over time are shown as horizontal bar charts, giving the impression of time moving forward (see Figures 9.10 and 9.11).

The three-dimensional effects are often very appealing to children, so it is important to ask them what the scales mean. If there is a third dimension, what are they measuring and where is the data? The same applies to the use of a variety of shapes instead of the default columns, is it the volume of the shape that has the meaning or the height of the top of the shape? As the teacher, you should challenge the use of the different representations in terms of their meaning and how they can be misinterpreted. Three-dimensional pie charts can also be used to tell a number of stories. Depending on the position of the largest sector, the three-dimensional presentation may magnify or reduce the size of the sector. By looking at the examples in Figure 9.12, you can see the three-dimensional shape is elliptical and not circular, so the front sector has both a width and a depth advantage over the remaining sectors.

Spreadsheets do not distinguish between discrete and continuous data, so it is important for the pupils to be aware of the correct type of graph for each type of information. Correlations can also be demonstrated graphically using spreadsheets. Again, their advantage is the speed at which the charts are generated, so that it leaves more time for the pupils to interpret the information and draw a line of best fit. Pupils can reverse the axes and experiment with different pairs of results looking for other patterns or relationships between variables.

For younger students, pictures can be inserted into an Excel graph which allows the teacher to mimic the production of a pictogram in whole-class teaching (see Figure 9.13).

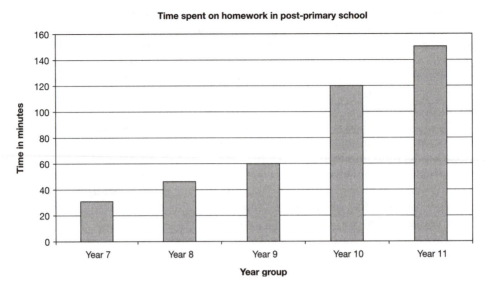

Figure 9.10 Using a columnar chart to illustrate upward growth or increases

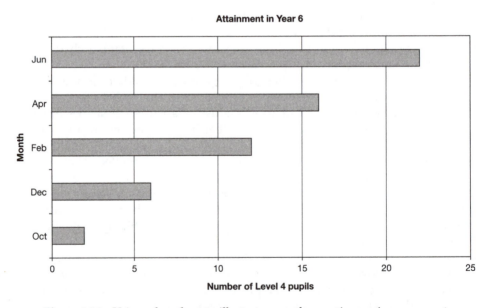

Figure 9.11 Using a bar chart to illustrate growth over time or improvement

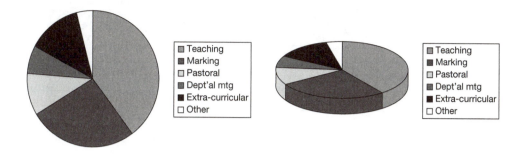

Figure 9.12   Comparing two-dimensional and three-dimensional pie charts

Difference tables

First and second order differences can be simulated in spreadsheets to allow pupils to work backwards and find an error. Once fixed, the remainder of the spreadsheet is automatically re-calculated, allowing the pupils to check that they have the right value. Using Undo will return the spreadsheet to its original state and allow the pupil to rethink his or her approach to the problem. The interactivity and speed at which feedback is offered to the pupils encourages them to remain on-task and highlights any difficulties that may be experienced at an early stage in the learning process rather than at the end when they sit the end of topic test (see Figure 9.14).

Another example of *working backwards* occurs in the Monkey Puzzle problem. It is worth investigating the time and effort required to solve this problem in the order in which it is presented and also working backwards using the knowledge that the solution is a multiple of 3. This task also highlights the fact that there can be more than one solution. How can you represent these solutions as a mathematical generalisation?

Statistics

A number of statistical functions are also present on spreadsheets, so if the aim of the lesson is to illustrate how pupils can distinguish between two sets of data with the same maximum and minimum values and the same mean, the teacher can quickly calculate the standard deviation to show the 'spread' of the numbers in each set. In terms of illustrating the purpose of the standard deviation, without requiring the pupils to understand how it is calculated, the spreadsheet function is ideal. As pupils progress through the mathematics course, more knowledge of statistics will be required, so many of the functions used in the spreadsheet package will need to be calculated manually too. In terms of demonstrating the statistical features, though, the spreadsheet functions are superb for whole-class discussions and revision of key concepts at the end of the topic.

Matrices

Matrices can also be manipulated in an Excel spreadsheet. By thinking of the matrices as special blocks of cells, the pupils can discover the rules governing addition and subtraction of matrices. Using simple examples of matrix multiplication, they may explore the

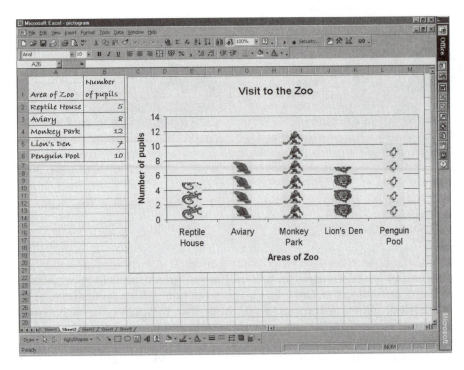

Figure 9.13 Example of a pictograph using Excel

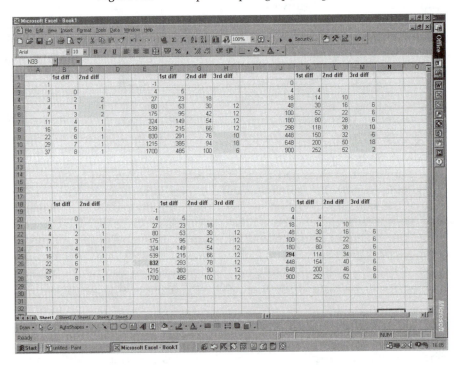

Figure 9.14 Using Excel to support work on difference tables

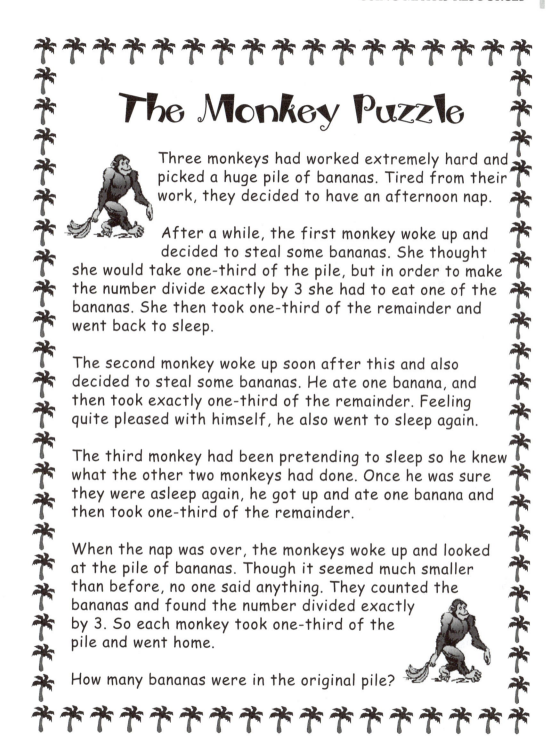

The Monkey Puzzle

Three monkeys had worked extremely hard and picked a huge pile of bananas. Tired from their work, they decided to have an afternoon nap.

After a while, the first monkey woke up and decided to steal some bananas. She thought she would take one-third of the pile, but in order to make the number divide exactly by 3 she had to eat one of the bananas. She then took one-third of the remainder and went back to sleep.

The second monkey woke up soon after this and also decided to steal some bananas. He ate one banana, and then took exactly one-third of the remainder. Feeling quite pleased with himself, he also went to sleep again.

The third monkey had been pretending to sleep so he knew what the other two monkeys had done. Once he was sure they were asleep again, he got up and ate one banana and then took one-third of the remainder.

When the nap was over, the monkeys woke up and looked at the pile of bananas. Though it seemed much smaller than before, no one said anything. They counted the bananas and found the number divided exactly by 3. So each monkey took one-third of the pile and went home.

How many bananas were in the original pile?

Figure 9.15 The Monkey Puzzle problem

relationship between the dimensions of two matrices and the resultant solution of the multiplication and also the rules for multiplying two matrices.

A more useful example of matrices in Excel is when the matrix approach is being used to solve simultaneous equations. Pupils at GCSE and Advanced level will be able to find the inverse of 2×2 and 3×3 matrices and then use the pre-multiplication method on both sides of the equation to find the solution for vector x as shown:

$$Ax = B \qquad A^{-1}Ax = A^{-1}B \qquad x = A^{-1}B$$

As stated, the 2×2 and 3×3 cases can be solved manually on paper. However, using a spreadsheet, it is possible also to determine the inverse of 4×4 and 5×5 matrices using

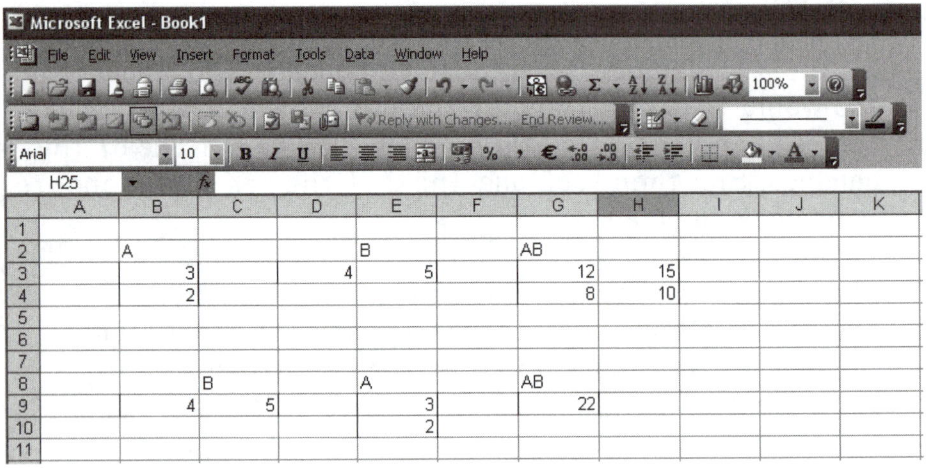

Figure 9.16 Using arrays in Excel to implement matrix algebra

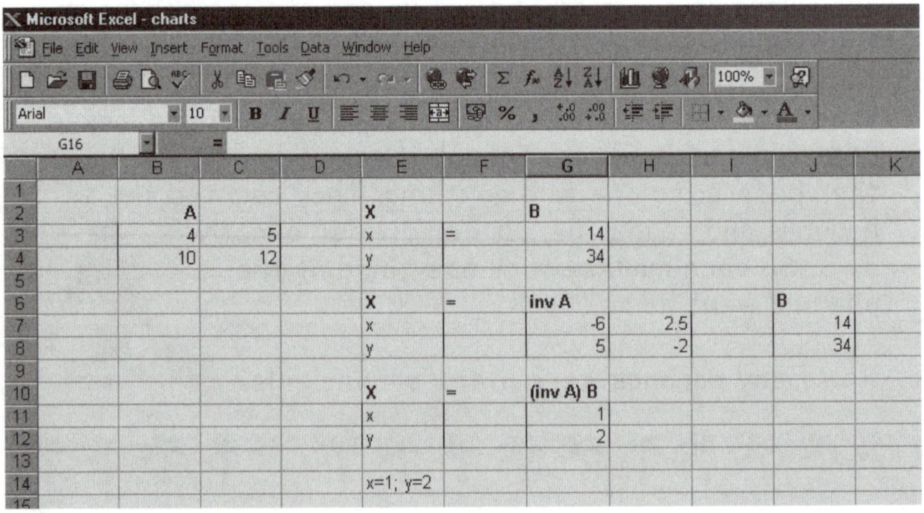

Figure 9.17 Using the matrix method to solve simultaneous equations

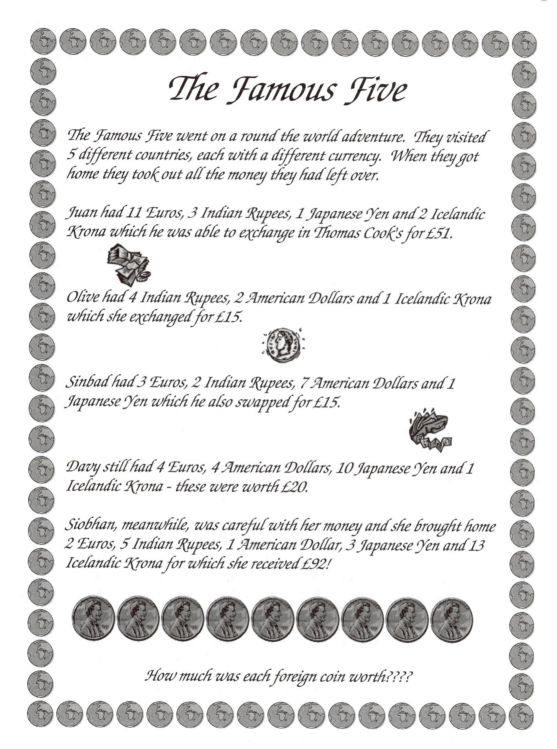

The Famous Five

The Famous Five went on a round the world adventure. They visited 5 different countries, each with a different currency. When they got home they took out all the money they had left over.

Juan had 11 Euros, 3 Indian Rupees, 1 Japanese Yen and 2 Icelandic Krona which he was able to exchange in Thomas Cook's for £51.

Olive had 4 Indian Rupees, 2 American Dollars and 1 Icelandic Krona which she exchanged for £15.

Sinbad had 3 Euros, 2 Indian Rupees, 7 American Dollars and 1 Japanese Yen which he also swapped for £15.

Davy still had 4 Euros, 4 American Dollars, 10 Japanese Yen and 1 Icelandic Krona - these were worth £20.

Siobhan, meanwhile, was careful with her money and she brought home 2 Euros, 5 Indian Rupees, 1 American Dollar, 3 Japanese Yen and 13 Icelandic Krona for which she received £92!

How much was each foreign coin worth????

Figure 9.18   Problem-solving in a context – 5 × 5 matrix

the function *minverse*. Since the mathematical process involved in solving the equations remains the same regardless of the size of the matrices, the pupils can be taken to a higher level of working, dealing with examples from real-life situations. By finding instances such as this, where ICT allows pupils to go beyond what they are normally capable of in the classroom, the teacher is making effective use of ICT as expected and required by 10/01.

Databases for handling data

The basic processes in Handling Data require pupils to be able to sort information into groups. The NNS encourages the use of Carroll Diagram, Venn Diagram and Sorting two-dimensional shapes as ICT support materials in the primary classroom. Other software for this age group includes Counting Pictures 2 (produced by Black Cat) and can be used to introduce the idea of databases at a simplistic level. Teachers can use existing topics and fields to collect data within the classroom – for example, the class database can be restricted to gathering data on pupils' hair colour and eye colour only. Using an interactive white-board and an optical (or wireless) mouse, each pupil can select the data relating to themselves by passing the mouse around the room. The class data can then be sorted and patterns observed using charts.

In more advanced databases, pupils will also use the Sort facility to arrange data in ascending or descending order. Pupils should be encouraged to establish the link between ascending and alphabetical order or increasing numerical order, while descending order is the reverse. The use of searches on single or multiple criteria can be applied to the data when testing hypotheses. The application of criteria will often demand the use of mathematical terminology or symbols such as 'greater than' or >, 'less than or equal to' or <=, and the Boolean operators: *not*, *and* and *or* when using multiple criteria.

Depending on the software package being used, additional information such as mean, mode and median may also be available from the data. Packages such as SPSS offer the full range of statistical approaches. However, this software would only be suitable for Advanced-level analysis in biology, geography or mathematics coursework. The most commonly used database software in schools (aside from integrated databases such as Works and MS Access) is Pinpoint. It comes in two forms, Junior Pinpoint for primary schools and Pinpoint 3 for post-primary pupils. Pinpoint allows the pupils to work through each stage, completing a survey using a built-in facility for creating a questionnaire, electronic storage of the results, a range of analytical facilities and charting options, plus the electronic production of a report that integrates the tables of data and the charts in an editor. The questionnaire design can include a number of different data types as defined by the pupils. When analysing the results, the use of Boolean operators can be used to extract subsections of data for analysis, such as gender or age groups. Cumulative frequency curves can be produced and the median and semi-interquartile ranges can be calculated and included in the report. Bar charts, line graphs and correlations are all available as ways of representing the information and drawing conclusions.

Work of this nature is best completed as a group task over an extended period of time. If linked to a local issue related to the environment, shopping, parking facilities in the town or road safety, there could be a real audience for the final report. Using this approach will allow pupils to design and complete a survey under realistic conditions. By suggesting a real audience for the report, the pupils will be able to take into account the level of language to be used, the importance of accuracy and sound interpretation of facts rather than hypotheses, and the use of a clear structure and presentation in the final report.

Graphs in Omnigraph

The Omnigraph software is often used for introducing graphs to children. However, it is not limited to pre-GCSE and many investigations have been created for use in Advanced-level mathematics. It can be used either as part of a classroom demonstration or for pupil-centred ICT work in the Computer Room. As an introduction to the topic of straight-line graphs, teachers can use Omnigraph to draw a number of graphs of the form $y = n$ and $x = n$ (where n is any number). Based on the features of these graphs, the pupils should be able to answer questions and draw conclusions about the lines. Words such as parallel, horizontal and vertical should be used and a worksheet containing blank axes for the pupils to draw their observations and suggestions for the shape of other lines of the same format will provide a suitable means of checking the pupils' understanding of the main features of the task.

A similar process can be used for lines of the form $y = mx + c$. By keeping m fixed and changing c, pupils will notice that the intercept of the graph and the y-axis changes with c. Next examples can be used where c is fixed and m changes (positive numbers only), so that the pupils see the slope or gradient of the line changing. By repeating the last example with negative values for m, the pupils should be able to predict the shape of graphs of the form $y = mx$ for positive and negative values of m.

Graphs of the form $y = ax^2 + b$ can also be produced quickly and accurately so that the role of a and b can be investigated for positive and negative values. It is quite possible that less able pupils will be able to understand and discuss these patterns as work of this nature is purely observational, requiring only the ability to notice patterns.

The benefit of using ICT for graphing is that it allows the pupils to visualise the mathematical process without spending large amounts of time plotting points and joining them together. The patterns can be viewed easily from the software and the key teaching points can be reinforced through questioning the pupils regularly. The inclusion of ICT in the lesson or series of lessons in this topic offers the less able pupils access to work normally reserved for the more able students or older students. Variations on the sine and cosine functions can also be covered using a visual approach.

Using graphics calculators

The work described in the above section can also be illustrated using graphics calculators. By pre-setting the values for m and c in the example $y = mx + c$, the recursive facility will display a series of lines representing each graph specified in the range using the same axes. Pupils will be able to identify the patterns on the graphics calculators in the same way as they did in Omnigraph. A similar approach can be used for graphs of the form: $y = ax^2 + b$. Dick (1996) highlights the importance of graphics calculators to work within

NINETY-NINERS

Do you know the answer to 6x99 ?   Well, it's time to learn your 99 times tables!

Using your calculator, start entering the following:

        1x99 =   What patterns can you see in the answers?
        2x99 =   1. _____
        3x99 =   2. _____
        4x99 =   3. _____
        5x99 =
Now try   Do the same patterns hold? _____
        6x99 =   What do you notice about 2x99 and 9x99 ?
        7x99 =   _____
        8x99 =   _____
        9x99 =
        10x99 =   Does this happen with any other numbers?
                                        _____

What happens when you choose numbers greater than 10?
Using your calculator find:
        11x99 =
        12x99 =   What patterns can you see in these answers?
        13x99 =   1. _____
        14x99 =   2. _____
        15x99 =   3. _____
        16x99 =   4. _____
        17x99 =

Using your conjectures, write down the answers to:
18x99 =   19x99 =   20x99 =
Check these answers using your calculator.

What happens when you choose numbers greater than 20?
Using your calculator find:
        21x99 =
        22x99 =   Does the same pattern hold? _____
        23x99 =
        24x99 =
        25x99 =

Write down the answers to:
26x99 =   28x99 =   30x99 =
Check these answers using your calculator.

Without using a calculator, can you write down the answers to the following:
42x99 =   55x99 =   97x99 =
68x99 =   84x99 =   79x99 =
What happens when you have a three digit number multiplied by 99?

Figure 9.19   Ninety-niners calculator activity for pattern recognition

a pupil's zone of proximal development through using the technology to remove the tedium and allow the pupil to focus on the higher-order thinking skills.

Whereas Omnigraph was used for a whole-class demonstration and discussion or for individual work in the computer room, graphics calculators can be used on an individual basis in the classroom without requiring the teacher to book additional facilities in advance.

The portability of graphics calculators is a distinct advantage for the maths teacher. In terms of paired or small groupwork, a limited number of calculators can be shared around a class and activities such as work on number patterns can be completed and discussed by the pupils. Instead of asking pupils to compute a number of long multiplication sums, graphics calculators can be used to look for patterns in the 99 times and 11 times tables. Pupils can consider 2-digit, 3-digit and 4-digit numbers in their investigation and the scrolling feature of the graphics calculator tabulates the answers and assists pupils in identifying common patterns in the results. A low level of algebraic notation can be used to generalise the pupils' findings.

In terms of teaching resources, the TI-82 has been one of the most popular graphics calculators for educational research studies. The interested reader is encouraged to consult the 'Supercalculators through the curriculum' website at www.infj.ulst.ac.uk/NI-Maths/CalcMenu.html for exemplar teaching materials currently available in Northern Ireland. Consultation of your LEA materials may also offer additional activities using newer versions of the graphics calculator.

LOGO and ZENO

In the LOGO environment pupils are encouraged to create mini-programs called procedures to move a turtle around the screen. This environment assists in developing the pupils' ability to estimate the size of angles and distances. They become aware of direction and position in the two-dimensional plane and may be able to transfer this knowledge to other situations. A number of micro-worlds also exist that help pupils to develop their problem-solving skills. Black Cat offers a version of LOGO with built-in levels of functionality suitable for use from Reception to Year 6. At the high levels, LOGO offers a simple introduction to programming using a language that is natural to the pupils. Commands (or primitives) such as `forward`, `backward`, `left` and `right`, control the motion of the turtle when distances and angles are included in the command lines.

The Zeno environment encompasses LOGO and extends into topics on the GCSE and Advanced-level mathematics syllabi. It is a windows-based package and the language (primitives) are as natural as those used in LOGO. The language appears on the left-hand side of the screen, while the drawings appear on the right. This format of the display encourages the pupils to look at the 'algebra' on the left and the corresponding 'geometry' on the right. As the commands are changed, the drawings also change. The immediacy of the feedback allows the pupils to learn from their mistakes without waiting for the teacher's assessment.

Like LOGO, the use of variables is introduced when creating simple procedures for drawing shapes. For example, the command `repeat 4[fd 100 rt 90]` draws a square of side 100, while `repeat 4[fd 150 rt 90]` draws a square of side 150 units. Therefore, a general procedure to draw a square of any size may be written as:

```
to square :side
repeat 4[fd :side rt 90]
end
```

The procedure is called *square* and it has one variable called *side*. To draw a square of size 120 units, the pupils would have to enter the command line `square 120`.

The locus of a point dependent on the movement of two other points can be illustrated as shown in Figure 9.20.

The position of the third turtle is the average position of the first and second turtles. By taking each side of the square in turn, you will see only three lines result because turtle1 and turtle2 are moving at the same speed but in opposite directions when the third side of the square is being drawn. By changing the speed of a turtle or the motion of either or both turtles, the pupils can investigate the locus of any turtle relative to two (or more) other turtles.

The notation used for the speed of the turtle introduces the pupils to the concept of vectors. (1|0) denotes movement in the *x*-direction, while (0|1) is the equivalent movement in the *y*-direction. (3|0) and (0|3) would be three times the above speeds but in the same directions – parallel to the *x*-axis and parallel to the *y*-axis respectively. To move at an angle of 45° to the vertical, (1|1) would be the notation used. However, it should be remembered that the speed would be $\sqrt{2}$.

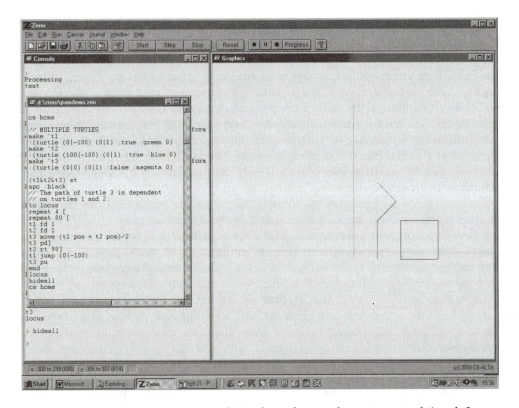

Figure 9.20   Locus – movement of t3 is dependent on the movement of t1 and t2

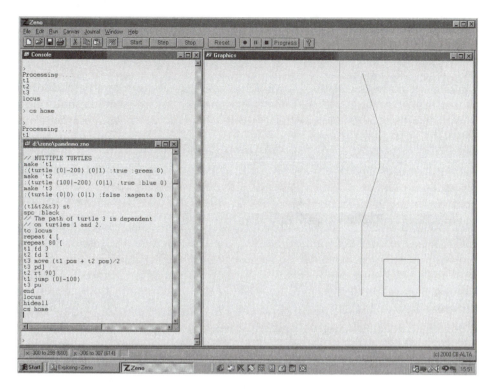

Figure 9.21 Changing the speed of t1 and the impact on the locus of t3

The link between matrices, transformational geometry and complex numbers can be illustrated particularly well using the Zeno environment. The matrix

$$\begin{pmatrix} a & b \\ c & d \end{pmatrix}$$

is written in Zeno as (a, b | c, d) where the | distinguishes between each row in the matrix.

In terms of transformational geometry, five primitives exist – one for each of the transforms: reflection (rf), rotation clockwise (rotateright or rr), rotation anti-clockwise (rotateleft or rl), enlargement (enl) and translation (xl). Each primitive requires more information, which can be summarised as follows:

Reflections: rf (x | y) a shape
　　Reflection of *shape* in the line through the point (x, y) inclined at a° to the vertical

Rotations: rr (x | y) b shape
　　Rotation in a clockwise direction through b° about the point (x, y) applied to *shape*

Enlargements: enl (x | y) s shape
　　Enlargement by a scale factor of s about the point (x, y) applied to *shape*

Translations: xl (u | v) shape
　　Translation by vector $\binom{u}{v}$ applied to *shape*

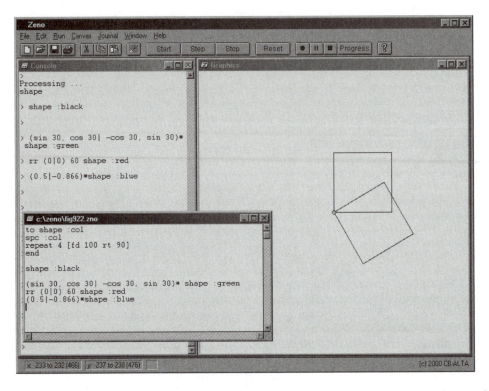

Figure 9.22 Exploring the link between matrices, transformational geometry and complex numbers

The complex number $4+5i$ is written in Zeno as (4|5). The modulus of this complex number can be found using **mod (4|5)**, while its argument results from the use of the command **arg (4|5)**.

The link between these three aspects of mathematics can be illustrated by considering the application of the following three commands to the square called *shape*.

$$\text{The matrix } \begin{pmatrix} \sin 30 & \cos 30 \\ -\cos 30 & \sin 30 \end{pmatrix} * \text{ shape}$$

the transformation **rr (0|0) 60 shape**

and the complex number $0.5 - 0.866i$ applied to shape **(0.5|-0.866)*shape**.

As shown in Figure 9.22, each command results in the same transformation of the square *shape*.

Using computer algebra systems such as Derive

Much of the 'real' algebra surfaces at GCSE and higher levels. However, Derive should not be viewed as a post-Key Stage 3 application. It is easy to use and addresses topics such as factorising and simplifying expressions, substituting values into equations and solving simultaneous equations. The discovery of Pascal's triangle and use of the binomial theorem can be achieved by expanding $(x + y)^n$ for values of n ranging from 1 to 7 and then looking for patterns in the coefficient of each term in the expression and the powers of x and y in each term. Derive can also be used to assist pupils in finding the factors of 180, say, to be $2^2.3^2.5$ or to simplify surds such as $10/\sqrt{5}$ or $1/(a \pm \sqrt{b})$.

The factors of a polynomial can also be revealed using the substitute command.

Cabri-Géomètre and proof

The application of proof can be demonstrated in terms of geometrical constructions using Cabri-Géomètre. As an introduction to Pythagoras' Theorem, this software allows pupils to experiment and interact with the sizes of the squares to confirm that:

The square on the hypotenuse = the sum of the squares on the other two sides

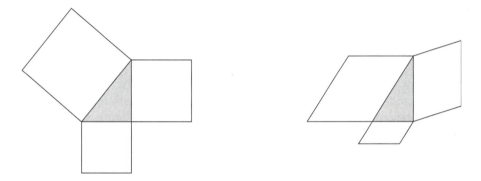

Figure 9.23   Investigating Pythagoras' Theorem

Pupils can extend this investigation to see if Pythagoras' Theorem holds for other quadrilaterals or regular polygons. The dynamic nature of Cabri encourages experimentation and discovery which would not be possible if pen-and-paper constructions were required for each test case.

Cabri also offers an insight into vertically opposite, alternate and corresponding angles when sets of parallel lines are created in Cabri. This work on angles can be extended into the sum of the interior angles in a quadrilateral or any polygon. Further investigations can be found in *Discovering Geometry with a Computer – Using Cabri-Géomètre* by Schumann & Green.

The internet as a teaching resource

For the pupils

The internet offers a variety of resources for teaching and learning. Data sets for use by schools for projects in handling data are available from www.CensusAtSchool.ntu.ac.uk.

The Maths Year 2000 website also offers a selection of games and ideas for teachers, as well as 'edutainment' for pupils. For interactive puzzles and logic games, www.cut-the-knot.com provides a wide spectrum of mathematical problem-solving games and puzzles, including interactive simulations of some of the old SMILE software and also an online version of the coursework task – The Towers of Hanoi. By working online, the pupils can discover recursion as a strategy for the most efficient solution to the problem. The number of blocks on the puzzle can be increased as the pupils refine their problem-solving tactics. The colourful and dynamic appearance of many of the maths sites encourages pupils to view the tasks as fun rather than boring mathematical investigations. Even drill and practice sites for mental maths are presented in an exciting and motivating context – with sky divers whose parachutes open when the correct answer is entered in the box, otherwise they crash into the ground! Care must be taken, however, to ensure that the pupils access only those sites suitable for their age and ability. Many sites will be designed for pupils working at a higher level and should be avoided by younger or lower ability pupils. For primary school children, www.primarygames.co.uk and www.my-maths.co.uk offer a good selection of activities such as a maths version of *Who Wants to be a Millionaire?* to promote mental arithmetic skills. The Grid Club website at www.gridclub.com is designed specifically for 4–11-year-olds and is an excellent resource for teachers, pupils and parents alike. There is a wide variety of activities and challenges for the pupils.

For the teacher

Teacher resources can also be found in a number of sites. The Becta website (www.becta.org.uk) provides an excellent selection of information sheets for teachers and also access to online resources, recommendations and reviews of software, and links to other good sites. School-based websites also provide an insight into the types of activities being completed in other schools and information on worksheets and effective tasks are often available for downloading. Mathematics associations such as ATM offer numerous downloadable resources such as spreadsheet files suitable for whole-class work on topics suited to the 11–16 age group or Flash Films for primary school pupils on mathematical ideas such as exploring halves and tanagrams. The NRICH website also offers a range of valuable resources and ideas for teachers. For teachers wanting to use the interactive whiteboard, MathsNet (www.mathsnet.net/campus/big.html) offers the BIG series of topics that use Java applets to offer interactive geometry demonstrations for shapes, graphs, transformations and various post-16 topics. For the primary school age group, number investigations such as the multiplication table and a cross-numbers task (both using Excel macros) are available on www.interactive-resources.co.uk alongside a number of other predefined whole-class activities designed for use on any interactive whiteboard.

Online versions of paper-based resources

Discoveryschool.com and many of the American websites also offer good starting points for investigative tasks. Mathematics Help Central (www.mathematicshelpcentral.com/graph_paper.htm) offers excellent resources such as a Graph Paper Printer program – so pupils can print out as much dotty paper as they like!

To take a quick and easy approach to creating word searches and crosswords containing the key terminology of a topic, www.awesomeclipartforkids.com comes highly recommended, or you could use www.puzzlemaker.com. Alternatively, you could explore http://puzzlemaker.school.discovery.com, and Funbrain at www.funbrain.com for quizzes that are marked automatically and the pupils' results sent to you via e-mail.

CD-ROMs for maths

A wide range of educational CD-ROMs is available from software houses such as AVP, Black Cat, Cambridge Publishers, Pearson Publishing, Chartwell-Yorke, and many more. Some packages are designed for revision and examination preparation where pupils are encouraged to work through the topics and the software marks, monitors and records their progress. Other CD-ROMs such as Maths in Motion, are better equipped for problem-solving and use with a class over an extended period of time. Skills such as planning, analysing, evaluating and predicting are developed in the context of high-performance cars, while a CD-ROM such as ActivStats offers an interactive learning experience combining teaching and assessment as the topics are completed. Many CD-ROMs are designed for the younger mathematicians and use adventure games in which pupils have to solve clues and complete calculations to move on to the next stage. Quite often, they mimic the high levels of interactivity and high-quality graphics that are typical of PlayStation games.

The role of games should not be underestimated as a learning experience. Pupils are learning mouse skills, manual dexterity, co-ordination and the ability to think quickly and make decisions on the spot. Games also have outcomes, so the pupils can have immediate access to the effects of their quick decisions. It is amazing how creative pupils can become when they cannot master a level and yet want to move on to the next one. Research skills improve dramatically as they try to discover the 'cheats' or password that will allow them to progress to the next level. By continually striving to work at the highest level possible, pupils are actually creating their own 'zone of proximal development' and using the 'cultural tools' of their friends or magazines to get the necessary passwords to assist them in the process.

Industry also sees education as a marketplace for promoting themselves and careers in their discipline. Most recently, the Royal Air Force and Shorts Bombardier have both created CD-ROMs promoting aeronautics as a career through curriculum materials. Since both CD-ROMs are available free of charge, and come with worksheets and educationally prepared teaching materials, the only investment needed from the teachers is time. Maths departments can pick and choose the topics that are covered well and address the Programmes of Study in the most suitable manner. Since there is no investment of money in purchasing this new resource, there is no pressure on every teacher to use it with a class. The RAF materials are more worksheet-oriented and suitable for use after a session on the computer. The Shorts-Bombardier materials take a more interactive approach and require access to the internet to gather resources and follow hyperlinks. The latter CD-ROM is looking at the Flight Experience from a problem-solving perspective – for example, it asks the pupils to re-design the interior of the plane to maximise the seating capacity while still meeting health and safety requirements. The more open-ended nature of these tasks makes them suitable for use as groupwork activities or paired work where work is completed over a longer period of time.

Hyperstudio

Apart from reporting on coursework or completing projects, pupils do not spend a large amount of time communicating mathematically. Much of the oral work in class depends on single word answers, phrases or quoting formulae. Hyperstudio could be viewed as an electronic storybook environment, so would offer an opportunity for young pupils to write about their mathematics or for older students to carry out a detailed piece of research on a specific aspect of maths such as fractals or chaos theory. Using a combination of pictures and descriptions, the pupils create an electronic project book with links between consecutive pages (for a linear project) or cross-referencing to a variety of pages via keywords. The types of projects depend on the intended learning outcomes and the skills you wish to develop. However, the pupils could choose anything from an electronic picture gallery of mathematical shapes to revision pages on mathematical topics. Even the life history of a famous mathematician or scientist such as Pythagoras or Euler with connections to a timeline showing the key points in his life, or an interactive test of misconceptions developed from sets of exemplars and non-exemplars for a topic can be created in Hyperstudio. By creating tests themselves, pupils have to understand and recognise the difficulties and mistakes frequently made by students. In many cases, it is easier to complete this task for a topic covered a year or two earlier in school rather than a current topic.

Mathematics outside the classroom

As described in the section on using digital cameras, it is often more efficient and convenient to bring the outside world into the classroom rather than take the pupils outside. Pictures of the occurrences of mathematics in the environment will focus the pupils' attention on a number of mathematical structures and processes and it may even encourage them to look more closely for their own examples of maths as they travel to and from school.

However, there are some cases where going outdoors is a necessity. In the PoS for Shape, Space and Measures, pupils are expected to create scale drawings, so a quick visit to a particular area of the school grounds, such as the playground, science or technology suite, computer room or home economics room (depending on the age of the pupils) will provide an opportunity for pupils to measure the overall shape of the building(s) and also the interior design and space needed for storage, equipment and resources.

The task can be extended to a real-life context by asking the pupils to make a scale drawing of their bedroom – real or imaginary – design the layout of a supermarket, children's playground or fitness centre to meet a set of minimum requirements. Pupils should be encouraged to visit their local supermarket, playground or fitness centre outside school hours and to gather information about the layout and any health and safety restrictions that may apply, and include these in their plan. In the supermarket, pupils should focus on the positions of perishable and non-perishable foods, refrigerated areas and the positions of the checkouts. The widths of the aisles and the places where queues develop should also be noted. In terms of the playground, the position of swings, climbing frames, roundabouts and slides should be noted. Again, the use of space for the children's safety and parental observation should be highlighted in group or class discussions. For the fitness centre, the location of changing facilities relative to the entrance/exit and the number of different rooms and the users' needs should be investigated. Areas that are used frequently will require easy access and rooms with specialist equipment may need an instructor nearby to offer assistance. Security issues, access for the disabled and fire exits need to be addressed in all plans. For the more able students, three-dimensional scale drawings, including the positions of windows for the interior designs, should be encouraged.

Most of this work will be integrated into the normal classroom activity. However, some aspects may require additional time, particularly if pupils are planning the layout of a public facility. Depending on the age and ability of the pupils and where the appropriate software exists for drawing in three dimensions, pupils should be encouraged to use it. Skills gained in technology and design classes should be transferred to mathematics when appropriate. In the same way, the skills developed in maths should be applied in science and technology lessons.

Sensor equipment and data logging

Most of the sensor equipment resides in the science departments in schools. However, a light gate and data logger would provide an excellent resource for investigating distance–time graphs, acceleration due to gravity or the motion of a simple pendulum. The sinusoidal wave motion of a heartbeat and the use of pressure pads to determine how high pupils can jump are viable uses of the sensor equipment and also interesting activities for both the primary and post-primary pupil. Measurements over time can be recorded and the shapes of the graphs can be justified and explained in the light of the circumstances and context of the work. Limitations may exist in the classroom, so these should be recorded in the findings and conclusions.

Pupils of all ages can work very effectively in 'discovery' mode using this equipment. They can create their own objectives such as 'How do I make the graph go flat?' when it is recording distance against time, or 'What happens to my heartbeat when I have been running?'. Many data-collection opportunities are missed during PE classes, so it may be worthwhile to involve the PE teachers in secondary schools in the collection of real data for a class to analyse and interpret. This may result in the use of a PDA to store sprint times or distances for the long jump.

In the primary school, using a 'circus' of activities for the different measuring devices will allow the pupils to work in groups collecting data and discussing the results after each activity. In the plenary session, all groups can give feedback on their conclusions, and shared outcomes and findings can be explained mathematically. Graphics calculators often come with 'Rangers' that can measure distances within a specified range and record the data. The data can then be shared across calculators and individual analysis completed on identical data sets.

Integrated Learning Systems (ILS)

The ILS seems to be more beneficial for the less able students who have demonstrated the greatest improvements in recent research (Underwood and Brown, 1997). It offers a range of questions of a drill and practice nature to pupils and records their achievements in a Pupil Record System. Areas of strengths and weaknesses are noted and the teacher can gain access to the reports via the Management System. Maximum impact is achieved in those schools that use the system most effectively – regularly and in short sessions. Pupils are motivated by the presentational effects of the software and can view their own progress and improvement that fosters their self-esteem and encourages them to try harder on each subsequent visit to the system. Pupils are also encouraged to take an interest in their own learning, remembering areas where they are experiencing difficulty and doing additional work or receiving additional help in this area before returning to the computers.

Work in this environment is not designed to release the teacher from dealing with these less able students. Instead, it is designed to assist teachers in focusing their time and attention on addressing the individualised needs of the pupil as discovered by the assessment system and displayed in the feedback. A typical ILS system available in a number of primary and post-primary schools is SuccessMaker.

The importance of mental maths

Without regular practice, pupils often 'forget' their basic number skills such as times tables, number bonds and 'tricks' for adding larger numbers together. The properties of shapes and the links between percentages and fractions when calculating discounts and increases in prices also require regular revision. Using Publisher, teachers can create a series of signs for displaying around the room. Pupils can be asked to determine the 'best price' for a particular item by calculating the various discounts available. The ability to compute sums quickly and accurately without the use of paper or a calculator is a basic life skill.

Pupils also need to be able to communicate accurately when discussing numerical issues such as the size of a kitchen, bathroom or bedroom when discussing the design and possible location of the built-in furniture. Even measuring windows for curtains requires accurate reading of tape measures.

Through the NNS and Key Stage 3 Strategy, more attention has focused on the role of oral work in the classroom. Pupils are given opportunities to talk about their work in maths to assist them in internalising the skills and making links across topics. Through interaction with their peers, pupils can extend their own knowledge and understanding of a topic and practise using the new terminology in the correct context.

Conclusion

With the rapid increase in the availability of interactive whiteboards, such as SmartBoards or Promethean boards in schools, DfES has commissioned a range of support materials to be piloted in schools. Maths Alive (supported by RM) is one pilot study that offers teaching materials tailored to the Key Stage 3 Strategy for maths and includes access to the recommended software such as Geometer's Sketchpad and Easiteach. Maths Alive also facilitates a departmental approach to using ICT for teaching and learning due to the ability to create and share resources and lessons electronically. For more information, consult the Maths Alive website (www.mathsalive.co.uk).

For more details on each item of software and its role in the maths classroom, the reader is advised to consult the following organisations and websites for resources:

Association of Mathematics Teachers	www.atm.org.uk/
Becta	www.becta.org.uk/
Chartwell-Yorke publishers	www.ChartwellYorke.com/
Granada Learning	www.granadalearning.com/
Grid Club	www.gridclub.com/
Maths Year 2000	www.counton.org/
NGfL (England)	www.ngfl.gov.uk/
NGfL (Scotland)	www.ngflscotland.gov.uk
NINE	www.nine.org.uk/
Pearson Publishing	www.pearsonpublishing.co.uk
SPA – Omnigraph resources	www.spasoft.co.uk/omnigraph.html

10 Mathematics in the primary school

Introduction

This chapter addresses the content coverage of the mathematics curriculum in the primary school classroom. All references to the use of ICT have been included in Chapters 8 and 9 and are not repeated here. The use of discussions, teacher-directed and pupil-centred activities and groupwork are highlighted in this chapter. For ease of discussion, the content will be grouped by ATs. However, teachers are encouraged to plan their teaching according to the Programmes of Study and it is assumed that the mathematical activities will be addressed in accordance with the requirements of the NNS.

Learning outcomes

At the end of this chapter you should be able to:

- appreciate the role of practical work in primary school maths;
- explain the types of work covered in the PoS for each AT in maths;
- discuss the pedagogical approaches used for teaching primary maths.

Language in maths

Language is often considered the greatest facilitator of learning. However, it is equally the greatest obstacle to learning. For young children, language is a new and often confusing experience. In the early years of school, pupils often use colour, texture, size, shape and the 'normal view' of an object to define particular objects such as a chair, teddy bear or a watch. When the object is a different size, shape or colour from the example already experienced at home or at school, the pupil may say it is a different object. At this stage in their cognitive development, pupils are unable to categorise objects according to properties, but instead group them by appearance. For this reason, mathematical language is particularly important. Words such as heavy, light, small, big, rough, smooth, and so on, need to be added to the pupils' vocabulary. Stories such as *Goldilocks and the Three Bears*, *The Billy Goats Gruff* and *The Three Little Pigs* assist young children in understanding the meanings of these words in a context, as well as helping them to count. Mathematics itself is a language, a means of communicating ideas (Jennings and Dunne, 1998).

The primary school is one of the first places where mathematics as a taught subject is encountered by young people. However, this is only the beginning of a long journey in the development of mathematical knowledge and enquiry. As a result, the primary school teacher needs to be aware of his or her role in the overall process of learning mathematics so that the core ideas that will be needed in later years will be firmly established at an early stage. The goal of the teacher is to apprentice children in mathematical language, symbolism, meanings and ways of thinking (Lerman, 1998).

Number and algebra

The PoS identifies four main areas for consideration: Using and applying number, Numbers and the number system, Calculations, and Solving numerical problems. Within each of these areas are a number of subcategories that offer continuity in the approach to teaching mathematics across the Key Stages. For example, in Using and applying number, the teachers are encouraged to focus on the three domains of problem-solving, communicating and reasoning. The depth and breadth of study is determined by the variety of pedagogical approaches adopted by the teacher, such as using practical activities, setting work in a real-life context, using ICT or calculators, and cross-referencing mathematical ideas in other subjects.

A vital part of the teaching process is to encourage and engage pupils in mathematical communication – sharing ideas, talking about mathematical concepts, using active learning or discovery approaches and many more. Chanting or singing songs are the most common form of mathematical communication in the early years of education, and are a good means of ensuring that all pupils experience a feeling of success. If the whole class is engaged in the chanting process, mistakes are not usually heard and the pupils learn from their peers and the teacher in a non-threatening environment. Counting forwards and backwards using songs and rhymes such as '1, 2, 3, 4, 5, once I caught a fish alive' and 'Ten Green Bottles' evoke a sense of fun and enjoyment in the maths classroom. Singing in this informal way leads to memorisation which opens the door to the written work based on the 'learned' material. Steady progression accompanied by increased levels of confidence and ability are easily secured using this approach. Chains of meaning (Walkerdine, 1988) can be introduced by counting on your fingers with young children, which offers concrete examples of the name of the number (two), an icon (two fingers) and the associated symbol (the digit 2). Using this strategy, the pupils can be introduced to the number system and its meaning before moving towards calculations.

The memorisation of number bonds and times tables assists pupils' development of mental arithmetic skills and, once internalised, it also frees up the working memory to concentrate on the additional higher level skills and concepts being taught. Askew and Wiliam (1995) stress the importance of 'knowing by heart' and the ability to 'figure out' using deductive reasoning. Pupils who can use both strategies progress more in mathematics. An over-dependence on counting methods limits pupils' development of deductive skills.

Automaticity also results from chanting and rote learning. Think which one of the following calculations is easier for you: 7 + 7 or 7 + 8? Doubles are rote learnt in the majority of schools, so most children will automatically recall the first one as 14, but are highly likely to look at the second sum and say, 7 and 7 are 14, add on 1, makes 15. They will 'see' the double and work from there. The same applies to number bonds adding to multiples of 10. Most children recognise 2 + 8 = 10, so when they are asked what 52 + 28 is, they will mentally rewrite this as 52 + 8 + 20 to get 80. Being able to use number bonds in this way for addition is an important part of understanding the number system (Thompson, 1999; Anghileri, 2001). Mental strategies such as partition and recombine in the case of 'near doubles', or for 'bridging through 10', should be encouraged by primary school teachers. As part of the main section of the lesson, teachers may wish to use flashcards to develop and enhance pupils' powers of identification of 'sums to 10'. In terms of explaining the sum 52 + 28, the NNS encourages the use of the Empty Number Line to illustrate the process of partition and recombine:

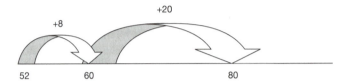

Oral work plays a role in understanding the language of mathematics in terms of the logical structure and sequence inherent in place value. By simply encouraging young children to count 'normally' with the suffix hundred, thousand, million, you can illustrate the structure of the digits in larger numbers. For example, one hundred, two hundred, three hundred, and so on can be easily grasped by the youngest pupils who know the number sequence from one to nine. Flashcards can be used to make the link between the spoken words and the actual numerical appearance of the numbers, thereby activating the auditory and visual learners (Gardner, 1993). Even addition in hundreds, thousands and millions can be achieved once simple number bonds have been committed to memory. Children who know that 2 + 3 = 5 will be able to say that 200 + 300 = 500. The same applies to other addition problems where the structure of the number can be reinforced – for example, two hundred plus fifty-seven is two hundred and fifty-seven or eight hundred and twenty plus three is eight hundred and twenty-three:

$$\boxed{200} + \boxed{57} = \boxed{257}$$

$$\boxed{820} + \boxed{3} = \boxed{823}$$

Subtraction can be treated in the same way – four hundred and fifty take away fifty is four hundred, or seven hundred and thirty-two take away thirty is seven hundred and two. Again, the logical pattern of the number is considered and the decomposition of the digits into the hundreds, tens and units is used to make oral work easy. Using calculators, pupils can be encouraged to 'zap' the digits by subtracting the hundreds, tens and units.

Alternatively, flashcards showing the addition and subtraction problems accompanied by separate cards giving the answer can be used for paired work to reinforce the whole-class teaching. By building on multiple addition problems teachers can facilitate the discovery of the associative and commutative laws by the pupils.

When the same number is added repeatedly, the concept of multiplication can be introduced and with additional practice, the commutative laws are uncovered in this area of mathematics too. Sometimes children understand multiplication as an array of dots. For example, 4 × 2 can be represented as shown:

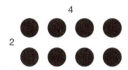

The pupils can then count the total number of dots in the array. This technique can also be used for multiplication of larger numbers when combined with the 'partition and recombine' rule:

32 × 54 =	50	4		
30	1500	120	=	1620
2	100	8	=	108
				1728

Division is usually represented as a 'sharing' or a 'grouping' process. For example,

8 sweets are shared among 2 children.
How many sweets does each child get?

Diagramatically, the 'maths story' can be illustrated as follows:

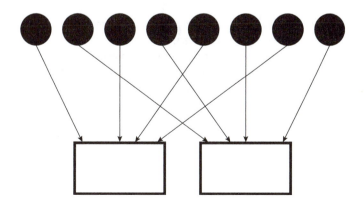

using the 'One for you, one for me' strategy to share the sweets. Alternatively, the pupils may ask, 'How many 2s are there in 8?', resulting in a grouping of 2 sweets at a time:

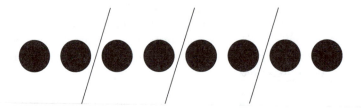

Finally, the Dutch 'chunking' method of repeated subtraction may be used.

Even as the pupils progress up the primary school classes, oral work still remains the first aspect of learning new skills in mathematics, whether it is fractions, decimals, percentages or even the properties of two-dimensional and three-dimensional shapes. If pupils cannot use the language of mathematics, they cannot communicate their ideas with others.

Maths stories

Once the chanting phase has been completed and the pupils understand the sequence of numbers to 20, the next stage is normally maths stories. A maths story requires the use of the correct mathematical operator to represent words such as 'add', 'add on', 'plus', 'subtract', 'take away', 'take' and so on. For example, pupils learn to write $3 + 5$ when a teacher says 'three add five' or $7 - 2$ whenever they are told 'seven take away two'. The chanting process and the maths stories often occur hand-in-hand as the pupils progress up the classes, so that the visual links are made with the words and the new terminology is associated with the new skill. Once the pupils have demonstrated individual mastery of the maths stories, teachers introduce real problems where pictures are used to represent the context of the maths story, such as the following example:

> There are eight houses, two are painted red and the rest are painted blue. How many blue houses are there?

These real problems can be extended as the pupils become more competent at the work, until the teacher reaches the stage where real-life problems are being used in the class-room. Problems of this type are like comprehension tasks where the pupils are required to extract the information from a few sentences and carry out calculations. Work in this format develops the pupils' thinking and reasoning skills, as well as continuing to rein-force the language of maths.

Challenging intuitive rules

Pupils do not arrive at school as 'a blank slate' (Bruner, 1996) with no prior knowledge of number systems. It is important to establish the starting point for each individual in the classroom so that assumptions regarding the existence of the necessary prerequisite knowledge are not ill-founded. Very often, pupils have created their own techniques for 'doing maths' such as counting the number of squares in a shape to determine its area. This method is likely to work for the majority of cases experienced in the early lessons on area that would leave the child reluctant to adopt a new approach of using a formula such as *area = length × breadth*. Why should a pupil reject his or her tried and tested method for something a teacher finds useful but seems to be much harder to do? Very often pupils continue to use their childish approaches long after more sophisticated techniques have been taught (Bruer, 1997). The only way to alter the pupils' method is by challenging their rule and demonstrating that it can fail. For instance, supposing the shape was still a rectangle, but measured 3.2 cm by 6.5 cm. How would the child count the squares now? In this case, the pupils couldn't 'take a bit from here and put it over there' to create a full square. Therefore, the pupils have to resort to the teacher's formula as this is their only alternative.

By building on examples such as this one with decimals, the pupils will become dependent upon the teacher's formula more than on their own methods and over time they will forget the 'counting the squares' approach as it is only suitable for particular cases. This strategy of challenging the pupils' 'rules' is not peculiar to area; it also applies to a variety of other topics addressed in Chapter 7.

Same value: different appearance

A second key idea in maths introduced in the primary school is that of '*keep the value: change the appearance*' (Jennings and Dunne, 1998). A first illustration of this idea occurs in number bonds when a teacher explains that $1 + 2 = 3$ and $2 + 1 = 3$. By introducing a large number of these examples, the laws of addition and multiplication can be shown to be commutative and also associative. Another occurrence is in the decomposition method of subtraction where pupils rewrite 34 as twenty fourteen in the following calculation:

$$
\begin{array}{r} 3\,4 \\ -\ 8 \\ \hline 2\,6 \end{array}
\qquad
\begin{array}{r} 20\ +\ 14 \\ -\qquad\ \ 8 \\ \hline 20\ +\ \ 6\ =\ 26 \end{array}
$$

The representation of fractions is another illustration of *keep the value: change the appearance* as pupils are often required to rewrite fractions in their lowest form or to take a common denominator before adding unequal fractions. Some examples of the application of this are:

$$
\frac{3}{12} = \frac{\triangle}{4} = \frac{6}{\triangle}
\qquad
\frac{1}{4} + \frac{1}{8} = \frac{2}{8} + \frac{1}{8} = \frac{3}{8}
\qquad
\frac{1}{4} + \frac{1}{5} = \frac{5}{20} + \frac{4}{20} = \frac{9}{20}
$$

A natural progression is the link to mixed numbers where pupils learn to recognise that

$$
\frac{5}{2} = 2\frac{1}{2}
\qquad
\frac{8}{3} = 2\frac{2}{3}
\qquad
\frac{30}{7} = 4\frac{2}{7}
$$

The final use of *same value, different appearance* occurs when percentages and decimals are introduced as special cases of fractions. Using flashcards, pupils can match the fraction, decimal and percentage as shown:

$$\frac{4}{10} = 0.4 = 40\% \quad \text{and} \quad \frac{8}{100} = 0.08 = 8\%$$

This matching process also highlights the interconnectedness of maths which is a key element of effective maths teaching (Askew *et al.*, 1997; Thompson, 1999).

Finally, representing information graphically, a maths story such as $x + y = 16$ can be found using the logical and structured approach of a table of values for x and y and then plotting these answers on a graph:

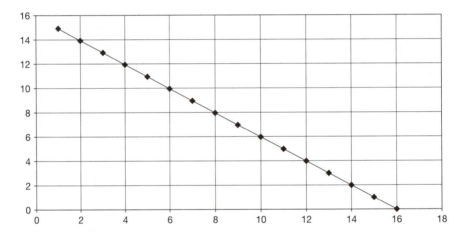

Chapter 7 on misconceptions reveals the pupils' misunderstanding of the points on the line not represented as ♦. Students tend to 'see' only the integer values as solutions of $x + y = 16$ (Hart, 1995).

Algebra can also be introduced in the early stages of learning without too much attention. For example, if teachers say that x and y represent any two numbers like those in the number bonds for 10 – e.g. $1 + 9, 2 + 8, 3 + 7$ – and so on, then the children will easily recognise a table (such as the one shown below) showing the headings x, y and $x + y$ as just representing a set of additional problems.

x	y	$x + y$
1	3	
6	4	
2	5	
3		7
4		9
3	5	
4	8	

The idea of inverse operations is also introduced through this tabular approach. For example, in row 4 in the table on the previous page, the teacher will encourage the pupils to say 'what do I have to do to 3 to get an answer of 7?' Questioning of this nature encourages the pupils to *count on* rather than subtract 3 from 7 or count back. Young pupils will quickly accept this notation and will be 'prepared' for algebra at a higher level with minimal fuss.

A similar approach can be taken for the other three operators – subtraction, multiplication and division. Again, links to the inverse of each operation are made with ease.

Positive and negative numbers

The final aspect of Number requiring careful attention from an early stage is the manipulation of positive and negative numbers. In many cases, a temperature scale is used to demonstrate the addition and subtraction process. However, this often adds to the pupils' confusion as a *change* in temperature is discussed, which also uses positive and negative signs. By working on distances above and below some base level, such as the ground or sea level, pupils seem to be clearer on the use of the $+$ and $-$ sign. By building on the strategy used for number bonds adding to 10, pupils are encouraged to look for instances of numbers adding to zero and then determining the amount above or below this zero level. For example, $-20 + 32 = -20 + 20 + 12 = 0 + 12 = 12$ or $7 - 12 = 7 - 7 - 5 = -5$. When both numbers are positive or both are negative, the pupils appear to be able to 'visualise' the distances extending upwards or downwards from zero.

Again, the Empty Number Line can be used to illustrate and explain these calculations:

$-20 + 32$

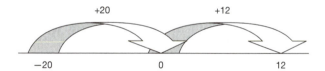

and

$7 - 12$

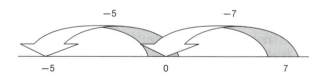

In the context of geometry, *keep the value: change the appearance* is used to demonstrate the link between Number and the area of a rectangular shape. The pupils will know that $3 \times 4 = 12$ and that $6 \times 2 = 12$, so two separate grids can be shown to have the same area if the length is multiplied by the breadth. From this, pupils can experiment with a number of 'pairs' of grids where the area remains constant but the appearance changes. By establishing patterns of this form, pupils will make the link with the algebraic notation $A = l \times b$.

A number of tiling patterns can also be investigated to find the patterns of coloured tiles or the number of straws to produce a shape.

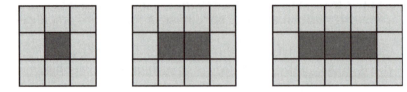

Measures

In the Programmes of Study, Shape, Space and Measures are grouped together as a single unit. Like Number and Algebra, there are four main subsections: Using and applying shape, space and measures (with the three themes of problem-solving, communicating and reasoning as before), Understanding properties of shape, Understanding properties of position and movement, and Understanding measures. This section of the chapter will focus on 'Understanding measures' and its breadth of study.

All measurement requires a scale. The concept of a scale can be introduced in terms of the pupils' choice of arbitrary unit (such as a footstep or pace, a handspan, or the height of a person, e.g. teacher). Measurements can then be made in terms of whole 'units' or perhaps parts of 'units'. For example, the pupils' desks may measure 6 hands by 9 hands. Once the pupils have grasped the idea of measuring a selection of objects using the same units, the teacher can move on to introducing the 'conventional unit' of a metre ruler. Parts of this standard measurement can be discussed and labels given to each of the 100 divisions – centimetres. Links can be made to literacy by discussing words like century, centipede and cents in US dollars or Euros, all of which have a link to the number 100. Pupils are therefore more likely to remember that 100 cm = 1 m and not the reverse.

Physical measurement

One of the common mistakes made by younger children (and often taken into secondary schools) is not knowing how to line up the zero mark on a ruler with the start of the line to be measured (Hart, 1995). It is important to distinguish between the ruler – a piece of wood or plastic – and the scale – a series of marks denoting particular measurements. A plastic ruler used with an overhead projector is an ideal way to illustrate the process of lining up the end of a line with the zero mark on the ruler. Only through a clear demonstration followed by individual practice will a child internalise the correct usage of a ruler. Similarly, the interpretation of each of the 'divisions' marked on the ruler must also be addressed and the need for accuracy and precision emphasised on a regular basis. Most of the problems that occur in reading a more complex measurement stem from an incomplete understanding of decimals. Pupils may be familiar with 6.5 cm being halfway between 6 cm and 7 cm, but they may not be able to transfer this knowledge when faced with a scale showing divisions of 0.01.

Once a clear understanding of units such as cm has been established, then pupils should be able to progress to units for areas (cm^2) and volumes (cm^3).

Angles and directions

In addition to distance, a second form of measurement also needs to be introduced and that is direction. Pupils should be introduced to the idea of turning, clockwise and anti-clockwise, through a particular angle. Full turns, half turns and quarter turns can be acted out in the classroom, both in a clockwise and an anticlockwise direction. This is particularly important for kinaesthetic learning (Gardner, 1993). Links can be made from this activity to the directions on a compass and the angles of 90°, 180°, 270° and 360°. The multiples of 45° and the labels for NE, SE, SW, NW can be addressed next before moving on to consider how to measure any angle. The use of a protractor may be taught in the same way as the use of a ruler. Using a clear plastic protractor on an overhead projector, the teacher can show the pupils how to line up the zero with one arm of the angle and then read off the angle using the outer or inner scale as appropriate. In most cases, teachers will measure the acute angles first, then the reflex angles (360° acute angle) and finally the obtuse angles. Again, reinforcement of the correct procedure through practice is a requirement for using these physical resources with accuracy. Typical activities may include role-play as a pilot of a plane or a ship using simplified maps of the local area. Alternatively, the more able students may be able to create a treasure hunt, giving the list of clues as directions.

Time

Reading the time can be introduced through the use of a clock (without batteries) so that the hands can be moved to any position. Like movement, full turns of one hour are usually discussed first, followed by the half and quarter turns of half past the hour and one quarter past or one quarter to the hour. Time is often referred to in the context of the child's day – what time they get up, go to school, have lunch, go home from school, go to bed. By having laminated cardboard or plastic models of a clock for each pupil, whole-class discussions on time can be completed, with the pupils positioning the hands to the appropriate time and then holding their clock up for the teacher to see. By using digital and analogue clocks, the vocabulary associated with time can be reinforced. Practical activities in PE and Science can be used to supplement the learning through the introduction of stopwatches to measure time to the nearest second. Conversions between the 12-hour and 24-hour clock can be achieved through discussion of timetables for trains and buses. Planning a trip is often the most enjoyable way of developing skills in this area while allowing for differentiation by ability in the groups. Number patterns of the seconds and minutes in multiples of an hour also make for an interesting activity. For whole-class teaching using the interactive whiteboard, an interactive clock can be found at http://arcytech.org/java/clock/index.html.

Graphs

The final type of measurement made at primary school is that of reading information from graphs – conversion graphs and distance–time graphs being the two most common ones at this stage in the National Curriculum. The concept of continuous data is addressed through the use of conversions between temperatures in °F and °C, exchange rates from pounds (sterling) to Euros or US dollars in the context of holidays or for finding infinitely many solutions to equations such as $x + y = 10$. Many pupils think that plotting points on a graph automatically means that these points can be joined together, so instances in which it does not make sense to join points should be illustrated at this stage so that pupils stop and think what the line between the two points actually means. Typical examples of not joining the points are when converting from British to American clothes sizes, investigating the class profile of the number of correct responses to each item in a test, plotting pupils' heights against their shoe sizes, and so on. Terms such as discrete and continuous data can be introduced if appropriate. Using scenarios based on holidays will provide a reason for pupils to read information from both the temperature and exchange-rate conversion graphs.

Distance–time graphs for simple journeys are often used in the upper years of primary school. In most cases, the time intervals are in hours to assist the pupils in interpreting the meaning of each of the stages in the graph. Used as a whole-class discussion, the pupils can develop their oral communication skills and mathematical reasoning when interpreting steep inclines and flat plateaux in these graphs. Ideas of constant speed and being stationary for a period of time may allow pupils to speculate what is happening during the journey – being on a motorway, sitting in a car park, a train stopping at a station, and so on. As long as the pupils recognise that these are hypotheses and nothing more, the teacher can encourage this form of creativity. Other forms of graphs will be discussed in the section on Handling data (see p. 170).

Shape and space

The Shape and Space Programme of Study offers an opportunity for pupils to use their imagination. Initially, pupils are encouraged to hold a variety of shapes, using their sense of touch to feel whether they are flat and to assist them in counting the number of straight edges and faces on the shape. Pupils are also using their sense of sight to visually absorb the appearance of the shape – the number of edges and number of angles in the shape as well as determining whether it is a flat (two-dimensional) or a solid (three-dimensional) shape. Through this close visual inspection of the shape, the pupils learn to identify differences between shapes and therefore to call them different names. With help from the teacher, pupils are encouraged to identify and also describe shapes using the correct terminology. Phrases such as a regular shape, parallel sides and right angles become part of the pupils' vocabulary when talking about shapes and, as time progresses, the use of diagonals and symmetry is also incorporated into discussions.

Identifying shapes

Pupils love to play games, so being a detective and using clues to guess the name of a shape may be used to engage the whole class in a learning activity. The teacher can began by playing lucky dip and choosing a shape from a box or bag. Without letting the pupils see the shape, the teacher then describes what she can feel – whether the shape is flat or a solid, the number of straight edges or sides, the number of angles and whether they are right-angles, the shape of the surfaces on a three-dimensional shape, and so on. The pupils have to visualise all the information to try to 'picture' in their minds the shape the teacher is holding behind his or her back. When all the clues have been given, the pupils can then guess the name of the shape. As the pupils become more proficient in guessing, the teacher can allow them to ask the questions to find out information about the shape or a pupil can play the role of the teacher responding to the questions from the class.

Using flat shapes initially allows the pupils to build up the sequence of questions and focus on a restricted set of names of shapes. Pupils can also work in pairs repeating the process and practising the use of the new terminology. They can also work backwards from the name of the shape to a list of its properties that emphasises the elegance and economy of the mathematical language – one six-letter word such as 'square' creates a list of over six properties! All representations of the shapes need to be highlighted so that pupils recognise a generic term such as triangle compared to a more specific example such as isosceles or equilateral. Similarly, they should appreciate that the word 'quadrilateral' encompasses parallelogram, rectangle, square, rhombus, kite and trapezium. Pupils need to be able to use the word that 'best describes' the shape – the one that offers maximum information. Using drinking straws, the teacher can work with the whole class as individuals, asking them to create a quadrilateral with no lines of symmetry, an isosceles triangle or a quadrilateral whose diagonals bisect at right angles on their desks. Informal assessment through observation will identify those pupils who require additional practice and the pupils who have mastered the language and properties of the shapes.

Creating shapes

Logo is often used to draw the regular shapes as it demonstrates the pattern between the number of sides in the shape and the exterior angle. Pupils can also investigate tessellations (tiling) through repeated drawing of the shape and the introduction of the idea of reflection or translation. Using ICT in this way allows the pupils to focus on the mathematics and not the drawing of the shape. More time is available for investigating different shapes as the drawing has been automated. Pupils will discover that some shapes tessellate (rectangles, squares and triangles) while others do not (pentagons). They may also discover that certain pairs of regular shapes tessellate (octagons and squares).

Once pupils are familiar with the two-dimensional shapes, they can use this vocabulary when they are talking about the solids. By applying their knowledge in another context, the pupils are reinforcing their understanding of each mathematical label. Finally, the pupils are encouraged to visualise what happens when shapes are cut along their diagonals, two-dimensional shapes first and then three-dimensional shapes. It may be necessary to have a number of shapes already cut so that the teacher can show the pupils what they should be imagining – particularly for the three-dimensional shapes.

The use of the co-ordinate system can also be achieved through fun activities such as adding a point to complete the shape on a grid of squares or playing detective and joining a series of points to produce a picture of a cartoon character or animal. A number of interactive websites offer games using co-ordinates in the first quadrant initially, moving to the other quadrants at the higher levels – for example, Connect 4 and Connect 5 (a game for two players) at www.mymaths.co.uk and follow the link to Games, and www.oswego.org/ocsd_web/games/BillyBug2/bug2.html where the pupils have to insert the correct co-ordinates to make the bug move to the food.

Handling data

The Programme of Study for Handling data at Key Stage 2 is composed of these topics: Using and applying handling data; and Processing, representing and interpreting data. The breadth of study suggests the integration of integer and non-integer values for the data, approximation and estimation, patterns and algebraic ideas, practical activities and context or other subjects as the basis for the problem-solving, the use of ICT and calculators for storing and representing the data in alternative formats.

Handling data is a clear illustration of Using and Applying Mathematics in real-life (or almost realistic) situations. The interpretation of data is an important skill across a range of subjects such as biology, geography, physics, history and social sciences. Mathematics allows pupils to develop the skills and knowledge to compute values to assist them in creating a clearer and more accurate understanding of the data in other subjects. Data alone is not information – information results from the combination of data and a context.

---

data + context = information

Data types

There are two main forms of data: discrete and continuous. Discrete data results from counting – for example, a survey of favourite pop groups or month of birthday, a traffic survey at an accident black-spot, a survey of the holiday destinations in the month of August. Discrete data are normally integer values. Continuous data occurs when measurements have been taken, such as people's heights or weights, time taken to travel to school or distance from home to the nearest sports centre. Different types of data are best represented in different ways. Bar charts and pictograms illustrate discrete data more effectively than line graphs since the lines joining adjacent points are meaningless. Continuous data is best represented by line graphs or grouped frequency tables and frequency polygons. Scatter graphs allow discrete relationships to be plotted as individual points and then a line of 'best fit' or regression line can be included through these points to summarise the overall trend of the graph.

Grouping data

The combination of activities whereby data is collected, represented and interpreted to form information is called statistics. By focusing pupils' attention on the final two steps – representation and interpretation of data – children will develop a better understanding of what types of questions need to be asked to obtain suitable and useful data. Initially, young children will sort data by size, colour or shape using criteria to group data before counting the number of objects in each group. The groups can be represented as Carroll or Venn diagrams.

Larger data sets can then be stored as a grouped table where the number of objects in each group is noted. By adding together the subtotals for each group, the total sample size can be calculated. This data can also be displayed in a suitable format as a chart or diagram.

Interpreting data

Once the pupils are familiar with a range of ways of representing data, it may be time to move towards developing the skills of interpretation. By giving pupils completed charts or tables of information, the teachers can encourage the creation of 'maths stories' to explain the data. There are two key questions: what can you deduce from the data? What do you not know? Pupils can comment on the most popular and least popular option and, in most cases, the sample size (by adding together the heights of the bars in a bar chart or by totalling the categories in a table of data). Unless stated in the title or legend (key), it is unlikely that the pupils will know the respondents' ages, time of day or year, ethnic background, and so on. When creating their maths stories, it is important to emphasise the difference between *facts* and *fiction*. Pupils should be encouraged to focus on the facts rather than hypothesise about possible reasons for the outcome of the survey. Using articles from newspapers, books and magazines or a video clip from television, instances where data has been inaccurately interpreted should be shown as non-exemplars. If possible, isolate examples where there have been dramatic consequences as a result of misinterpretation.

Representing data

Much of this work will be completed orally as a whole class or working in pairs. By selecting data that has been gathered for a specific purpose and making this purpose explicit to the students, teachers will motivate the class to think about the information and how it could be represented effectively. By selecting different audiences to whom the information will be reported, teachers can show how the data can be made to tell a particular story. Illustrations of changes in scales, lack of labels on axes, use of two-dimensional pictures or three-dimensional columns in charts can all be used to exaggerate specific aspects of the data. It is as important to recognise the misrepresentation of data as it is to be able to interpret correctly presented information.

The use of descriptive statistics to talk about the data set has already been mentioned. For the older students, summary statistics may be introduced where larger data sets can be described using 'averages'. Pupils should be aware of how to calculate the mean, the median and the mode. They should also be able to make sound judgements on which of the three is most appropriate in different contexts. Later in their school life the pupils will also need to discuss the 'spread' of the data in terms of standard deviations (this is not usually addressed in the primary school).

Probability

The final area of handling data relates to probability. Most children can rank events in order of likelihood from impossible, to evens, to certain. Depending on their level of competence in Number, pupils should also be able to relate 'evens' to a 50:50 chance, 50 per cent chance, 0.5 or ½. Using practical experiments where group results are pooled for whole-class use, pupils can simulate the throwing of a dice 1,000 times to determine the probability of scoring each of the six numbers or tossing a coin 1,000 times to determine the probability of obtaining a 'head'. Since these probabilities can be calculated mathematically, the pupils learn that they are theoretical probabilities, whereas weather forecasting is experimental probability and therefore less accurate. In terms of real-life situations, children should be exposed to games where the probability of winning is very low so that they are not fooled into thinking they have an 'even' chance of winning or losing due to the presence of only two outcomes. The application of this finding can then be applied to situations such as the National Lottery!

Conclusion

The primary school years are the time when pupils learn to love or hate mathematics, where feelings of despondency and failure first surface, and where misconceptions are often formed and never lost. The role of the primary school teacher is thus particularly important, so the use of a range of encouraging, motivating and engaging tasks and activities is required to ensure that the appropriate level of reinforcement of core skills is achieved by all pupils. The nature of the primary classroom allows the teacher to make the important links between mathematics and the other subject areas. Mathematical literacy can be embedded into the normal routine or the National Literacy Hour in the form of spelling the names of new shapes, reading a comprehension and extracting the numerical information, filling in the blanks in a paragraph that requires a high level of mathematical analysis or constructing a logical argument and presenting it orally to the class. Gathering, interpreting and representing information correctly is a useful skill in the context of geography and science. There are numerous software packages available to support the primary school teacher in a number of the topics mentioned in this chapter. The National Numeracy Strategy has identified suitable software for use with this age group and further details can be found in Chapter 4.

11 Investigations and problem-solving in GCSE coursework

Introduction

This chapter aims to introduce the reader to the variety of mathematical problem-solving tasks available for different ability levels of the pupils. The links between the Processes element of the National Curriculum, and the requirements of GCSE coursework are highlighted, as is the use of structured tasks for pre-GCSE work. Mathematical investigations are frequently used in the primary school classroom to engage and motivate the pupils. Much of the early learning in maths utilises practical activities where the pupils have hands-on experience of counting, grouping, selecting by criteria, sorting, identifying patterns, modelling and controlling the motion of a 'Roamer' to discover distance, direction and angles. However, as pupils progress through the school, less use may be made of practical activities and more emphasis placed on textbooks to practise skills and reinforce knowledge. Consequently, when pupils reach the end of Key Stage 3, there may be lower levels of enthusiasm for discovery and investigation in maths, leaving the GCSE teachers to find and rekindle the 'detective' in the pupil.

The following sections illustrate the role of investigations in preparing students for GCSE coursework and offer a number of examples of the incline of difficulty that exists across the standard tasks in use in schools.

Learning outcomes

At the end of this chapter you should be able to:

* identify the use of linear, quadratic, cubic expressions in an investigation;
* identify other mathematical formats in a generalised solution;
* organise a series of investigations by increasing difficulty;
* use structured tasks to illustrate the generic approach used to complete an investigation;
* encourage pupils to annotate their problem-solving work effectively;
* assess coursework against the predefined criteria and understand the purpose of moderation.

Mathematical investigations

Like the 'knowledge' aspects of the National Curriculum, Ma1: Using and applying Mathematics extends from the basic identification of objects according to size or shape to in-depth investigations of mathematical relationships. Pupils are encouraged to adopt a structured problem-solving approach – using a top-down or bottom-up design – by breaking the task into manageable parts at each stage of the problem-solving process. Ma1 or the Processes in Mathematics in the NI Curriculum considers the application of mathematical knowledge in the context of everyday life and encourages the transfer of mathematical knowledge and skills into other subject areas or situations that relate to other areas of the curriculum.

There are three main themes for Processes in Mathematics:

- making and monitoring decisions to solve problems;
- communicating mathematically;
- developing skills of mathematical reasoning.

(CCEA, 2000)

The parallels in the National Curriculum are:

- problem-solving;
- communicating;
- reasoning.

(Curriculum Online, 2003)

Within the NNS and KS3 Strategy, mathematical processes are referred to as *Using and Applying Mathematics*. The incorporation of thinking skills has also been added to this area of mathematics. Five categories of thinking skills are embedded in the National Curriculum: information processing skills, enquiry skills, creative thinking skills, reasoning skills and evaluation skills (DfES, 2001). Thinking skills are not restricted to mathematical investigations but should be integrated into everyday classroom activities. This chapter focuses on pupils developing their thinking and problem-solving skills for mathematical tasks lasting in excess of one week.

Making and monitoring decisions to solve problems

Initially, pupils require assistance in choosing the appropriate approach to solving a problem, so teachers will often guide pupils at this stage and then allow them to work independently trying out and checking their ideas. With increasing levels of experience, the pupils become more adept at selecting a suitable approach to the task and implementing it. The process of planning the problem-solving strategy leads pupils to use skills such as identifying the variables and controlling variables to determine their effect. Reasoning and questioning also develop and pupils start asking themselves 'What would happen if. . .?' questions to assist them in understanding the problem. By generating hypotheses and testing them in this way, pupils reveal more information that often solves some of the subproblems identified earlier in the planning stage. A number of approaches can be applied to the problem such as trial and improvement, working backwards and looking for patterns. After each experimentation, the problem is reviewed again – suggestions are made and refinements implemented before repeating the process. Monitoring and regulating the process are the key elements of successful problem-solving (Kroll, 1988) that need to be recorded in the written work associated with the task. Evidence of generating and testing hypotheses is an important stage in reaching an overall generalisation for the solution.

Communicating mathematically

Being able to communicate mathematical ideas is a skill in itself. Low-level communication revolves around the oral discussions and exchange of views that occur in class. However, as pupils develop their ability to think logically, then diagrams, flowcharts or a sequence of events showing each intended step in the problem-solving process become more frequent additions in the planning stage. Graphs and symbols illustrating the pupils' findings are also advantageous in encouraging pupils to look for patterns in their results. Tables of data from the test cases designed to investigate trends or hypotheses are often included in the written documentation. Through testing these hypotheses, conclusions can be drawn that explain the discoveries to date and additional, relevant test cases can be identified and examined to ensure that all the avenues of the problem have been addressed before coming to a final conclusion. The conclusions to the individual subproblems are then evaluated and justified for accuracy. An overall general conclusion summarising all the subparts can be created and explained with clearly constructed and precise reasons.

Developing skills of mathematical reasoning

The ability to communicate ideas is linked inextricably with mathematical reasoning. The first stage in reasoning is to identify the variables that exist in the problem and to control them so that only one variable is changed at any one time. A number of examples or test cases are required to create a table that facilitates the 'pattern spotting' stage. This then leads to a prediction or hypothesis that can be represented symbolically. The testing process incorporates both verification and also testing using counterexamples to disprove the 'theory'. Suggestions, reasons and justifications for the outcome are all required at this stage in the problem-solving process. The use of 'If . . . then' reasoning can be supplemented by 'What would happen if. . .?' testing to investigate the hypothesis and look for inconsistencies in the outcome. Using substitution and clearly structured arguments, the hypothesis can be evaluated and justified or rejected in the light of the testing. Ultimately, the generalisations for each subproblem identified in the planning stage should come together to form an overall general solution with (perhaps) a number of restrictions or conditions. The final form may be in algebraic, graphical or geometrical, or statistical format depending on the type of investigation. The validity of the results should also be considered and proved if possible.

GCSE coursework requirements

As part of the GCSE course, 'all candidates are required to submit two coursework tasks, one of a practical nature and one of an investigative nature' (CCEA, 2000b, p. 9). Each task is supervised by the teacher and is completed during normal classroom time with a maximum of four hours being available in total. Teachers devise and assess the tasks using the predefined criteria. No pupil should be given a task that is deemed to be outside the mathematical competence covered in the examination tier to which he or she is working at that point in the course. Pupils should be given every opportunity to show what they know, understand and can do in maths.

The practical task endeavours to encourage the pupils to look at real-life problems by modelling the key aspects and highlighting the limitations of the process. Using the mathematics covered in the Handling Data PoS, pupils can carry out a survey or implement some form of data capture to provide a real data set for analysis. Alternatively, downloading a dataset from a website such as the Census At School (www.CensusAtSchool. ntu.ac.uk) would offer a larger and more representative sample for analysis leading to more reliable conclusions. Where spreadsheets have been used, pupils should print out the completed spreadsheet and also the formulas for assessment. Other forms of ICT such as graphing packages may also be used to assist in the analysis, interpretation and representation of the data.

Exemplars of approved tasks for the NI Curriculum, complete with data sets and matched to the GCSE tiers of entry, can be downloaded from the CCEA website (www. ccea.org.uk/gmaths_coursework_guidance/index.htm).

Task 11.1

Look on the website of your local examining authority. Are there predefined tasks available for use in the classroom?

Task 11.2

Ask the Head of Department in your placement school for some past GCSE coursework with the marks awarded. Discuss the reasons for allocating particular marks and how the student could have improved the work.

Typical investigations and the incline of difficulty

Investigative tasks

New York Cop and Other Investigations (Bell *et al.*, 1988) offers an excellent selection of structured tasks to develop pupils' skills at solving problems before they embark on their assessed coursework. Solutions involving linear equations are normally introduced first as the patterns are easier to identify. Then the quadratics (particularly n^2) and the cubics are used before considering other sequences of numbers such as the Fibonacci series, Pascal's triangle or the use of the highest common factors. Using the Virtual Teacher Centre, the NGfL, TRE or the NINE site, links to websites containing coursework tasks and often exemplars of pupils' work can be found that will illustrate the volume and standard of work required from pupils at this level. Alternatively, you can contact your local examinations authority for exemplar coursework materials as these will also contain the teacher's and moderator's comments.

Linear solutions

Two common examples of a problem with a linear solution are Pict's Result and the Areas and Perimeters task in *New York Cop* (Bell *et al.*, 1988).

> Pict's Result asks pupils to investigate the creation of shapes on a pin board. In particular they should look for the relationship between the area of the shape A, the number of pins on the perimeter of the shape P, and the number of interior pins I.
>
> > (*New York Cop*, 1988, p. 74)

This task can be structured as follows:

- Using a nine pin board, create as many different triangles as possible.
- Find how many different shapes can be made using only 4 pins.
- Using a nine pin board, find how many shapes can be made with an area of two units.
- Find how many shapes can be made on a nine pin board which also enclose exactly one pin. Record the area and number of pins on the perimeter of each shape.

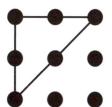 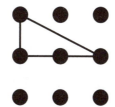 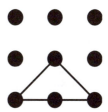

(Source: *The Active Maths Pack* by Hodder & Stoughton, 1989)

The *Areas and Perimeters* task asks pupils to control the number of dots inside the shapes and to record the area and number of dots on the perimeter for each shape drawn. By starting with one dot inside the shapes, the simplest form of the equation is revealed to be A = ½P. The pupils can then move to investigating zero, two, three, etc. internal dots.

Using the basic formula already discovered, the pupils will be able to build in the impact of the number of internal dots into the equation.

The use of square dotty paper is particularly beneficial to pupils for this task. It is important to remind the pupils that they must include their diagrams on the square dotty paper alongside the tabular summaries of the findings in the report. An interactive website exists at www.cut-the-knot.com/ctk/Pick.html, which may be used to assist the pupils in generating their tables of results.

Barriers is another example in which the square dotty paper assists the pupils. In this task the pupils are asked to investigate a barrier system for fencing in sheep or other animals. The barrier system is composed of posts (the dots) and fences (straight lines joining posts in a horizontal or vertical direction only).

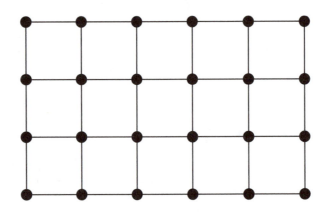

This barrier system is 5 units long and 3 units wide, securing an area of 15 square units. The aim is to find the association between the number of posts (P), the number of barriers (B) and the area enclosed (A). The inclusion of one or two walls as part of the enclosure adds to the problem. To determine the minimum number of posts and barriers for a given area, it can be shown that the shape of the enclosure needs to be as square as possible. If one wall is included, then the enclosure should take maximum advantage of the wall and make the side of the enclosure parallel to the wall as large as possible.

The *Barriers* task can be extended further to include cubic equations if the pupils investigate the number of square enclosures (of varying dimensions and positions) that can be formed within a square or rectangular boundary.

Variations of this task can be found in the Resources section of the ATM website. Different types of dotty paper for investigations can be downloaded from www.mathematics helpcentral.com/graph_paper.htm.

Quadratic solutions

Figurate numbers provides an excellent introduction to number patterns. Again using the square dotty paper, the triangular and squares numbers can be illustrated diagrammatically:

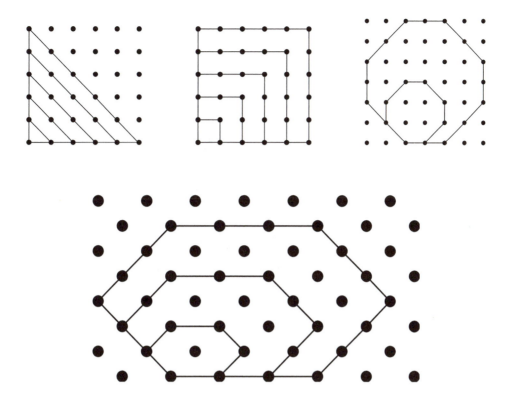

The isometric dotty paper can be used for the pentagonal, hexagonal and octagonal numbers. By increasing the size of the shape in each case, the total number of dots in the shape can be represented algebraically. The results of this task are particularly helpful when identifying and generalising the number patterns in other tasks. Links can also be made between the position of the figurate numbers and the diagonals in modified Pascal's triangles:

Triangular numbers

					1					
				1		1				
			1		2		1			
		1		**3**		3		1		
	1		4		**6**		4		1	
1		5		10		**10**		5		1

Square numbers

				1		2				
			1		3		2			
		1		**4**		5		2		
	1		5		**9**		7		2	
1		6		14		**16**		9		2

Pentagonal numbers

				1		3			
		1		4		3			
	1		**5**		7		3		
1		6		**12**		10		3	
1	7		18		**22**		13		3

Based on the patterns revealed in the above sets of formulae, pupils should be able to hypothesise the formula for the n-othogonal number.

This task can be extended to three dimensions to include the tetrahedral numbers and the pyramidal numbers. In each case the base area is increased and a pattern can be revealed between the number of dots in the three-dimensional shape and the number of horizontal 'levels'. Level 1 is a single dot, level 2 is the basic minimum shape with 2 dots on each side, level 3 is the next level up with 3 dots on each side, and so on.

Another commonly used task is *Growing shapes* (CCEA, 2002). This investigation considers the growth of a square initially from a single square at stage 1 to a square with four additional squares attached to each of its exposed sides (stage 2), and so on.

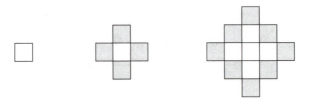

The investigation looks at the relationship between the stage in development and:

- the new growth area (the number of squares added to the exposed sides of the previous shape);
- the perimeter of the new shape;
- the total area of the shape.

By completing the investigation in this order, the incline of difficulty of each of the generalisations can be maintained. This task can be extended to investigate the patterns that occur in other shapes, such as the growth of hexagons, since they tessellate too. Finally, a three-dimensional perspective can be investigated by looking at the growth of cubes.

A *Mystic Rose* is created by joining together each point to every other point on a circle as shown below (p. 181). The investigation looks at the link between the number of points on the circle and number of lines. As shown, the pattern becomes the triangular numbers.

The *Mystic Rose* investigation is a good introduction to the *Handshake* problem where every person at a party shakes hands once with every other person at the party. These tasks can also be used to prepare pupils for the *Tournament* task where every team plays every other team twice (once at home and once away). If there are *n* teams, how many matches will be played? Based on their previous work, the pupils should be able to spot the triangular numbers doubled in this situation.

(Source: Shell Centre for Mathematical Education,
University of Nottingham, 1984)

Cubic equations

A Cube investigation taken from *New York Cop* (Bell *et al.*, 1988) illustrates the progression from linear to quadratic and finally to cubic equations. The Cube investigation asks the pupils to think about a $3 \times 3 \times 3$ cube that is painted on the outside. The painted cube can be taken apart to show the 27 unit cubes which have a different number of faces painted. The unit cubes located at the corners of the painted cube have three faces painted, the unit cubes on the edges between the corners have two faces painted, while the cubes in the centre of one face of the painted cube have only one side painted. At the very centre of the painted cube, there will be a single cube with no paint on any of its faces. By changing the overall size of the painted cube from $3 \times 3 \times 3$ to $2 \times 2 \times 2$, $4 \times 4 \times 4$, $5 \times 5 \times 5$ and so on, and looking only at the cubes with two faces painted first, a pattern can be found between the length of one side of the painted cube (L) and the number of cubes (N) in total. Similarly, a link exists between the number of cubes with only one face painted (M) and the dimension of the overall painted cube (L). Finally, for overall painted cubes with sides in excess of 2 units (if L>2), cubes will exist with no paint on any of their faces, the link between these cubes (X) and the length of one side of the painted cube (L) forms a cubic expression. The total number of each type of unit cube (M, N, X and the corner cubes) can then be expressed as a function of L.

Other formulae

The Snooker investigation (SMP, 1985) looks straightforward, but pupils often find it difficult to explain the patterns. In this task, a snooker table has corner pockets only. A ball is struck from the bottom left-hand corner (D) with sufficient force that it exits at one of the pockets (C). In the diagram below, the table has size 2 by 5 and the ball travels at an angle of 45° at all times, traversing the small squares in the diagram. The investigation is to determine how the size of the snooker table affects the number of rebounds off the sides and at which pocket the ball exits.

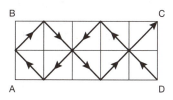

The first stage of this investigation considers the change in exit corner when the table has dimensions x by 6 where $x = 1, 2, 3, 4, 5, 6, 7, 8, \ldots$ Next, the pupil looks at a random selection of table dimensions to see if a pattern can be established between the size of the table and the exit corner. Then the number of rebounds is investigated for tables with sides that have no common factor apart from 1. This process is repeated for tables with dimensions that have a common factor. Finally, the pupils investigate the traversal of the smaller squares in the examples already drawn.

The pupils should discover a link between the odd and even dimensions of the table and the exit corner, taking into account the impact of the highest common factor. They should derive a result for the number of rebounds and also the number of squares crossed when the dimensions of the table are co-prime or have a common factor.

New York Cop (Bell *et al.*, 1988) is an investigation based on the rectangular, block layout of the streets in New York. The police wish to have total supervision of all the streets using as few police officers as possible. If one police officer can see all that is happening down the length of one block, but cannot see past a road junction, how many police officers are needed to patrol a street system of size R by L?

Like the cube investigation, there are different 'categories' of vision. Officers standing on a corner can see only two streets (T), officers standing along an edge can view three streets (Y), while officers standing at the cross-section can observe four streets (X).

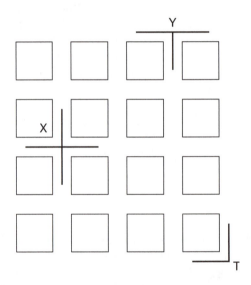

By splitting the task into arrays with an odd number of rows (R) and an even number of blocks wide (L), a formula can be generated for this subproblem. Similarly, an even-by-even array can be investigated, leading to a new formula. Finally, the even-by-odd array and the odd-by-odd array can also be checked to ensure that all eventualities have been addressed in the solution. The overall generalisation will be dependent on the dimensions of the array, in terms of even or odd numbers. Software exists to assist pupils in developing their table of results.

Other tasks also exist that require the use of Pascal's Triangle or the Factorials button on a calculator. By browsing through the booklets produced by the Institute of Mathematics and its Applications, Learning and Teaching Support Network, NRICH, Becta, NFER, and their associated websites, a number of other investigations can be found or adapted from work completed in schools or universities. Examining Boards also provide exemplars of marked coursework that often offers a new slant to an old problem such as Max Box.

Task 11.3

Try some of the above structured tasks yourself. What proportion of your time was spent completing the task? How much time was spent writing it up?

Practical tasks

As stated earlier, two coursework tasks must be submitted at GCSE level. The following are typical examples of the practical tasks used by schools in NI:

- Book investigation – compare two books by counting the number of vowels, consonants and letters in a line.
  Mathematical skills: Representation of information in a variety of contexts and working out statistical averages.

- Arbelos – to draw an arbelo, take any line AB and any point C between A and B. Draw the semicircles with AC and CB as diameters, then draw a semicircle with AB as the diameter. Investigate the perimeter of the shape and area enclosed between the shapes.
  Mathematical skills: Calculating the perimeters of semicircles and the areas enclosed. Using graphs to determine the maximum possible area that can be enclosed (no knowledge of calculus at this stage).

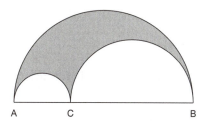

- The Towers of Hanoi.
  Mathematical skills: Discovering recursion. This task can be completed using the interactive website at www.cut-the-knot.com/recurrence/hanoi.html which will allow the pupils to control the number of discs on the pole at the start of the task. Number of moves is an exponential growth.

- Guttering: Most houses have semicircular guttering. Is this the shape that will carry most water? (CCEA, 2002a)

Mathematical skills: being able to work out the cross-sectional areas of shapes, including those requiring the use of trigonometric functions. Ability to use a computer graphing package to represent the results.

- The use of the CensusAtSchool database (www.CensusAtSchool.ntu.ac.uk) for statistical analysis based on a large-scale survey.
  Mathematical skills: Generating and testing hypotheses of subgroups such as age, gender, socio-economic status, and so on. Charts and analysis completed using Excel functions.

- Strawberry Box (CCEA, 2002)
  This is similar to the MaxBox problem discussed in Chapter 9. Pupils investigate the optimum volume of a box to hold strawberries, given a piece of square card of side 24 cm. Ideally, students should consider more than one shape of container, e.g. cubes, cuboids, cones, cylinders, and so on.

- Test marks (CCEA, 2002)
  - *Mathematical skills*: Pupils are given a data set to analyse in Excel. Basic descriptive statistics are used to describe the data and then sampling by gender, subject, year or class can be investigated. Correlations, grouped frequency tables, frequency polygons, cumulative frequency graphs with quartiles marked, and Box and Whisker diagrams should be used by the able students. A regression equation with three dependent variables is the ideal outcome.

- Car Survey/Driving tests (CCEA, 2002)
  Mathematical skills: Using a given data set, pupils generate and test hypotheses such as 'the mileage is proportional to the age of the car'. Basic descriptive statistics, correlations, grouped frequency tables, frequency polygons, systematic sampling or stratified samples are encouraged for the higher tiers. Pupils working at the uppermost tier should generate hypotheses with three dependent variables.

Marking GCSE coursework

An example from the Northern Ireland Council for the Curriculum, Examinations and Assessment (CCEA) will be used as an illustration. Other QCA examination boards will have a similar structure.

Coursework submitted to the CCEA has a maximum of 8 marks available for each of the three traits – making and monitoring decisions to solve problems, communicating mathematically, and developing skills of mathematical reasoning – making a total mark of 24 for each coursework task. Depending on the perceived difficulty of the task, restrictions on the marks available to a pupil may occur – for example, for a *simple* task (roughly equivalent to the Foundation Tier) the maximum mark that may be awarded in any strand is 3. Other task categories are *substantial* – in which the task can be broken down into subparts (a maximum of 6 marks are available in each strand) and *complex* where there should be at least three variables or features for which a maximum of 8 marks are available for each assessment strand. This means that the three bands of the mark scheme are utilised in full and differentiation in scores parallels the difficulty of the task and is easily justified by the teacher. Pupils should include clear tables and diagrams of the examples they have used to create their hypotheses and their writing should guide the marker through their thinking process. Reasons for each stage in the coursework should be stated clearly. Using the assessment criteria, all pupil scripts should be annotated clearly by the teacher to indicate the aspects of work that led to the awarding of a particular mark on each strand. A 'best fit' between the pupils' work and the criteria is used, the reliability of which is dependent on the teacher's professional judgement and the moderation checks completed by the examination awarding body.

The use of internal moderation between teachers in the same school is advocated to ensure consistency of standards. The first teacher (the pupil's teacher) marks the work and then a second teacher blind-marks the same piece of coursework. Where disagreement in the scores awarded occurs, the two teachers meet and discuss how they came to their individual conclusions. The agreed mark is then included on the mark sheet. External moderation by the examining body ensures consistency across schools.

The use of ICT in GCSE coursework

In many of the practical tasks the pupils are looking for the maximum or minimum value to solve a problem, such as the maximum volume of a box or the minimum amount of raw materials to produce the box or tin. In these cases, the pupils do not have the necessary calculus skills to determine the maximum or minimum value, so graphing is their only alternative. Using Autograph, Omnigraph or an Excel chart, pupils can represent their data more effectively than in a table, so they can determine the location of the maximum or minimum value at a glance. This also means that the pupils can re-visit their spreadsheet to increase the accuracy of their result by increasing the number of decimal places in the identified range of solutions.

Interactive websites can also be used to support the task or offer an introduction to the types of thinking required in approaching work of this nature. The immediacy of the feedback keeps the pupils motivated and since they have minimal levels of recording to do, the pupils are more likely to experiment with new ideas in their approach to solving the problem. Many of the tasks originally produced as part of the SMILE series of maths software are available online as interactive web pages. For example, the Toads and Frogs puzzle can be found at www.cut-the-knot.com/SimpleGames/FrogsAndToads.html or Diagonals at www.cut-the-knot.com/Diagonals.html. These sites offer a good starting-point for pupils prior to completing one of the written tasks described above. The *New York Cop* task also has an associated software package that can be used to generate the examples for inclusion in the coursework.

Task 11.4

Search for other websites that relate to paper-based coursework tasks recommended by your placement schools, university tutor or local examinations board.

Depending on the type of coursework required by the examining boards, some schools may find that tasks based on open-ended investigations using Logo or Zeno may meet the assessment criteria. For instance, the link between matrices, transformational geometry and complex numbers can be demonstrated graphically in the Zeno environment using a low level of language. Singular matrices can also be studied using Zeno and generalisations drawn from the graphical output linking the gradient of the line with the ratio of the rows of the matrix (Cowan *et al.*, 1998).

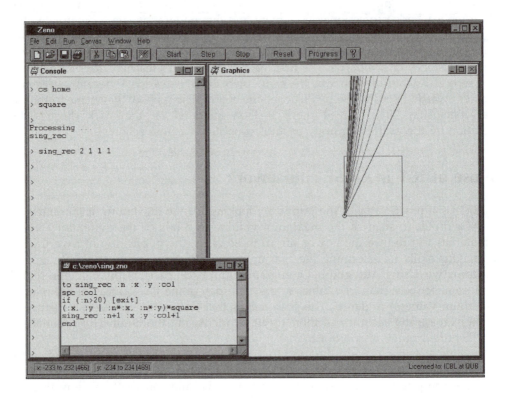

Conclusions

It is likely that the use of ICT in GCSE and Advanced-level coursework will increase dramatically over the next few years. The use of ICT as a tool for learning in the class-room should automatically transfer to the problem-solving environment and therefore into coursework. Ideally, pupils should reach for the laptop in the same way as they currently use a calculator. However, it may be necessary to 'write' such usage into the criteria for coursework before all teachers make it a reality.

Perhaps the future of coursework will be the use of ICT to take the students beyond the mathematics currently covered in the syllabus and to complete real-life investigations for businesses or industry with the added incentive of having a real audience for their written report.

12 Key Skills and mathematics

Introduction

This chapter considers the role of Key Skills in the GCSE and Advanced-level curricula for mathematics. It is split into five main sections: the background and purpose of Key Skills; the structure of Key Skills; assessing Key skills; integrating Key Skills into the mathematics specifications at GCSE and Advanced level, and finally the organisation of Key Skills across a school.

Learning outcomes

By the end of this chapter you should be able to:

- state the six Key Skills areas, differentiating between the 'core' skills and the 'wider' Key Skills;
- explain the assessment of Key Skills;
- list ways of integrating Key Skills into your mathematics teaching;
- evaluate the organisational strategies available to schools regarding the delivery and responsibilities associated with implementing Key Skills across a Sixth Form.

The background and purpose of Key Skills

Sir Ron Dearing's (1996) *Review of Qualifications for 16–19-year-olds* identified some key issues regarding public opinions about the skills and standards of young people's education on leaving school. A repeated concern expressed by employers and commentators alike was:

> The need to improve standards in the skills of communication and the application of number amongst young people . . . Many commentators, and employers in particular, have stressed the importance of developing the wider skills including inter-personal skills, particularly team-working, presentational skills, a problem-solving approach

and the ability to 'manage one's own learning. In a society which needs increasingly to be committed to life-long learning, this last is a key to all the rest.

(p. 46)

Concerns were also expressed about the speed at which pupils were expected to specialise in a limited number of academic subjects. Compared to other European nations, the post-16 qualifications were deemed restrictive and limited pupils' development of skills and range of experiences which may be needed in later life. Early specialisation in three A-level subjects was seen as potentially damaging a pupil's future career options (Crowther Committee).

Confusion also existed for employers who were unclear of the equivalences of the academic, vocational and occupational routes into industry. It was widely accepted that the academic route was not suitable for all students, but there lacked a parity of esteem between academic and vocational qualifications (Dearing, 1996). To promote lifelong learning, the 'image' of the vocational route had to be improved so that both learners and employers placed an appropriate level of 'value' on the resultant outcomes of this mode of study. As part of his *Review of the Curriculum for 16–19-year-olds*, Dearing aimed to lessen the 'vocational/academic divide' in post-16 education. Public opinion regarded the traditional academic route to university via A-levels as the 'Gold standard', while alternative routes, such as GNVQs and other vocationally based qualifications, were deemed to be substandard. To redress this situation, Dearing introduced a set of skills, often incorporated into the vocational qualifications, called *Key Skills*.

The Learning and Skills Development Agency (2001) described Dearing's reforms as follows:

The reforms were intended to make post-16 study broader and more flexible, encourage young people to study more subjects, provide easier combinations of academic and vocational study and have an entitlement that includes key skills, tutorial and enrichment.

As an incentive to all pupils, the Key Skills qualifications were to be awarded UCAS points, thereby increasing their currency for entrance to university courses. Each Key Skill at Level 3 was worth 20 points, so a student possessing the three core Key Skills was awarded 60 points – the equivalent to a grade A at AS-level or a grade D at A-level. Motivation to include Key Skills in the school or sixth form college provision was improved by declaring the inclusion of Key Skills results in national performance tables.

What are Key Skills?

The Key Skills were to encompass the existing generic skills developed during the completion of A-level and GNVQ courses, such as the ability to:

- discuss the subject content;
- research information in libraries or on the internet;
- select, analyse and evaluate evidence to form a convincing argument;
- use evidence to test, support or refute an argument;

- construct and test hypotheses;
- present information, findings or conclusions in an appropriate way;
- plan and revise personal work schedules and goals;
- tackle problems effectively;
- work in pairs or groups.

The focus was increasing teachers' and pupils' awareness of the broader skills being developed in the natural progression of the subject being studied – it was not deemed to be the case that 'key skills were being introduced into A level'; 'Key skills were to encourage the use of active learning and to help students take responsibility for their own learning' (CCEA, 2000a, p. 2).

The selling points for Key Skills were described in the QCA (2000a, p. 2) documentation to all schools as follows:

Key Skills:

- are valuable in their own right, for higher education and for employment;
- are intrinsic to A-level programmes;
- enhance A-level programmes;
- are crucial for lifelong learning;
- attract FEFC funding;
- attract UCAS points;
- are subject to inspection by OFSTED and FEFC;
- are welcomed by HE institutions;
- are valued by employers;
- are part of the National Training and Education Targets.

The six Key Skills

All post-16 (GCSE and Advanced-level) subject specifications or syllabi for teaching from September 2000 have the six Key Skills areas included in their structure. These are:

- Communication (Comm);
- Application of Number (AoN);
- Information Technology (IT);
- Working with Others (WWO);
- Improving own learning and performance (IOP);
- Problem-solving (PS).

The first three skills in the list are termed the 'main' or 'core' Key Skills, while the remaining three are the 'wider' Key Skills. These six Key Skills are generic and should be transferable across subjects and in the workplace. They are viewed as being indicative of the need to be adaptive and flexible in education and industry. Five levels exist for each Key Skill. Levels 1 and 2 are mapped into the GCSE course specifications, while Level 3 is addressed at Advanced-level. Degree courses are tailored to Level 4, while Level 5 has only one Key Skill – Personal Skills – encompassing all six skills listed above and is applicable to postgraduate courses and qualifications.

Key Skills occur naturally in our everyday lives. We use them regularly to 'make things happen', 'solve problems' and 'to get things done'. The QCA (2001) Key Skills for developing employability report makes a convincing case for Key Skills:

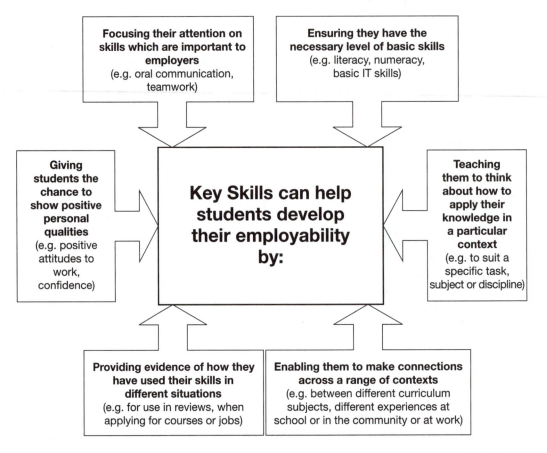

Figure 12.1   Key Skills and their role in contributing to employability (Source: QCA/001/752)

The structure of Key Skills

Each Key Skill Unit has specific content for each of the five levels. Within a Unit there are three parts – A, B and C.

- Part A defines 'What you need to know' for that Key Skill. In essence, it presents the skills and knowledge associated with the Unit.
- Part B describes 'What you must do' and is subdivided into two sections: the Elements and the Performance Criteria for each Element. In each Key Skill Unit, the Elements can be summarised as: Planning the task, Developing the process and Presenting the outcomes. Students must be able to produce evidence for every criterion in this section in their portfolio.

- Part C offers guidance to the student on the types of activities that might be used to develop the Key Skill, including the sources of evidence that may be included in their portfolio.

Task 12.1 Access the Key Skills guidance materials for students

Obtain a copy of the folder and documentation offered to students for the award of Key Skills. Browse through the leaflets illustrating Parts A, B and C.

Try to obtain access to a student's portfolio submitted last year. Look at the quantity and quality of the work included in each section. Using the criteria, check for 100 per cent coverage of Part B.

Assessing Key Skills

The 'core' Key Skills are assessed by a combination of external test, addressing parts of the content listed in Part A of the Unit, and by a portfolio of evidence, illustrating the pupil's competence in Part B of the Unit. Pupils must pass both assessments to be awarded the level. The 'wider' Key Skills are assessed by portfolio alone.

The portfolio

A portfolio is 'a file or folder for collecting and organising evidence for assessment' (CCEA, 2000a, §1, p. 6). Evidence can be in the form of written work completed for the teacher within the context of a particular subject such as project work or coursework, a written report, an oral presentation of findings that has been video-taped, a transcription of an interview, photographs, models, witness statements or testimonials from external people. Students can gather this evidence from any area of their life, including their school subjects, part-time jobs, sports teams or other extra-curricular activities. All evidence must be 'authentic' – that is, recent (no more than two years old), relevant and signed by the witness or named person who can verify the accuracy of the statement. Every teacher has a role to play in assisting pupils in developing their Key Skills, regardless of whether the particular subject maps directly to the generation of the required evidence.

The portfolio is internally assessed by the designated teacher(s) and also internally verified by the Key Skills co-ordinator or another designated and trained Internal Verifier (IV). The awarding body then request a sample of portfolios for external moderation.

The external tests

The external tests are set and marked by the awarding body. At Levels 1 and 2, each test lasts 60 minutes and comprises short answers or multiple-choice questions. At Level 3, the test is 90 minutes in duration and is composed of more open-ended questions in which the candidates have to apply the knowledge listed in Part A to a given situation(s). The questions are drawn from the content specified in Part A of the Unit. Sample tests and guidance materials are available from the QCA website at www.qca.org.uk/nq/ks/ key-skills-data/example_tests_index3.asp and www.qca.org.uk/nq/ks/guidance_specs.asp respectively.

| **Task 12.2** | Access the exemplar tests and past papers for the 'core' Key Skills |

Go to the QCA website and download some Key Skills tests for each of the core Units. Assess your own ability by completing the tests within the given time. Ask a friend, tutor or colleague to mark the tests for you.

Exemptions

Exemptions exist for students following some GCSE and A-level courses – for example, ICT. Depending on the subject specification, full exemption from both the test and the portfolio can be given. However, in most cases it is only exemption from the written test. The GCSE mathematics specification states that pupils awarded grades A* to C are exempt from the external test at Level 2 in Application of Number, while pupils achieving grades D to G are exempt from the Level 1 test in Application of Number. Full details and regular updates of the exemptions are provided on the QCA website (www.qca.org.uk/) or at www.keyskillssupport.net.

Key Skills and teaching pedagogy

'Key Skills can be done as part of the subject teaching' (CCEA, 2000a), with the main focus being their integration into the current schemes of work for mathematics and other subjects. It was not the intention of Dearing to add additional burdens on the teachers' or pupils' already extensive workload. Key Skills were not designed to be 'bolt-on' tasks, but were created to recognise, develop and reward current good practice in existing teaching methodologies. It was recognised that pupils need to be actively engaged in their own learning process. They should be able to discuss mathematical ideas coherently and with confidence. They should be able to work as a group, solving complex problems where the combined expertise of the group adds value to the finished product and they should have the knowledge and ability to research topics and access other sources of expertise outside the classroom, such as the internet, using e-mail to request information from people or organisations and identify instances of conflicting viewpoints that are worthy of further investigation.

As a teacher, the integration of Key Skills into your scheme of work or lesson plans will enhance the way you teach. By varying your teaching style to embed the opportunities for developing your pupils' communication skills or IT skills, you will produce a highly motivated and energised classroom of pupils who are absorbed in their work and keen to play an active role in each stage of the learning process. With suitable choices of tasks and activities, the pupils will view mathematics as an integral part of their life, thereby understanding the role of differential equations or mechanics in the context of their environment. They will start to reflect on their own ability to solve problems, to remember strategies used in the past to solve similar problems and begin to monitor their progress in mathematics over an extended period of time. Consequently, the pupils will also start to identify their own (and others') strengths and weaknesses, allowing them to define their own learning goals and become autonomous, and possibly lifelong, learners.

The teacher's role in the classroom will also change – you will no longer be the source of all the knowledge, but will be an active facilitator of learning experiences, offering numerous and varied opportunities to develop Key Skills while still covering the subject matter on the syllabus. However, a balance between the traditional teaching of the underlying skills and content will be matched with the provision of alternative perspectives and ideas on the topic. You should not be responsible for the production of the evidence and the development of the portfolio – this is the role of the student. Nevertheless, you should be willing and able to assist pupils offering advice and perhaps remedial support if necessary. In some cases, you may need to address areas of subject knowledge deficiency such as a lack of familiarity with statistics or the inability to interpret results. Often, these problems are dealt with in a group context where the teacher provides additional classes addressing the content of Part A in Application of Number in timetabled classes. This arrangement is particularly valuable when the external tests are looming.

All GCSE, AS and A-level specifications now include 'signposts' to the Key Skills opportunities. Exemplification of the types of opportunities for developing and generating evidence of each of the Key Skills are flagged in an Appendix to the main subject specification. Teachers are encouraged to integrate the ideas into their pedagogy. However, it may not be possible to fulfil every instance in each Key Skill.

Task 12.3

Locate the Key Skills section of the GCSE and/or A level specification you will be teaching. Check that your teaching strategies are in keeping with the intended opportunities for Key Skills development.

Key Skills in GCSE mathematics specifications

In GCSE mathematics specifications, the 'signposts' to Key Skills are included in the Appendix. The opportunities in the specification refer to the evidence requirements of Part B in each Key Skill and typical opportunities should arise through normal classroom teaching. The majority of instances result from coursework-type activities, such as investigations in which pupils are required to solve extended problems often relating to everyday life. The signposts are divided according to the Key Skill and the following suggestions are summarised from the CCEA GCSE specification for examination in 2003.

For Communication, the suggestions include:

Element 1: Discussing and presenting ideas as a group or class; using mathematical notation and language in written and oral presentations, including graphs and charts to explain the techniques used in the task.

Element 2: Searching for information – on the internet, CD-ROMs, newspapers, books; reading and summarising the main points in the materials to suit the purpose of the task.

Element 3: Reporting the outcomes of the work in a style and format appropriate for the audience, and including images or charts where appropriate.

For Application of Number, the suggestions include:

Element 1: Data retrieval from a variety of sources such as the internet, databases or CD-ROMs, timetables, timelines, graphical representations of information. Select and interpret the relevant information before summarising it as a flow chart.

Element 2: Carry out calculations depending on the data – use scale diagrams for measurement problems, statistical 'averages' for handling data, algebraic expressions for generalising a table of results, or decimals, ratios and percentages for number-based tasks. In each case, measures of accuracy and feasibility determined by mental checks should be included.

Element 3: Interpretation of results of an investigation. One example offered was 'the properties of a linear function of the form $y = ax + b$' as it facilitated the requirements of a table of results, graphical representations, charts and diagrams. The straight line graphs could then be extended to investigate inequalities to solve linear programming-type problems. The inclusion of pie charts, bar charts, line graphs, pictographs or scattergrams could be used to represent the outcome of the data-handling activity in the previous section.

For Information Technology, the suggestions overlap somewhat with those in Application of Number, highlighting the opportunity for cross-referencing tasks as evidence of different skills:

Element 1: Search for and select information for a purpose using technologies such as the internet, CD-ROMs, prepared datasets, and so on. Demonstrate an awareness of the benefits and limitations of the new technologies.

Element 2: Carry out a data-handling exercise where data is accessed from a variety of sources, organised and recorded using data capture forms or other pupil-designed recording sheets, analysed and presented in a suitable format for the audience, including graphs and tables as necessary.

Element 3: Merge datasets for comparative purposes and display the results in a variety of formats: graphically as charts, numerically in tables or diagrammatically in flow charts. Choose a range of ICT tools appropriate for the task such as graphics calculators, spreadsheets, data-analysis functions and presentational packages.

For Working with Others, the suggestions relate once more to a data-handling exercise such as that identified above and include:

Element 1: Working as a group to plan and share responsibilities for problem-solving tasks. The strategy should be agreed in advance and subgoals defined at the outset.

Element 2: Act responsibly on the allocated task, collaborating, co-operating and exchanging results for collective analysis. Use shared resources to ensure that the separate data sets can be collated in the final stage.

Element 3: Compare individual results and then collate the combined data set for individual analysis and reporting. Reflect on the effectiveness and value of the overall groupwork process.

For Improving Own Learning and Performance, the suggestions include working alongside the teacher to:

Element 1: Plan and improve the pupils' mathematical skills by setting realistic short-term and long–term goals and targets. By pupil reflection on progress to date that will inform the likely gains in the realistic planning of targets.

Element 2: Learn how to take responsibility for personal learning by following the plan with support as necessary from others. Plan and manage time effectively to meet goals and improve progress. Be open to suggestions and advice from others. Know when to ask for support and when to make decisions alone.

Element 3: Review progress at agreed time periods, checking that targets are met and redefine new goals to further improve personal performance.

For Problem-solving, the suggestions include:

Element 1: Understanding and representing the real-life problem as an equation (or set of equations) where assumptions are clearly defined and limits are set. Plan a number of suitable problem-solving strategies, trying to anticipate the difficulties in advance.

Element 2: Use trial and improvement methods, reflecting on the effectiveness of the methodology with an appropriate person and using any support or advice offered.

Element 3: Determine if the plan has been effective and the solution accurate – for example, if solving simultaneous equations, then substitute the answers back into the original equations. Evaluate the problem-solving strategy used, highlighting personal strengths, weaknesses and what has been learned from the activity.

It should be clear from the above outlines that practical coursework activities, particularly relating to data handling and analysis, would be valuable additions to the classroom in terms of generating Key Skills evidence that could be cross-referenced across almost all Units. If carefully planned and controlled, the individual and group dimensions could be met in a single extended task or project. It should be noted, however, that the pupils may not always recognise where the evidence can be garnered, so the teacher should ensure that appropriate and accurate records of all discussions, agreements and targets are recorded by each member of the group.

Task 12.4 Design a task for GCSE pupils that incorporates as many of the Key Skills criteria as possible

Plan the structure and organisation of an extended task for GCSE pupils that incorporates as many of the Key Skills criteria as possible. Choose a topic that is of interest and relevance to the pupils. Check the internet for the availability of suitable materials or resources and include this suggestion in your discussion with the class. Design the worksheets and teaching notes you will require in order to use this task in the classroom. If possible, try to use the task while on teaching placement.

Integrating Key Skills into the planning of A-level mathematics

Despite the calls for all teachers to build opportunities for pupils to generate Key Skills evidence from normal classwork, some pupils remain in difficulty when demonstrating their competence in some of the Key Skills. In most subjects, opportunities arise naturally for pupils to develop and consequently generate the required evidence. However, there are some traditional lessons in which the students remain the passive recipients of knowledge with little opportunity to become actively involved in the lesson. In these cases the scheme of work for the subject requires 'modernisation'. It is a relatively easy task for an experienced teacher to reflect on instances when each of the Planning, Implementing and Evaluating stages occur for each Key Skill. Using a grid, all the natural occurrences of evidence can be marked, leaving gaps where opportunities need to be built in to the existing scheme of work. As mentioned earlier, not all of the subjects can offer all of the Key Skills. However, by attempting to address as many Key Skills as possible, the teacher is likely to expand his or her teaching repertoire and so benefit professionally from using these new techniques.

On identifying the gaps in the provision of Key Skills, the teacher can either consult the booklet of given tasks (QCA, 2000a) and identify the ones to 'plug the holes' or design his or her own tasks based on personal knowledge or experience of particular aspects of graphics calculators or software.

Key Skills in AS and A-level mathematics

Due to the modular nature of AS and A-level mathematics, a number of tasks have been specifically designed for pupils to complete, depending on whether they have chosen the AS or A2 modules in pure mathematics, Statistics or Mechanics (QCA, 2000a). Most of the tasks require between two and four hours of classroom time, plus the same amount of self-directed study for research and writing up results. There are two pure maths activities, three statistics activities and five mechanics activities. None of the tasks address the reading aspect of Communication, three tasks do not use ICT, four tasks omit Opportunities for Working with others and only one task addresses one element of Improving Own Learning and Performance, and the same task deals with two parts of Problem-solving. It will probably strike the reader as being strange that Advanced-level mathematics has so few opportunities to meet the requirements of the Problem-solving Key Skill. The following tasks are taken from the QCA Key Skills documentation for A-level mathematics produced in 2000 and aim to offer suggestions for possible activities in the maths classroom. For full details, consult the folder entitled *Adaptable learning materials and practical guides: Key Skills in A Levels: mathematics.*

Pure maths tasks

Both pure mathematics activities address graphical functions building in opportunities to develop and create evidence in parts of Communication, all aspects of Application of Number, IT and Working with Others. Neither Problem-solving nor Improving Own Learning and Performance are deemed to be included in these tasks. The first task investigates the effect of simple transformations on the graph $y = f(x)$ such as $y = af(x)$, $y = f(x) + a$, $y = f(x + a)$ and $y = f(ax)$. Use of a graphics calculator is recommended for this investigation. Pupils are required to predict the shapes of a number of predefined graphs and then to check their predictions using a graphics calculator or data sensor equipment. Each graph should then be described using the appropriate mathematical terminology and then the process repeated for another function. A mixture of print-outs and hand-drawn graphs are required as evidence of the skills covered. Finally, the pupils are encouraged to submit a report and oral presentation of the results.

The second task examines the methods available for solving equations that cannot be solved algebraically. This task straddles both AS and A2 material. Again a graphics calculator is required, plus access to a computer graph-plotting package. Where numerical methods to determine the solution are being used, a spreadsheet is also recommended.

All tasks are structured so that pupils are encouraged to use a variety of methods to find the solution, thereby matching the Key Skills criteria. Where possible, more open-ended suggestions of tasks are included to facilitate differentiation for the more able student.

Statistics tasks

The three statistics tasks address the topics: Collection and analysis of data, Data collection and presentation, and Sample means. The first task is suitable for AS Statistics students, while the remaining two require a higher level of statistical expertise and should be covered in A2 classes.

The first of the statistics tasks asks the pupils to design some experiments that generate data on reaction times – e.g. how quickly a student can catch a falling ruler. This activity requires the students to generate a large data set using appropriate methods of data collection, representation and analysis. Due to the size of the sample required, the pupils will work in groups generating subsamples before pooling their results. Consequently, this task addresses two aspects of Communication, all aspects of Application of Number, IT and Working with Others. No skills in Problem-solving or Improving Own Learning and Performance are included in this task.

The second statistics task is directly relevant to pupils wishing to study at university. This task asks pupils to investigate higher-education opportunities, looking at issues such as entrance requirements for a particular course, number of students – undergraduates and postgraduates – employability, special features such as placements, proportion of firsts awarded, drop-out rates, course duration, accommodation and travel costs, social events and local entertainment, and others. This activity requires some initial collaboration with other people interested in the same course, so it contributes to the planning element of Working with Others. Due to the need to set personal targets and goals, plus the requirement to investigate a number of options, some development of IOP and PS will occur. Both AoN and IT are addressed in full, while most of Communication is covered.

The final statistics task addresses the same Key Skills as the second statistics task, apart from the contribution to IOP and PS. This task also involves practical activity as pupils collect data from a normal population and then investigate the distribution of sample means. For S3 module students, the task can be extended to include the Central Limit Theorem.

Mechanics tasks

The first two mechanics tasks address most of the IT Key Skills elements; however, the final three tasks make no use of ICT. All five tasks cover the criteria for AoN and most of Communication. The first mechanics task investigates co-planar forces in equilibrium using practical techniques and some groupwork. Mathematical modelling using pulleys and weights combined with Newton meters, for measurement purposes, is used to generate the data for the diagrams representing the equilibrium positions. Using a mixture of scale drawings and trigonometry, the pupils can demonstrate balancing the forces vertically and horizontally.

In the second mechanics task the pupils design an experiment to investigate the horizontal distance travelled by a projectile as the direction of the initial velocity changes. Modelling assumptions and experimental error can be integrated into the discussion of the results.

The final three tasks relate to a children's playground. The topics of moments, horizontal circular motion and the inclined plane are investigated through the medium of designing a safe see-saw, a safe roundabout taking into account angular speed and centripetal force, and a slide with and without friction. Using mathematical modelling, a practical generation of actual data can be produced for each task. These outcomes are then analysed, hypotheses generated and conclusions drawn. Based on the results, recommendations for the design of the playground equipment is included in the written report.

Task 12.5 Complete one of the Level 3 tasks

Look at the mathematics resources provided by your local Key Skills examining authority and select one of the Level 3 tasks. Work through all aspects of the task and generate an exemplar solution for showing to your students.

The organisation of Key Skills across a school

Some A-level students struggle to generate evidence across the core skills and wider Key Skills due to their choice of subjects. Therefore, it is imperative that schools and colleges have a 'back-up' plan for dealing with these cases. Three models of the organisation of Key Skills have been developed for consideration by school management teams: the cross-curricular approach, the specialist approach or the pick-n-mix model (CCEA, 2000b). Each system has its own values, so it remains a school management decision to determine which approach is most fitting for the staff and pupils within the school.

The *cross-curricular* approach distributes the workload across a number of subject teachers who are expected to collectively co-ordinate the provision of all Key Skills in the school by identifying which subjects will offer which Key Skills. In an ideal world, this arrangement would ensure 100 per cent coverage. However, it requires all the teachers to be committed to offering the allocated Key Skills opportunities. It is also difficult for all subject combinations to be addressed, so this design may encourage the specification of restricted subject combinations and A-level choices, based on the need for Key Skills evidence.

The *specialist model* advocates that specialist teachers are timetabled for teaching Key Skills subject knowledge and are also responsible for the supervision and marking of the students' portfolios. The advantage of this model is that schools can be sure that Key Skills provisions are of a high standard and that specialist teachers have the expertise to offer remedial help and advice to students. In the case of ICT, this structure also prevents a gridlock in the booking of the computer suites by subject teachers. Against this is the possible over-burdening of small groups of staff such as the maths teachers, the ICT teachers and the English or literacy teachers. The model also gives the impression that Key Skills are detached from the A-level subjects and will be viewed as additional work by the pupils. This impression is at odds with the intentions of Dearing. A final disadvantage of this model is the chaos which results when the teacher, who has assumed full (and often sole) responsibility for a particular task, decides to move school.

The final model is called the *pick-n-mix approach* since it is a combination of the best aspects of the above two models. In this model, the departments co-operate with one another, cross-referencing the location and subject areas of the Key Skills evidence. The specialist teachers may offer classes in preparation for the external examination, while the portfolios are developed with the subject teachers. Often, the specialist teacher is approached for a 'set task' if a student has identified a gap in his or her portfolio of evidence and, after consultation with the subject teachers, still has no means of achieving the evidence. The role of the school's Key Skills Co-ordinator is a highly complex one for this model.

Conclusion

Despite the bad publicity surrounding Key Skills and the low pass rates that have been reported for some external tests, it is clear that the integration of opportunities to develop Key Skills while completing their AS- and A-level courses is of benefit to most pupils. In many schools, A-level teachers are the more experienced members of the maths depart-ment who have established effective methods of delivering the A-level subject knowledge.

By having to integrate Key Skills into their teaching, these teachers are now revising their pedagogy and reflecting on alternative teaching strategies to achieve the same outcomes. Pupils are therefore benefitting by having a wider variety of approaches to the subject content and are also receiving opportunities for developing their skills as independent learners in preparation for university or working life. The two major disadvantages of this system are the lack of acknowledgement of Key Skills by universities in terms of UCAS points and the time-consuming nature of the new teaching pedagogies in an already over-crowded curriculum.

13 Teaching mathematics and special educational needs (SEN)

Introduction

This chapter addresses the issues surrounding teaching children with special needs in mainstream education. It offers an insight into the range of special needs – both low-ability and gifted children – and also the variety of teaching strategies used to assist them in their learning. Practical assistance on planning and preparing a maths lesson is suggested and information is offered on the process of assessing children with SEN. The impact of ICT in teaching children with learning needs is also reviewed in the light of the requirements for 'inclusion'.

Learning outcomes

By the end of this chapter you should be able to:

- define special educational needs;
- list the types of special needs;
- adapt your lesson to take account of children with SEN in the class;
- build differentiation into the resources to be used with children with SEN;
- use ICT to assist children with learning needs;
- plan for and understand the needs of gifted children in your class;
- understand 'inclusion' in terms of teaching and assessment.

What is SEN?

Special educational needs (SEN) is the term used to describe the requirement for additional educational provision compared to the 'norm'. For the majority of people, SEN implies a lack of ability, but it should be remembered that gifted pupils also have special needs as they are progressing at a much quicker rate than their peers and so require 'additional educational provision' too. As a teacher, you must acknowledge the needs of these children so that both ends of the ability 'continuum' receive the preparation and separate attention they may need in your lessons. In this chapter, SEN in terms of low ability will be discussed first, followed by a section highlighting how to deal with gifted children in your classroom and the types of provision they require for effective learning.

Quite often the phrase 'learning difficulty' is used instead of special needs particularly if the problem is subject specific. A pupil is said to have 'special educational needs' if

(a) he has a significantly greater difficulty in learning than the majority of children his age; or

(b) he has a disability which either prevents or hinders him from making use of the educational facilities of a kind generally provided at an Ordinary school.

(NI Order, 1986, para. 33(2))

A revised SEN Code of Practice came into force in January 2002 together with the SEN Provisions of the SEN and Disability Act 2001 and the Education (Special Educational Needs) (England) Regulations 2001. This new Code of Practice replaced the existing one issued in 1994. The new Code gives children the 'right to have their voices heard and be part of the decision-making process on their educational future' and offers encouragement to the 'partnerships between parents, schools, Local Education Authorities, health and social services and voluntary organisations that are crucial to the success in raising the achievement of all children'. Overall, the aim is to offer a better deal to all children with special educational needs.

It is important to note that the majority of pupils with special needs are in mainstream education. Due to the government's requirements for inclusion, only a small proportion of children with special needs are in special schools. Most pupils have minor problems which can be dealt with in the normal classroom setting using differentiation in the teaching methodology. Therefore, all teachers should have a basic knowledge of the issues relating to SEN and how to cope with them in the classroom environment. The inclusion statement highlights the need for teachers to ensure that their lessons and teaching styles are:

* relevant;
* motivating;
* appropriate to the individual needs of the child.

Types of special educational needs

'Learning difficulties' can cover a wide range of special educational needs ranging from those associated with profound and multiple learning difficulties to those typical of moderate learning difficulties or subject-specific problems. Typically, pupils with learning difficulties are unlikely to achieve above level 2 by the age of 16.

The types of special needs vary from pupil to pupil. Some pupils may have only one special need, while other students are faced with a host of problems. The following classification system has been adapted from Alsopp and Luth (1999):

* severe learning difficulties (SLD) (for example, autism, Asperger's Syndrome, multi-sensory impairment);
* moderate learning difficulties (MLD) (such as poor literacy and numeracy skills);
* specific learning difficulties (SPLD) (typically, dyslexia and dyscalculia);
* emotional and behavioural difficulties (EBD) (often temporary, resulting from bullying, bereavement or abuse);

- physical impairment (requiring wheelchair access);
- sensory impairment (for example, (partially) deaf or blind children);
- exceptional ability or gifted children.

Every school (including grammar schools) now has a Special Educational Needs Co-ordinator (SENCO) who is responsible for ensuring that a school policy exists to deal with pupils with special needs. This person offers support and advice to teachers, pupils and parents in relation to the planning, delivery and assessment processes within the National Curriculum. Since the majority of problems are related to literacy and/or numeracy, the SENCO works closely with the Literacy and Numeracy co-ordinators within the school to ensure that the three school policies complement each other. As a teacher, you will also have access to the help and advice of these people when dealing with cases of special needs in your classroom. However, the ultimate responsibility rests with you, the teacher, to maintain an inclusive approach to your teaching using differentiation whenever necessary to ensure the delivery of the statutory entitlement to learning for *all* pupils.

Inclusion

The revised National Curriculum for England and Wales pays particular attention to the responsibilities of schools to provide a broad and balanced curriculum that is deemed inclusive in terms of gender, race, religion and disability.

There are three principles for inclusion:

- setting suitable learning challenges;
- responding to pupils' diverse learning needs;
- overcoming potential barriers to learning and assessment for individuals and groups of pupils.

(QCA, 2000)

In the sections that follow, these three principles of inclusion are embedded in the context of teaching mathematics.

Coping with children with SEN in mainstream education

This section aims to give a few pointers on how to deal with pupils who have special needs in the mathematics classroom. It is not a definitive guide, nor does it offer the answer to all the problems; instead, it is intended to provide a starting point for thinking about what you do in the classroom, how you prepare, plan and teach a lesson, and how you could improve the process.

Lesson planning

As with all lessons, it is important to be fully prepared before you enter the classroom. Ensure that you have clearly defined aims and key learning objectives in your lesson plan with a thoughtfully structured approach in the presentation phase of the main part of the lesson. Think carefully about the prerequisite knowledge for the lesson and build in checks at an early stage (introduction) to clarify that the pupils will be able to cope with what follows. Now look at the examples you will be using – is there an incline of difficulty? Are the examples in the introduction matched to the work to be completed by the pupils? Have you emphasised the criterial attributes sufficiently? What check have you made on the pupils' level of understanding? So far, this seems like the preparation for a normal lesson, but now we will consider our special needs checks on:

- language;
- presentation;
- difficulty;
- quantity.

Language

In terms of each type of learning difficulty, language plays an important role for every learner. Pupils with literacy problems may be unable to read and follow detailed instructions in textbooks or on worksheets. For this reason, the teacher must make all the instructions explicit verbally, as he or she is completing a worked example with the class. High levels of questioning and interaction with the pupils provide good opportunities to discuss, reason and exemplify the process of 'showing your working' and solving the problem. Oral work is particularly valuable in addressing the needs of learners with poor literacy skills and also those pupils with visual problems. However, it is important to remember that the hearing-impaired student may not be keeping up with the lesson if you rely too heavily on this teaching style. So:

- keep your instructions concise and clear;
- use short sentences in your description of the work to be completed and reinforce important points both orally and on the board;
- do not overuse new vocabulary and always offer an alternative phrase to ensure that the pupils understand the meaning of new terminology.

Presentation

For the pupils with hearing difficulties, remember to produce an overhead transparency or Powerpoint slide summarising the main teaching points. If you are using the overhead projector or data projector, make sure the work is presented clearly and of an appropriate size for reading. Try to encourage pupils with hearing or visual problems to sit in areas of the classroom where they have a clear view of you, so that they can see any visual aids you may show and also to allow lip-reading if necessary. Be aware of reflections from lights or windows on the (interactive) whiteboard. Pace the lesson to allow pupils with a hearing impairment sufficient time to copy down any notes from the board or OHT. Ideally, you should keep this activity to a minimum and follow it with the application phase so that other pupils in the class can continue to work alone once they have completed the notes. This will allow you to keep the information on screen for longer without delaying the lesson.

Introduce new vocabulary with the use of diagrams and, where possible, include illustrations to emphasise the main teaching points or to highlight new terminology – for example, in circles: circumference, arc, diameter, radius, sector, segment and tangent. Choose the colour of the text and diagrams carefully, taking into account contrasts and colour blindness. The presentation of the work should be engaging but not distracting from the purpose. If mathematical puzzles or games require the use of colour or observation skills, then make sure that the text or diagrams are sufficiently large for the visually impaired – e.g. fraction dominoes, identifying shapes, lines of symmetry.

Worksheets should be word-processed, and the font should be sufficiently large and clear to be read by the visually impaired. If the handouts are notes summarising a topic, make frequent use of headings and subheadings to break large areas of text. Include plenty of white space and put a border round important definitions or equations.

Difficulty

Within the worksheet, start with relatively easy questions or problems similar to those you have completed on the board with the class. Build an incline of difficulty into each worksheet to keep the pupils motivated and on-task. However, make sure that the gradient is not too steep! Pupils will become de-motivated if the work is too easy or too hard, so gradually increase the difficulty so that each question is within the extended grasp of the students. By leading them steadily from the easy to difficult questions, the pupils will feel encouraged by their own achievements and this will increase their self-esteem. This is particularly important if you have pupils with emotional and behavioural difficulties (EBD) in your class who have short attention spans and low levels of self-esteem. This type of pupil becomes bored easily, so worksheets need to be interesting yet engaging without being too difficult and causing confusion.

Quantity

The quantity of work set may spark off misbehaviour in a classroom of able pupils. Be realistic in the volume of work set – it is better to have extension materials available for pupils who finish earlier than others than to dishearten students by expecting them to complete a whole exercise in ten minutes. When dealing with children who have EBD, encourage them by providing a variety of tasks all addressing the same set of maths skills. For example, start with five mental arithmetic or oral questions, followed by five drill-and-practice items before moving to contextualised questions and eventually problem-solving items. To maintain their concentration span, motivation and interest, this type of teaching can be mixed with paired work or groupwork to add variety to the lesson. In many cases, the less able pupils will feel a sense of achievement when they finish a worksheet and will be very happy to ask you for another one. Develop the self-esteem of pupils with SLD, MLD or SPLD by providing them with slightly longer and more difficult worksheets each time.

It is also worth bearing in mind that 'What is good practice for SEN is good practice for all', so think about these four aspects in all your lessons, not just those where you know of pupils with SEN.

Groupwork and pupils with SEN

Pupils with SLD and often severe EBD are taught in special units on the school campus or in special schools if they have multiple-sensory impairments or severe disabilities. SEN pupils in mainstream education typically have single and often specific problems that can be dealt with using a sensitive and controlled approach. To overcome some of the problems being experienced by these pupils in mainstream classes, teachers can use groupwork to provide a means of informally assisting the pupils with learning difficulties. For example, a pupil with literacy problems may be highly skilled in creativity and original thinking. He or she can 'see' solutions to problems in a different light from other students and therefore would have an important role to play in the groupwork situation when someone else can write down the ideas for him or her.

Similarly, a pupil with EBD may excel at mathematics when allowed to work in a context with few rules or routines such as working in a group to solve an open-ended problem. Misbehaviour is often a sign of frustration – either from the work being too hard or too easy. Being part of a group often sustains the pupil's attention and even offers an 'audience' when he or she is attention-seeking. If the EBD pupil is withdrawn and silent in class, then working as part of a group may help to develop his or her self-confidence in achieving success in mathematics, leading to a willingness to contribute to mathematical discussions.

Groupwork is also advantageous for the pupil with visual or hearing difficulties as the smaller group setting will allow for repetition of discussions and the use of diagrams to illustrate the theory or problem-solving process. Each pupil can also assume a responsibility for a particular part of the work, if necessary, ensuring that everyone's contribution is valued.

Clearly, groupwork assists the teacher who has a number of pupils with learning difficulties in his or her class as the responsibility of speaking individually to each one is sometimes unmanageable within the classroom context. By ensuring that each group contains no more than one of these pupils and that the members of the group are aware of the pupil's difficulty and how to assist that pupil without making him or her feel inadequate, each pupil with SEN will receive the extra attention they require either from the teacher or from their peers.

At the opposite end of the scale, gifted pupils may also feel 'different' from their peers and may also wish to be accepted for their 'normal' qualities rather than their mathematical excellence.

Disadvantages of groupwork

There are a number of advantages in using groupwork; however, disadvantages also exist at times. As pupils get older, they are not always willing to accept the pupil with SEN into their group as they are concerned that the person will 'hold them back'. This feeling is particularly dominant if they have had no previous experience of children with learning difficulties. The pupils with special educational needs can therefore feel isolated and rejected from class activities. However, other class members who have accepted the pupil with learning difficulties in primary school continue to 'look after' him or her during their secondary school education. These pupils are able to see the person and not the learning difficulty.

The teacher plays an important role in encouraging the integration of the pupils with SEN into the classroom activities and discussions. By demonstrating the best way to treat these pupils so that their self-esteem is preserved and they have a positive learning experience, other pupils in the class will begin to understand how to work alongside pupils with special educational needs.

Learning Support Assistants (LSAs)

For some pupils with SEN, one-to-one attention is the only means of ensuring progression. As a teacher, you are responsible for the whole class, so it may be difficult to ensure that these pupils gets sufficient levels of one-to-one attention. Consequently, some schools invest in additional teaching assistance or learning support assistants (LSAs) for these pupils. Making good use of help is an area that requires a certain amount of organisation and planning and is one of your teaching competences. If the LSA is employed to sit with the pupil offering extra explanations relating to the work then you must ensure you have briefed the assistant in advance of the lesson. It is vital that he or she employs the same teaching methodology as you so that there is a consistency of approach to the rules or algorithms being practised in the lesson. Alternatively, it may be to your advantage to deal directly with the pupil so that a continuity of approach and monitoring of progress is achieved, particularly if you are involved in drawing up the Individual Education Plan for each pupil with SEN. In this instance, the LSA can manage the rest of the class as they complete the work you have set.

Sometimes, the additional help is provided in another school in the area so that specialist numeracy or literacy assistance is administered to a group of students rather than on an individual level. In these cases, arrangements are made for the pupil to be out of class for a certain period of time on a regular basis. Transport is also provided to and from the school.

What are dyscalculia and dyslexia?

Dyscalculia is a condition affecting the pupil's ability to acquire arithmetical skills. Research by Gordon (1992) describes dyscalculia as:

> a developmental lag in the acquisition of numerical skills, can be manifested in many ways, including the inability to recognise number symbols, mirror writing, and a failure to maintain the proper order of numbers in calculations.
>
> (Gordon, 1992)

Pupils experiencing this condition struggle with simple number concepts, facts and procedures. Purely dsycalculic learners may have cognitive and language abilities in the normal range, so they excel in non-mathematical subjects.

Dyslexia is an inability to process language which may also affect areas of mathematics such as sequencing and number patterns, orientation and time/organisational ability, and memory. They find it difficult to do mental calculations quickly and tend to 'learn by heart' the techniques for solving problems rather than understand the mathematical processes. Dyslexic learners benefit from the use of physical objects and visual methods. They often use a multi-sensory approach, adopting rhymes, colour-coding and mnemonics to help them remember the 'rules'.

For further information on dyscalculia and dyslexia, consult DfES (2001) and Henderson (1998).

Assessment and SEN

This section investigates the responsibilities placed on teachers to assess pupils according to the National Curriculum requirements.

With regard to assessment arrangements for these students, it has been accepted that certain criteria can be ignored when making judgements against the level descriptions, particularly when it is clear that the pupils will not be able to achieve mastery of the criteria due to the nature of their problem. The National Curriculum highlights the following areas of mathematics as being potential barriers to progress and states that some pupils may require:

- specific help with number recall or the interpretation of data presented in graphs, tables or bar charts, to compensate for difficulties with long- or short-term memory or with visual discrimination;
- access to tactile or other specialist equipment for work relating to shape, space and measures, to overcome difficulties in managing visual information;
- help in interpreting or responding to oral directions when making mental calculations, to compensate for difficulties in hearing or with auditory discrimination;
- access to equipment or other resources, such as ICT, to overcome difficulties in thinking and working in the abstract.

In assessment:

- when judgements against level descriptions are required, those should, where appropriate, allow for the provision above.

(QCA, 1999, p. 82)

Benefits of ICT for children with SEN

Teaching and learning

Multimedia is a powerful educational resource in any classroom. With its combination of textual, visual and sound facilities, multimedia resources are ideal for engaging pupils with a variety of learning difficulties. Pupils with dyslexia or difficulties in reading textual information find multimedia a particularly beneficial mode of presenting information as there are few large chunks of text, plenty of visual images and quite often sounds, video clips or animations/simulations to demonstrate principles or concepts. Similarly, pupils with hearing problems are not dependent on listening to instructions and explanations from teachers when using ICT. Using the computer offers them the independence and freedom to work at their own pace and access information in the way that best suits their requirements. The interactive nature of the software benefits pupils with SEN as the 'cause-and-effect' relationships are immediately evident, which motivates even the most reluctant of learners. Mouse-clicks on key words or to select an area of the screen results in a change in the information presented, thereby encouraging the pupils to continue this behaviour. Keyboard overlays and a variety of accessories are available for users with limited dexterity, while the new voice-activated software is becoming increasingly more sophisticated, allowing pupils to dictate their work to overcome literacy difficulties.

Software applications are being produced for a range of ability levels and ages. For example, First Word is a beginner's version of MS Word, Junior Pinpoint is a database package for primary school children, and the Black Cat software offers spreadsheet, database, word processing, Powerpoint and drawing packages designed specifically for the younger pupils. Powerpoint can be used to introduce pupils to the idea of presenting their work as a story using a sequence of slides or pupils may wish to use Hyperstudio. One opportunity for a multimedia presentation in maths is a report on 'The everyday instances of symmetry'. Pupils with literacy problems could include clip-art or pictures taken using a digital camera or scanned from a book as illustrations to explain the types of symmetry that exist such as line or rotational symmetry. Other presentation topics could be based on the history of a famous mathematician, such as Pythagoras, instances of mathematics in society such as looking at the natural occurrences of the Golden Ratio, which may involve scanning in images of paintings or architecture, or the applications of probability in everyday life, e.g. the Lotto.

Logo-based systems allow pupils to experience motion first-hand by controlling the movement of a turtle around a fixed area. The use of commands to set directions, turning and distances encourages the pupils to use skills of estimation and to develop their spatial awareness while maintaining a fun element to the task. The ability to order events in a logical sequence to achieve a goal is a worthwhile learning experience and Logo is ideal for practising these skills.

Research (Underwood and Brown, 1997) into the use of Integrated Learning Systems (ILS) such as Successmaker, revealed the positive impact such computer-based systems have on pupils with SEN. Compared to other pupils, children with SEN demonstrated a much higher rate of improvement using these systems than when experiencing traditional teaching. The drill and practice nature of the software encourages these pupils to use their existing knowledge and since the computer is non-judgemental, they are more willing to try to answer a question with the knowledge that they could get it wrong without their teacher knowing. The journalling facility, however, records such instances so that the teacher can offer additional tuition on this topic before the next session on the ILS. The pupils are administered a range of items addressing literacy or numeracy. However, as most of the numeracy items are read to the students, the teacher is unable to gauge how this pupil would have performed on a paper-based test where the ability to read a question is imperative.

Assessment

The role of ICT in assisting pupils in learning new subject knowledge, skills and concepts is obvious as CD-ROMs and other teaching resources tend to adopt a hierarchical structure such as computer games that encourages pupils to keep trying harder to achieve the next 'level'. Research (Cowan, 2003 and Cowan and Lynch, in press) into the use of voice-overs and scaffolding to assist primary school pupils with dyslexia, literacy or numeracy problems, EBD and physical disabilities discovered that dyslexic pupils' assessment performance increased substantially as they understood the question fully. Similarly, pupils experiencing problems with the 'basics' made effective use of the Vygotskian prompts for each question to obtain 'hints' relating to the mathematical techniques needed to solve the question. With each selection of a 'hint' by the pupils, the marks needed to pass the test increased slightly, depending on the perceived helpfulness of the prompt to the pupil. The Angoff (1971) standard-setting technique, used to determine the cut-score of the original test, facilitated the recalculation of the passing score based on the use of prompting. The electronic tests (Cowan, 2003) also found that pupils with EBD remain focused on their work for longer time spans and enjoyed using computers due to the inter-active feedback at all stages. In conclusion, computerised testing benefited pupils with special educational needs.

Task 13.1

Find out about the types of learning difficulties being experienced by the pupils in your classes. Speak to the SENCO regarding the impact of these learning difficulties on their performance in mathematics. Make a list of suggestions on how you could deal with these problems in each topic you are teaching.

Task 13.2

If possible, try to gain access to a special unit and observe the teaching of a mathematics lesson. What were the lesson objectives and how did the teacher ensure he or she had met them?

Task 13.3

Select a worksheet which you designed yourself for use in class. Using the three principles of inclusion, evaluate your own worksheet and suggest improvements. Are there any basic improvements that would apply to all your teaching resources used by pupils?

Gifted children

The DfES (2002a) reports refer to 'able' pupils as 'gifted and talented' when the pupils' ability is beyond conventional expectation. EiC defines 'gifted and talented' pupils to be the top 5–10 per cent of pupils in a school. 'Gifted' usually refers to having a high ability in academic subjects, while 'talented' is associated with high ability in a creative or expressive art or sport. The Key Stage 3 Strategy advocates opportunities for enrichment, extension and acceleration in a gifted pupil's classroom.

How do you recognise that a child is a gifted mathematician?

Gifted children are often missed in a busy classroom and may become bored and rebellious if the work is not challenging them, so they are often mistaken for children with EBD due to their disruptiveness and persistent shouting out of the answers in class. Mathematically able children are logical thinkers and often take shortcuts when finding a solution to a problem. They absorb new information quickly and can use symbols and mathematical notation with ease. They are quick to notice patterns in numbers or sequences (DfES, 2002b) and can transfer problem-solving techniques from one problem to another. When faced with adversity, they are dedicated and persistent in their search for a solution. Sometimes these children are not exceptional when using drill and practice methods in numerical calculations as they are often too focused on the problem as a whole and make careless mistakes.

In identifying able mathematicians, schools tend to consider the child's performance in tests, examinations, classwork, homework, previous teachers' experiences of the child, the child's own perception of self and the parent's perceptions of the child's ability in maths. Regular re-assessment of the situation and an effort to observe the pupil's attitude and performance in a variety of maths activities in class is required before coming to a final decision.

Classroom work for able children

Across Key Stages 1 and 2, teachers can use the level descriptions for the next Key Stage to guide the content coverage for the able maths students. Using the National Numeracy Strategy, it is relatively easy to extend the objectives in terms of depth and breadth, setting more complex and detailed tasks for the able pupils in the class on the same general topic as other members of the class. The pace of coverage of the content can also be increased for these children, leaving them with more time to develop their higher-order thinking skills and mathematical reasoning through problem-solving activities. Similarly, the Key Stage 3 Framework for Mathematics allows for accelerated learning with Year 9 pupils addressing the depth of content normally typical of GCSE pupils.

The main focus of the lessons should be to provide enhancement and enrichment to the basic activity. They should be encouraged to research and investigate the *why* and *how* in certain tasks. The application of mathematics in other subject areas would offer an open-ended and perhaps more interesting approach to problem-solving and would further enhance the child's enjoyment of the subject. Tasks that focus on making comparisons, evaluating outcomes and suggesting reasons and critical comments on the findings, may be more suited to some learners than others. By increasing their level of independence in mathematical tasks, the pupils will grow mentally to become confident and successful mathematicians. The use of discussion and questioning also assists pupils in developing their communicative skills when explaining their thought processes and reasoning to others in the class. As the teacher, you can plan to ask these pupils higher-order questions in the class discussions such as 'Can you explain your calculation?', 'What are the stages in solving . . . ?', 'What evidence can you find to support . . . ?', 'I wonder why . . . (speculation)', 'What would happen if . . . (predictions)?', 'Tell me more about . . . (elaboration)' (NNS, 1999 and KS3 Strategy, 2002).

It is important not to leave the high-ability pupils with a large quantity of work pitched at the same level as the rest of the class. Start pupils at an appropriate level of difficulty, use challenging questions to deepen thinking and extend or open up tasks to enrich the learning experience (DfES, 2002b). The emphasis is on quality and not quantity of work completed in the lesson. Teachers are advised to incorporate more demanding and thought-provoking questions into the classwork or worksheets that require the gifted pupils to use their knowledge or adapt the new skills being practised. These pupils also need attention, support and direction to prevent them from becoming disillusioned with the more difficult work being administered to them. Discuss targets with the able students and encourage them to set themselves long-term goals to achieve over a few weeks. Encourage sustained work by the pupils on an extended task and allow the pupils to plan and monitor their own progress over this time, increasing their independence and level of responsibility for their own development.

By using a range of tasks comprising different levels of difficulty but addressing the same topic or theme within the one class, the three-stage lesson advocated by the NNS and KS3 Strategy can be maintained. The gifted student can report back on his or her findings from a more open-ended task or can be asked to explain why a finding is true. He or she can also be called upon in the class to offer an alternative strategy for solving a problem. Every student will learn from each other and their self-esteem will be fostered. All the students can celebrate their success together, regardless of ability level.

As with the low-ability pupils, high-ability students can also make effective use of the internet and CD-ROMs for problem-solving activities. Internet sites containing investigations and puzzles are available in a user-friendly and interactive format. Speeded activities for mental arithmetic as well as logical puzzles that require the discovery of patterns or sequences of events are available. The use of CD-ROMs allows a real-life situation to be simulated and the results from the pupils' decisions demonstrated on screen. Using the feedback, the pupils can revise their ideas and make a more informed decision the next time. In some cases, the pupils are required to pass on their knowledge and expertise to the next group, thereby enhancing the pupils' communication skills by using mathematical terminology in everyday life.

Organisation of gifted pupils in the classroom

The NNS recommends three main avenues to deal with a gifted *primary* school student in the classroom:

- keep the child with his or her peers and set the pupils into groups of equitable ability levels. Use high levels of differentiation in the classwork for each group;
- move the child up a class in an accelerated or fast-track route;
- bring in additional assistance to offer support or simultaneous teaching at a higher level.

As the class teacher, you must weigh up the advantages and disadvantages of each scenario. Keeping the child in the normal classroom environment with his or her friends will maintain feelings of security and consistency. As a teacher, you can monitor the pupil's progress alongside equally able children and can alter the pace of the work instantaneously if required. Placing the pupil in an accelerated class will allow him or her to continue to progress rapidly alongside other students (who may be a year older) of the same ability. Bringing in additional help to offer a flexible and supportive environment for the child will also benefit the student who has the undivided attention of this 'alternative' teacher.

The disadvantages are also clear to be seen. Setting the pupils may result in a gender bias at each end of the scale, thereby reinforcing stereotypes and demoralising the students who are not in the top group.

The fast-track method needs to be treated with caution. For this scheme to work effectively, schools need to have an overall policy for this form of teaching to ensure that the materials and contexts are suitable for the younger students and are independent of the links to areas of the curriculum that have not been covered by these pupils. The age of the pupil is also a concern as young children develop quickly, so one year's difference in age may mean a large difference in maturity. Children must be ready to cope with the accelerated system socially and emotionally, otherwise it could be detrimental to their personal development. The question of what happens to the child in the final year of schooling also requires a school policy decision.

Finally, a good interrelationship between the teacher and the LSA for the gifted child needs to be maintained so that the pupil's progress can be monitored and reviewed regularly. The LSA should also be qualified to deal with gifted children and know how to support and challenge them academically.

Underachievement of gifted pupils

Many pupils do not wish to have the extra attention associated with 'giftedness' and so play down their skills to mix in with the rest of the class (DfES, 2002b). Their work may be uneven in its quality, with excellent performance initially and then a drop in performance as they become 'noticed' as being good at maths and pleasing the teacher. Cycles of top-quality work may be followed by periods of poor performance or even missing homework assignments. Peer pressure and bullying are some of the main causes of talented pupils underachieving, particularly in the post-primary sector (DfES, 2002b).

As part of the strategy for Inclusion, pupils need to understand that different people have different strengths in a variety of subjects and it is not fair to pick on these students because they are doing well in an area that interests them. The teacher has to be careful not to emphasise outstanding performance in front of the rest of the class, particularly if there is a history of bullying in the school. By assigning pupils to specific tasks requiring a higher level of expertise than other tasks, the gifted pupil will soon realise that you have pinpointed his or her expertise but are not making it public. As time progresses, both the pupil and the teacher establish a mode of working that is effective and beneficial in encouraging and extending the pupil's performance.

Summer schools for gifted and talented students are now being funded by DfEE as part of the *Excellence in Cities* campaign. This programme is targeted at 16–17-year-olds to encourage them to consider a university education on leaving school. Some 450 secondary schools are involved in the initiative, which caters for the top 5–10 per cent of students in geographical clusters of schools within an LEA. Similar programmes are organised for 10–14-year-olds, amounting to almost 5,500 summer schools in total.

In a bid to determine the standing of the UK's best 9- and 13-year-olds internationally, QCA has introduced World Class Tests in maths and problem-solving that can be taken online or downloaded as test booklets for use in class. Further details on this initiative can be found at www.qca.org.uk/ca/tests/wct/. Gifted pupils should also be encouraged to participate in national events such as the National Maths Challenge run by the UK Maths trust – further details are available from www.mathscomp.leeds.ac.uk. Other more informal challenges can be found on websites such as www.nrich.maths.org and www. mathsnet.net. Organisations supporting teachers of gifted children include:

- QCA at www.nc.uk.net/gt/mathematics.
- Mathematical Association at www.m-a.org.uk/tc/enrich.htm.
- Excellence in Cities at www.xcalibre.ac.uk.

Task 13.4

Select a worksheet that you designed yourself for use in class. How would you adapt it for use with a group of gifted students?

Conclusion

Working alongside and assisting pupils with learning difficulties is a valuable learning experience for the rest of the class. It highlights the problems experienced by other children and encourages pupils to accept people for what they can do rather than what they cannot do. Being patient and understanding, giving everyone the opportunity to contribute and accepting alternative viewpoints are skills used in everyday life. By learning and working with pupils in their class who have learning difficulties, other pupils will often see skills that they themselves do not possess such as the strength of character and commitment in these students to overcome their difficulties.

14 Assessment

Introduction

Why do we assess pupils? Is assessment the same as testing? What are the main forms of assessment? How accurate are they? This chapter offers an overview of assessment, including the compulsory forms of assessment in mathematics curricula from Key Stage 1 to Advanced-level. Item types and test characteristics such as validity and reliability are also discussed in the context of defining what is being assessed in a test.

Learning outcomes

At the end of this chapter you should be able to:

- explain the purpose of assessment;
- discuss the types of assessments used in schools;
- identify different item formats in tests;
- understand validity and reliability and its importance in testing;
- list the compulsory assessments carried out in relation to mathematics.

Why do teachers assess their pupils?

Assessment is an integral part of teaching and learning. When planning any lesson, teachers have a set of instructional goals or key objectives that they intend to meet by the end of the lesson. In order to evaluate the effectiveness of their teaching, teachers must create opportunities to 'assess' pupils against these objectives. This can occur in a variety of ways: questioning pupils, the use of exemplars and non-exemplars, marking classwork, setting homework, carrying out practical activities such as investigations or problem-solving in real-life contexts. The feedback from pupils (orally and in writing) offers valuable information to a teacher who is evaluating his or her lesson. This form of assessment is called 'assessment *of* learning' (Black and Wiliam, 1998).

A second reason for assessing pupils is to obtain diagnostic information related to students' needs. The teacher needs to know if the pupils are ready to move on to the next stage in the learning process or if he or she needs to recap on the current work to remove any misconceptions or problems being experienced by the pupils. Sometimes, homework assignments reveal individualised problems that are not always apparent in the normal classroom setting. Such problems should be addressed on a one-to-one basis. This more formalised type of assessment highlights the need for additional teacher intervention in the learning process.

Another method of determining the pupils' level of understanding of a topic or area of subject knowledge is to test the pupils formally during a lesson. The results of tests also illustrate two important facets of teaching: the appropriateness of the learning goals to the pupils' age and ability; and the effectiveness of the instructional methods and resources in covering the topic. As part of the NNS, teachers are encouraged to *Assess and Review* (DfES, 2001) lessons at the end of each half-term to establish the pupils' ability to sustain learning.

Assessment is not just a technique to ensure improved student learning; it also contributes to improvements in the teaching and learning process. Formal assessment should complement the informal methods of assessing pupils' progress and not replace them.

So far, we have discussed the role of assessment from a teacher's perspective, but how do the pupils learn from this process?

The role of assessment for pupils

Pupils benefit from a range of assessment techniques in a variety of ways. Through informal questioning at the start of the lesson, pupils can refresh their memories on what they already know and what they have just learned. Often, they gain an insight into what they are about to learn. Discussions are a particularly powerful method of learning due to the presence of informal peer tuition. Pupils can assess their own strengths and weaknesses against those of their friends and peers, which often increases levels of motivation. The use of questioning in the plenary helps pupils to reinforce the new concepts and skills covered in the session and to emphasise the importance of recalling these key facts in the future. The use of exemplars and non-exemplars are a valuable means of achieving this end-point, particularly when they address the criterial attributes of a concept or technique.

Through assessment, pupils can also gauge their own progress and level of understanding within a topic. The ability to self-assess is an important skill (Schunk, 1996; Perry, 1998; QCA, 2001). Determining progress is particularly prevalent when homework is submitted for marking at regular intervals. The feedback from teachers should always be informative, positive and helpful to a pupil, thereby boosting self-esteem and interest (Butler, 1998; Pollard *et al.*, 2000) and raising standards (QCA, 2001). Pupils benefit little from a cross against an incorrect calculation with no words of advice regarding what was wrong. Instead, teachers should annotate exactly where the mistake occurred and offer an explanation why the pupils' work was incorrect. This type of detailed feedback on assessed work is often referred to as 'assessment *for* learning' (Black and Wiliam, 1998). Less formal and more continuous assessment of this nature is called *formative* assessment. The more formal methods of assessment such as tests that are usually carried out at the end of a topic or section are referred to as *summative* assessment. This final stage in the teaching process is designed to summarise and assess all the key aspects – skills, concepts and knowledge – relevant to the topic. The results from this type of assessment give the pupils an overall awareness or 'summary' of how well they have understood and mastered the content domain. It also provides opportunities for pupils to reinforce or establish cognitive links (Minsky, 1975; Rummelhart, 1980) between what is sometimes seen in class as a series of disjointed pieces of information with few interrelationships. By bringing the topic to a close, the pupils can view an overall and complete picture of the content domain as a whole unit.

Other uses of assessment information

Assessment information also has a role outside the classroom in terms of information to parents on their child's progress and also information for departments, school governors and curriculum developers. In most cases, this type of assessment would be the formal yearly examinations which result in reports being sent to parents. However, some schools also encourage parental involvement in homework assignments, which improves home–school links and keeps the parents up-to-date with their child's progress throughout the whole year rather than leaving them dependent on twice-yearly reports from the school.

Formal school examinations also allow school governors and departments to monitor the overall achievement of an entire year group since all the pupils sit the same examination papers at the same time, unlike class tests which may be designed by individual teachers or may be common to all the classes but administered on a test-as-needed basis. Departmental decisions and planning on schemes of work, content and depth of coverage of topics, GCSE examination tiers, setting or streaming of pupils and other aspects of the departmental management process are often based on the results of these examinations. The senior management team would also view these examinations as predictive of the national examination results – for example, end of Key Stage assessment, GCSE, AS- and A2-level examinations. Consequently, results play a role in target-setting within the school. For guidance and formulas used to predict achievement, consult the QCA website or the DfES Standards site for access to national figures.

Formal assessment of teachers

Pupils are not the only members of a school being assessed. Alongside the regular monitoring of the educational provision by the school's governors, once every four to six years the Office for Standards in Education (Ofsted) inspects schools with the aim of 'improvement through inspection'. Each of the whole-school policies is reviewed, including those for numeracy and assessment. In every subject, the Ofsted inspectors investigate pupil attainment against national standards, pupil progress in relation to prior attainment, teaching provision and resources, curriculum and assessment, plus a range of other aspects of school life. Departmental documentation such as Schemes of Work, development plans, units of work and even individual teacher's lesson plans and recording of assessment outcomes are all scrutinised by the subject-specific inspector. Classroom observations of lessons are also completed and scored on a 7-point scale, ranging from excellent to very poor, on each of the four categories: teaching, attainment, response and progress. Teachers at both ends of the range are identified and receive individualised feedback. They are also observed on a second occasion to confirm the validity of the inspector's first judgement. Written reports on all observations are made and verbal feedback is given to the teachers. Unlike the support from the Local Education Authorities (LEAs), this feedback is not in the form of advice or a conversation on issues in teaching mathematics that could be used as personal development by the teacher, but rather it is usually couched in Ofsted terminology and is bland.

The final summary report of the inspection process for the whole school is issued at the end of the five days. The inspectors' judgements cannot be challenged, only factual details on the school can be corrected if necessary. Based on the final report, areas of weakness or areas that could be improved as identified by the Inspectorate become priorities for the Principal and Board of Governors. Within 40 days of receiving the final report, the School's Action Plan is compiled as a response to the inspection. Often, the LEA will assist schools or departments in meeting their plans through the allocation of additional funds to improve the teaching facilities or to offer support and encouragement to particular subject departments in translating the 'Ofsted speak' into attainable goals in the classroom.

All Ofsted reports on schools become public documents once they are published on the internet (www.opne.gov.uk/ofsted/ofsted.htm) and therefore prospective parents can make judgements on the suitability of the school for their child. As a prospective teacher in the school, it is useful to read some of these reports prior to commencing your teaching placement or applying for a job. For further details on self-evaluation against the specific expectations of a post-primary mathematics department, consult the Ofsted support material entitled *Inspecting Mathematics 11–16 with Guidance on Self-evaluation*.

Summary

Overall, assessment is a vital part of the learning process and its value to both teachers and pupils should not be ignored. Consequently, the creation, administration, marking and feedback from testing should be completed with care (Ofsted, 1995) and the resultant implications of the testing process fully understood. Although not popular with teachers, the Ofsted inspections are effective in focusing a school's attention on continuously improving the teaching provision for pupils and therefore driving up standards of achievement, particularly in examination years. It also allows Principals, the Board of Governors and LEAs to make comparisons between and across schools with similar pupil intakes and educational provisions. Collectively, these reports also offer the government ongoing evaluation data on current educational policies.

Types of assessment

There are three main phases in teaching in which assessment can be carried out, as shown in Table 14.1. In each case, a different type of assessment is used, depending on the purpose or functional role it serves in terms of classroom practice.

Readiness assessment refers to the determination of the prerequisite knowledge and skills needed by a pupil before embarking in a new topic, content area or development

Table 14.1 Types of assessment in each phase
(Linn and Gronlund, 1995)

Teaching phase	Type of assessment
Before instruction	Readiness
	Placement
During instruction	Formative
	Diagnostic
After instruction	Summative

of a skill. This type of assessment may be carried out informally through questioning or classroom activities and/or formally via a test.

Placement assessment addresses the possible match between prior knowledge and the learning objectives of a topic or series of lessons. If pupils have already covered some of the intended learning outcomes, the teacher need only remind pupils of the skill or concept without actually re-teaching it. This form of assessment is particularly relevant to the Key Stage 2 to Key Stage 3 transition of pupils between schools.

Formative assessment allows both pupils and teachers to monitor progress on a daily basis and to adjust the teaching strategies accordingly from day-to-day, depending on the response of the class to the teaching techniques used. This type of assessment is not used to grade a student's ability, but is specifically designed for monitoring progress, encouraging pupils and confirming mastery of some skills and highlighting areas of weakness that require additional attention.

Diagnostic assessment is the term used to reveal recurring problems experienced by pupils and to plan for remedial action to correct them. It usually refers to problems that still occur after corrective action resulting from the normal formative assessment feedback. Specialised tests are available to identify these problems.

Summative assessment occurs at the end of a teaching and learning phase. Unlike formative assessment, this type of testing results in a grade or score being awarded to the pupils based on their performance in this test. All the remaining objectives for a unit or topic are normally addressed in this type of assessment and the pupils' levels of mastery of the content domain are recorded. More accurate results are obtained if pupils are given more than one opportunity to demonstrate their capabilities and if more than one context for assessment is given – for example, practical, written work, experimental reports, problem-solving, surveys, and so on (Messick, 1989). It is the summative assessment results that are transferred from the primary to the post-primary school during the transition to Key Stage 3. However, single overall grades in maths offer little information on the pupils' strengths and weaknesses in each area of mathematics.

Criterion-referenced and norm-referenced testing

Although tests are often referred to as norm-referenced or criterion-referenced tests, it is the measurement and interpretation of the *results* that are norm- or criterion-referenced, not the tests themselves. This distinction will be clarified when we consider the definitions of the two terms.

Criterion-referenced tests measure student performance against the intended learning outcomes – for example, SATs – while norm-referenced tests are typical of the national examinations such as GCSE and Advanced-level examinations where students are awarded grades according to their rank or percentile score. For the latter type of assessment, it is imperative that the test separates the students according to their ability. Therefore, very easy items and very difficult items are removed from the test because they offer little or no information about the candidates, since the majority of students will respond correctly or incorrectly respectively. The majority of items are focused at or near the 'average' level of ability and a large content domain is usually addressed by the test.

Criterion-referenced tests do not aim to rank order candidates by ability. Instead, they report the extent to which a pupil can correctly complete a task. For example, the pupils can perform a specific learning task such as counting from 1 to 100, or a percentage-correct score can be reported such as 'the pupil correctly multiplied two 2-digit numbers in 70 per cent of the cases given', or 'the pupil has met the minimum standard for mastery of a pre-defined domain such as scoring at least 40 out of 50 in a test'. Criterion-referenced tests usually address a small and limited domain, the item difficulty matches the learning objective so may range from easy to difficult, and the results of the test describe what the pupil can or cannot do relative to the clearly defined and restricted test domain (Linn and Gronlund, 1995).

What is assessed in tests?

The majority of testing falls into three categories: *knowledge*, *understanding* and *application*. A fourth type of assessment does exist, and is called *performance-based assessment*. However, it is normally reserved for the assessment of higher-order thinking skills such as analysis, critical thinking, reporting and reasoning, which are normally associated with open-ended problems set in real-life contexts (Linn and Gronlund, 1995). In the majority of classrooms, teachers tend to focus on what the pupils know, understand and can do. In some cases, the use of contexts is used to intensify the 'problem' so that pupils have to identify the correct technique for solving the problems. Different types of items are used in a test for different purposes.

Task 14.1

In the sections that follow, look at the types of questions and decide if they are aimed at assessing *knowledge*, *understanding* or *application*.

Short-answer items

Completion

> The longest side in a right-angled triangle is
> called the _ _ _ _ _ _ _ _ _ _ _ .

Simple calculation

Find angle A in the following triangle:

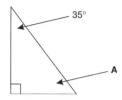

Simple calculation

If $a = 5$ and $b = 2$, calculate $2a + 3b$.

Multiple-choice question

The name given to a triangle with two sides the same length is:

A   equilateral
B   scalene
C   right-angled
D   isosceles

Matching

In the diagram below, letters are used to denote the angles. Use the letters to produce examples of each type of angle listed:

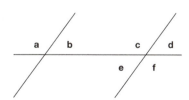

Vertically opposite angles are _ _ _ _ _ _ _ _ _ _ and _ _ _ _ _ _ _ _ _ _ _ .

Corresponding angles are _ _ _ _ _ _ _ _ _ _ _ and _ _ _ _ _ _ _ _ _ _ _ .

Supplementary angles are _ _ _ _ _ _ _ _ _ _ _ and _ _ _ _ _ _ _ _ _ _ _ .

Complementary angles are _ _ _ _ _ _ _ _ _ _ _ and _ _ _ _ _ _ _ _ _ _ _ .

An obtuse angle is _ _ _ _ _ _ _ _ _ _ _ .

An acute angle is _ _ _ _ _ _ _ _ _ _ _ .

True/false

Read each of the following statements. If the statement is correct, circle TRUE; if the statement is incorrect circle FALSE.

25% of 12 is 3	TRUE	FALSE
50% of $\frac{6}{8}$ is $\frac{3}{4}$	TRUE	FALSE
If 0.2 multiplied by a number is 4, then the number is less than 10.	TRUE	FALSE
In this diagram, angle *a* is smaller than angle *b*.	TRUE	FALSE

Restricted response

State the distributive and associative laws, giving an example of each.

State Pythagoras' Theorem.

Offer a reason for your answer to part (a). [Commonly seen in a multi-part question]

Structured response

A group of girls visiting New York were each allowed to take £250 spending money. If the exchange rate was US $1.65 to the pound (sterling), how many US dollars was this?

One girl spent US $297. How much is this in pounds (sterling)?

Extended response

I wish to travel a journey of 30 miles. I have travelled 15 miles and have $\frac{1}{3}$ of a tank of petrol. Do I have a problem?

Task 14.2

Look at one of the end-of-Key Stage tests, a GCSE examination paper and an AS- or A2-level test paper. Can you identify a question similar to each of the above types in these papers? What do you notice about the types of questions administered as you progress up the age range? Why do you think this occurs?

Test characteristics

Validity

The three essential qualities of a test are its validity, reliability and usability (Linn and Gronlund, 1995). *Validity* refers to the extent to which the results of a test are interpreted appropriately for a particular purpose – that is, it is not the test that is valid but the interpretations resulting from the test (Linn and Gronlund, 1995). Validity is not an all-or-nothing concept, but is better considered in terms of 'degrees' on a continuum such as high validity, moderate validity and low validity.

Face validity refers to the relevance of a test item to the context in which the testee is working – for example, a pupil could relate to the following question:

> You have 30 sweets which you want to divide equally among three friends. How many sweets do they get each?

If a carpenter was taking this test, the question would read:

> You have 30 nails which you want to divide equally among three workers. How many nails do they get each?

In each case the maths remains the same – namely, 30 divided by 3 – but by adopting an appropriate context, the question seems to assume greater relevance to the test-taker. This is particularly evident in the TTA Numeracy tests where all the mathematics items are situated in the context of teaching. For further support for this test, consult *Achieving QTS: The Numeracy Skills Test* published by Learning Matters.

It is important to base the testing process on an accumulation of evidence from various sources (Messick, 1989). Consideration should be given to the interpretation of the test results, as only the teacher can judge the validity of a test since he or she has a broader and more extensive knowledge of the pupils' true capabilities due to the observational evidence accrued over time.

Reliability

Reliability is a measure of the consistency of assessment outcomes. It is a necessary but not sufficient condition for validity – that is, results can be reliable and consistent but are completely worthless if they have no meaning or validity (Linn and Gronlund, 1995). Like validity, it is not the test instrument that is reliable, but the results of the test. Reliability refers to a particular type of consistency – for example, it may be the need for consistency over time, over a number of topics or tasks, over different markers, and so on.

High levels of reliability are needed if the interpretations of the test performance and resulting decisions are important or final (such as national examinations), irreversible and have lasting consequences (such as obtaining a place at university). If the reason for testing is low-stakes, such as monitoring pupils' progress, where the resulting decisions can be changed and the consequences have only temporary effects such as revisiting a topic before moving on to new material, then lower reliabilities can be tolerated.

Interrater reliability (Linn and Gronlund, 1995) is used to establish whether the same score would have been awarded had a different marker assessed the work. Pre-training using exemplar materials is often given to the markers of high stakes tests such as GCSE and Advanced-level examinations to ensure that all assessors are working to the same scoring rubric and to the same degree of stringency. When a rater (normally, the classroom teacher) is noticeably lenient or favours a particular student due to some prior knowledge of that person's ability, the 'halo effect' occurs (Popham, 1990) .

The reliability of a test can be influenced by a number of factors. In general, the longer the test, the more reliable it will be due to the increased number of opportunities for pupils to demonstrate their knowledge and the increased likelihood of correct and incorrect guesses to unknown items that cancel each other. The longer test also increases the extent to which the content domain can be covered, thereby reducing chances of pupils receiving only the topics they are most familiar with. Generalisability theory also advocates the use of multiple tasks or contexts to demonstrate skills and concepts (Messick, 1989). It should be noted, however, that these assessments need to spread the students' scores, thereby distinguishing between the weak student and the mathematically able pupil. Tests of this nature are highly reliable, which reduces the influence of the standard error of measurement on the pupils' scores. Objective tests increase the interrater reliability since scoring rubrics can be applied easily and accurately in these cases.

Usability

Usability is the name given to the practicalities of assessment within a busy timetable or teaching schedule. The main aspects influencing decisions on the usability of a test are its ease of administration and scoring, the time requirements in terms of lost teaching time, the level of interpretation needed to understand the outcomes of the test and the cost of the test if published tests are being used (Linn and Gronlund, 1995). The directions for the administration and use of a test should be concise and clearly stated, as should the instructions for the pupils.

Problems associated with tests

The main criticisms linked to tests are directed towards the effects of testing on pupils and the problems that may be inherent in test items themselves. Norm-referenced tests rank pupils from the most able to the least able in the class or form. This often leads to categorising or grouping pupils according to ability or, in more extreme cases, streaming or setting pupils within a form. With this re-organisation of classes comes labelling, which has a negative impact of the pupils and often the teacher, particularly in relation to the lower end of the ability range. Pupils lose their self-confidence and have a low self-esteem believing that they are inadequate, innumerate or incapable of coping with the mathematics at this level. Teachers can also be influenced by poor test results or being assigned to teach one of the low-stream classes. Sometimes, a teacher will reduce his or her expectations of the pupils, 'watering down' the maths associated with various problem-solving activities and setting mundane drill and practice homework rather than challenging tasks within the extended grasp of the pupils. Naturally, pupils pick up on the lower expectations and don't try so hard, resulting in a self-fulfilling prophecy (Rosenthal and Jacobsen, 1968) whereby those who are expected to achieve less do indeed achieve less than their higher stream peers. However, it is important for teachers to remember that the converse is also true: those who are expected to do well do actually surpass all expectations of them (often including their own). Therefore, it is a teacher's duty to believe in his or her pupils and to encourage them to develop and improve, despite the knock-backs resulting from streaming or labelling.

Problems in the test

Differential item functioning (Dorans and Schmitt, 1993) is the terminology associated with the differences in the performance of a single test item by two groups of pupils – these groups could be boys and girls, ethnic minorities, and so on. Bias in items will affect the validity and reliability of the test as a whole, so it is important to pilot items in advance to establish if some items are functioning adversely for subgroups of the test population. Items that stereotype the perceived gender roles in society may distort a pupils' performance in a test. In the same way, ethnic minorities are often under-represented in test items that may have a detrimental effect on these students' self-esteem and performance in the test. The same holds for the cultural context inherent in some mathematical problem-solving cases and the language register used in these situations.

Gender issues in assessment

In the past, the mode of assessment of science and maths was deemed more suited to boys than to girls. Bannister (1993) revealed that boys exhibited superior performance in multiple-choice type questions, while girls excelled in open-ended tasks and essay-writing activities. The introduction of coursework in GCSE maths offered a mechanism to facilitate the preferred learning style of girls and therefore assisted in addressing the imbalance in assessment techniques that were viewed as favouring boys and may have been the cause of the perceived underachievement of girls in the 1970s and 1980s. In more recent years, concerns are being raised at the dramatic over-performance of girls at GCSE in maths and science subjects – questions about over-correcting the gender imbalance and feminising the sciences are now being asked.

Underachievement in maths

Teachers often account for a boy's poor performance by commenting on his potential. Although boys are considered by teachers to have 'more potential' than girls, Younger and Warrington (1996) revealed that teachers tend to under-predict boys' grades at GCSE but over-predict girls' grades. They tend to predict outcome rather than potential. With current research focusing on the underachievement of boys in a number of disciplines, teachers are more likely to select boys as underachievers than girls (Jones and Myhill, in press). Consequently, the underachievement of girls in national tests has been overlooked, rendering them almost invisible, while attention is focused on finding ways to address the underachievement of boys (Osler *et al.*, 2002; Plummer, 2000). In addition to the gender effects in assessment processes, Cooper and Dunne (1999) found that the use of context in national maths tests in the UK was disadvantaging working-class children. As teachers, we need to be mindful of the variety of factors that may influence or inhibit a pupil's learning and be aware of the potential problems associated with tests at a local or national level. Although teachers' attention is being directed to the underachievement of boys in maths, this should not be to the detriment of monitoring the progress of the girls in the class. The girls may be performing well, but are they still achieving their full potential?

Compulsory assessment in mathematics

This section focuses specifically on assessment in mainstream education from ages 4–18. All end-of-Key Stage assessment is a combination of teacher assessment and the statutory written tests supplied by QCA. Teachers will have been continuously monitoring and recording pupils' progress over the academic year, so they will have made judgements on the pupils' attainment in each of the ATs in maths. The following sections focus solely on the statutory assessment requirements. The assessment arrangements associated with special educational needs pupils is dealt with in detail in Chapter 13.

From 2003, there will be 'more questions on the end of Key Stage tests which require pupils to use their skills on Using and Applying Mathematics' (QCA, 2003). This reflects the new Curriculum 2000 changes and the emphasis of the NNS and Key Stage 3 Strategy.

The Foundation Stage Profile

The Foundation Stage Profile replaces Baseline Assessment of pupils aged five years old. By the end of the Reception Year, a Foundation Stage Profile should have been created by the teacher summarising each pupil's competence in the six areas of:

* personal, social and emotional development;
* communication, language and literacy;
* mathematical development;
* knowledge and understanding of the world;
* physical development;
* creative development.

Mathematical development consists of three categories: numbers as labels and for counting; calculating; and finally, shape, space and measures. Each category has a maximum of 9 points listed in a pseudo-hierarchical level of difficulty. Points 1 to 3 are basic skills needed for progression towards the early learning goals, points 4 to 8 are mapped onto the early learning goals, while point 9 demonstrates the pupils' ability to work consistently at a greater depth and breadth than required by the early learning goals. The content of each category is summarised in Table 14.2.

Table 14.2 Summary of the content of mathematical development (adapted from *The Foundation Stage Profile Handbook*, QCA/03/1006)

Mathematical development category	Points 1–3	Points 4–8	Point 9
Numbers as labels and for counting	Pupils are familiar with numbers up to 6, including counting.	For numbers up to 10, pupils can count objects, recognise numerals and order numbers and problem solve.	Pupils recognise, count, order, write and use numbers up to 20.
Calculating	Pupils are familiar with the concept of addition and subtraction, recognise differences in size of quantities, can add or subtract one from numbers up to 5.	Pupils understand the physical process of addition or subtraction, can accurately calculate ±1 for numbers up to 10, have basic problem-solving skills.	Pupils use a range of strategies for addition and subtraction and have some mental recall of number bonds.
Shape, space and measures	Pupils play with objects or shapes and can match or sort them into groups.	Pupils identify patterns, use comparative language for size and position, can name flat shapes and complete basic problem-solving tasks with shapes.	Pupils use mathematical language for describing two-dimensional and three-dimensional objects.

In each of these categories, the teachers record evidence of pupils' achievement of a particular point on the scale through classroom-focused tasks completed alone or in small groups. 'Best fit' descriptions of the child's achievement are reported to the parents and the Year 1 teacher at the end of Reception Year. For further information, consult *The Foundation Stage Profile Handbook* (QCA/03/1006), which is available via the QCA website.

End-of-Key Stage examinations

Stemming from the Dearing Review of the Curriculum (1996), all pupils undergo end-of-Key Stage examinations at the age of 7, 11 and 14. In Key Stage 1, only mathematics and English are assessed, while in Key Stages 2 and 3, the three areas of mathematics, English and science are assessed at the end of each Key Stage, with ICT added for Key Stage 3 pupils from 2004. Each pupil is awarded a National Curriculum level which represents his or her current standard of achievement in that subject. Reports on *The Standards at Key Stage 1 in English and mathematics* and *The Standards at Key Stage 2 in English, mathematics and science* are available annually from the QCA website and contain details on

Table 14.3 Summary of end-of-Key Stage National tests in Mathematics

	Key Stage 1	*Key Stage 2*	*Key Stage 3*
Assessment medium	Level 1: task	Levels 3–5 – 2 papers (with/without calculator)	Levels 3–5, 4–6, 5–7, 6–8 – 2 papers for each (with/without calculator)
	Levels 2–3: tests	Mental arithmetic Extension paper for L6	Mental arithmetic Extension paper for L8
ATs assessed	Number mainly plus questions from Shape, Space and Measures and Handling Data	Number and Algebra: 50% Shape, Space and Measures: 25% Handling Data: 25%	Number and Algebra: 50% Shape, Space and Measures: 25% Handling Data: 25%
Possible pupil outcomes	W – working towards L1; Levels 1; 2A, 2B, 2C, 3	N – lower than compensatory L2 band; Levels 2, 3, 4, 5, 6	N – lower than compensatory level; compensatory level of one level below that of paper; Levels 3, 4, 5, 6, 7, 8
Government expectations	Level 2 by age 7	Level 4 by age 11	Level 6 by age 14

the pupils' performances on each question in these National tests (see Table 14.3 for a summary).

Areas of difficulty by Key Stage

Key Stage 1

The problem-solving questions often cause more difficulties than standard calculations or knowledge of number questions. In handling data, the use of a scale or a symbol that does not represent the natural numbers causes problems in interpretation – for example, a symbol that represents two objects in a pictogram or instances where one square in a chart is not equal to a frequency of one on the scale.

Key Stage 2

Most pupils adopt the vertical approach for addition and multiplication when a calculator is unavailable. The use of decimals in calculations often leads to problems for pupils who also tend to struggle more when calculating percentages of numbers than fractions of numbers. As in Key Stage 1, maths set in a problem-based context is still a concern for the less able pupils. The tests reveal the inefficient use of calculators by the majority of pupils and how the pupils cannot always interpret the display in relation to the required answer – e.g. 15.9 is often recorded as £15.09 by pupils. Similar problems occur with questions involving time.

In relation to Shape, Space and Measures, the most common problems arise when the pupils are asked to visualise a net of a three-dimensional shape or work out the position of a shape after rotational symmetry about a point other than the centre. Reflection symmetry, particularly in a vertical line, is found to be easier than rotational symmetry. Clarity appears to exist between area and perimeter by the end of Key Stage 2. However, the conversion between the 12-hour and 24-hour clock remains an area that requires further attention. In Handling data, the interpretation of information from a pie chart and the sizes of its sectors is problematic as pupils do not always appreciate the significance of the overall number or sample size represented by the pie chart. Explanations or offering reasons why a particular statement is true or false are found difficult at this stage. However, the same question can be answered correctly if it is asked in the usual manner such as 'What is the probability of scoring two when throwing a fair die'? compared to 'Why are scores of 2 and 4 equally likely on a fair die'?

Pupils working at levels 3 and 4 often find the mental arithmetic test more difficult than paper-based tests, possibly due to the content being designed to assess levels 3–5 in the one test. Finally, the use of mathematical terminology needs to be reinforced throughout all attainment targets so that pupils are aware of the differences between the vertices, faces and edges of a cube.

Key Stage 3

In some questions, the known pupil misconceptions associated with that topic are dealt with in a direct manner by asking pupils to offer explanations to back up a hypothesis or statement. As in Key Stage 2, these items are answered poorly by the lower ability pupils within the 'tier'. However, as the pupils advance in their mathematical ability, they also become more proficient at applying the theory to the problem posed, which leads to a more coherent and detailed response to these types of open-ended questions.

The problems being experienced by pupils at Key Stages 1 and 2 continue into Key Stage 3 in many cases. Issues surrounding place value in decimals, the links between fractions, percentages and decimals, variables in algebra and the effective use of a calculator prevail in feedback from these tests. Additional areas of weakness at the higher levels include work on linear equations and the equation of a straight line, index notation and simplifying expressions, including quadratics and the difference between surface area and volume.

At the end of Key Stage 3, the majority of pupils are working at level 6. However, recent reports have shown a significant increase in the numbers of pupils gaining levels 7 and 8.

Task 14.3

Look at an Assessment Unit (AU) or end-of-Key Stage test for the Key Stage in which you will be teaching and match each of the questions with the common misconceptions experienced by pupils of this age. Design a revision scheme for your pupils that will assist them in addressing these misconceptions.

Gender differences in performance in these tests are reported as being slight, question-dependent and non-significant. As part of the preparation for the end of Key Stage examinations, pupils in Years 7 and 8 (the first two years of post-primary education) can sit optional tests that reflect the content and structure of the statutory assessment system used in Year 9.

GCSEs and entry tiers for examinations

In the current structure of the National Curriculum, differentiation by ability is embedded in the assessment process. Three tiers of entry are offered to pupils sitting GCSE mathematics exams: Foundation, Intermediate and Higher level. Although National Curriculum levels are not used above Key Stage 3, it may assist the reader to equate these tiers, roughly, to levels 5–6, 7–8 and 9–10 respectively to get an idea of the depth and breadth of content covered. Due to the inherent increase in the mathematical ability of successive tiers of students, the Foundation level examination allows candidates to achieve grades ranging from D-G, Intermediate level awards grades B–E, while the Higher tier facilitates grades A*–C. Based on a combination of pupils' past performances and examination results, a decision on the tier of examination entry is made between the pupils, teachers and parents of each individual student. Both teachers and pupils need to be realistic about the tier of entry that best suits the child's needs as there is no point in entering a pupil for a higher-level paper than he or she is capable of answering if it may be detrimental to the child's performance, particularly where the grades are restricted. Pupils who do not meet the minimum score for the lowest grade in the tier are recorded as unclassified and do not receive a certificate. The majority of teachers look at the central grade in the range and decide whether or not the pupil is capable of achieving a B, C/D or E/F grade. Based on this decision, the tier of entry is decided. Pupils may only be entered for one tier.

There are six papers available at GCSE level: two for each tier and parallel papers are administered at the same time. Papers 1, 3 and 5 are parallel non-calculator papers assessing all the ATs for mathematics but at different levels. Similarly, Papers 2, 4 and 6 are the parallel with-calculator papers assessing each AT at a variety of levels. Each written paper is worth 40 per cent of the available marks. The remaining 20 per cent of marks is assigned to the two Internally Assessed Components (worth 10 per cent each), taking a maximum of four hours of class time each. One task is of a practical nature, focusing on Handling Data and set in a real-life context, while the second task is of an investigational nature, combining Using and Applying Mathematics plus one of Number and Algebra or Shape, Space and Measures (CCEA, 2001).

The practical task is marked against the categories:

- Specify the problem and plan.
- Collect, process and represent data.
- Interpret and discuss results.

(CCEA, 2001, p. 70)

It is advisable to use statistical projects rather than ones focused on probability if the students wish to be awarded high scores for their coursework. The use of primary or secondary data sets is acceptable and ICT can also be built into the data collection, analysis and reporting where appropriate. Exemplars of suitable coursework tasks are usually available by contacting the examinations body.

The investigational task is assessed under the headings:

- Making and monitoring decisions to solve problems.
- Communicating mathematically.
- Developing skills of mathematical reasoning.

(CCEA, 2001, p. 70)

Annotations should be included on the submissions and reasons why particular marks have been awarded should be identified on the assessment sheets for each piece of pupil coursework. Within the mathematics department, internal moderation of marks will normally occur to ensure that all the teachers are assessing to the same sets of standards and with equal rigour. External moderation by the examining board will occur during the month of June.

Task 14.4

Complete a structured investigation yourself, noting the skills and teaching points that you will need to address in advance of using this activity with your class.

Find a complementary open-ended investigation that extends the skills already covered in the structured task. Use this with your class and mark them against the GCSE criteria stated by the awarding body for the school.

Advanced-level mathematics

Post-16 mathematics has a prerequisite of GCSE mathematics, normally grade C or above. Ten modules are available from which four are chosen for an A-level and two are completed for an AS-level qualification in mathematics. Depending on the combinations chosen, a pupil can achieve an A-level or AS-level in Pure Mathematics, Mathematics, Mechanics or Further Mathematics. The same module cannot be used for two separate qualifications.

There are two schemes of assessment: linear and non-linear. In both cases, four papers are taken, lasting 1½ hours each. The papers used for the linear and non-linear examinations are identical in format and standard, but are administered at different times of the year. Each paper comprises up to eight compulsory questions with varying mark allocations per question. Each paper carries the same weighting, with marks being awarded for method – mathematical style and technique – as well as for the accuracy of the calculation. In both assessment modes, pupils must take at least two papers after late February in their final year of A-level study. These two examinations are called the 'terminal exams' and re-sits are not possible for these two papers if the terminal exams are worth 30 per cent of the final result. In all other cases, the best score in a paper (whether first attempt or re-sit) is taken as the score for inclusion in the final calculation of the grade (CCEA, 2001).

At Advanced-level there are no formal coursework requirements. However, the new Key Skills requirements deal with this issue directly.

Key Skills and Advanced-level mathematics

Like the GCSE course, an appendix of information is available for highlighting the range of opportunities existing within the curriculum (modules) for the development of all six Key Skills. At Advanced-level, the focus is on Level 3, with grades A–C offering exemption from the paper-based assessment paper for Application of Number. More detail on Key Skills is available in Chapter 12.

Free-standing mathematics units

As an alternative to Key Skill Application of Number, nationally accredited Free-Standing Mathematics Qualifications (FSMQ) are offered for post-16 students by awarding bodies such as AQA, EdExcel and OCR. The Free-Standing Mathematics Units were designed to complement the Application of Number Key Skill. They are available in three levels:

- Foundation (equivalent to GCSE Mathematics content for grade D or below).
- Intermediate (incorporates GCSE Mathematics content for grades A*-C).
- Advanced (includes the mathematics content compatible to AS/A level or Advanced GNVQ/AVCE).

In terms of existing qualifications, each free-standing maths unit is equivalent to an AS- or A-level module or to a GNVQ unit. Three FSMQ units are equivalent to an AS-level and six FSMQ units are the equivalent of an A-level. However, a student cannot aggregate three FSMQ units with an AS-level qualification to achieve an A-level.

The FSMQ units focus on a similar content in terms of mathematical knowledge, skills and understanding as that of Key Skill Application of Number. The assessment process comprises a portfolio of evidence, plus a written examination. The portfolio is graded: Pass, Pass+, Merit, Merit+ or Distinction, according to a set of 'best fit' criteria. The examination is graded from A–E and a combined grade is given, encompassing the achievement in the portfolio and examination. This is reported as a grade between A and E.

Within the portfolio, three themes must be demonstrated:

- Structuring and presenting work.
- Working accurately.
- Interpreting mathematics.

Each theme is awarded one of the following grades: Pass, Merit or Distinction. Transitions from Pass to Merit to Distinction are made according to prescribed criteria which demonstrate increasing levels of independence in the student's work for theme one, increasing degrees of accuracy in the work for theme two and finally, increasing levels of generalisability in the outcomes of theme three.

Clearly, not all portfolios will be awarded the same 'grade' in each theme. A set of rubrics have been generated to ensure that all students will be treated equally in terms of the overall qualification awarded for the portfolio.

The examination paper for the Foundation level lasts one hour, whereas the Advanced-level paper is 1½ hours' duration. These examination papers are available twice yearly: January and June. Sample tests plus curricular guidance can be downloaded from the QCA website: www.qca.org.uk/.

Current changes in assessment and implications for the future

The TIMSS Study

Although the purpose and design of the TIMMS test was not to elicit the expertise of the 'best' students in each country, the results of these tests are viewed as a measure of the overall performance of the 'average' pupil from the country and hence low performance by pupils leads to assumptions of low levels of education, particularly in the 'basics' such as numeracy. Research (Keys et al., 1996, Harris et al., 1997) indicates that the types of questions administered in TIMSS and other tests of this nature are atypical of those used in National Curriculum assessment in schools in the UK. There is an over-emphasis on low-level skills such as recall of knowledge and few questions require the use of problem-solving compared to end of Key Stage assessment tests. Similarly, all 'topics' (understanding number systems, fractions and proportion, geometry, mensuration, data interpretation and probability, and algebra) are treated equally in terms of the proportion of questions in the TIMSS tests, which is not representative of the content of the National Curriculum and therefore the associated assessment procedures used in schools. As with all assessment, pupils are not 'test-wise' to this format and style of assessment and it is hardly surprising to discover that they are underperforming as a result. From a teacher's perspective, it is clear that pupils require preparation for the variety and types of questions used in assessing mathematics so they can demonstrate their full mathematical ability without the presence of construct irrelevant variance resulting from unfamiliarity with the delivery of the questions.

World Class testing

World Class Tests have been introduced in response to pupils' performance on the TIMMS tests (Keys at al., 1996; Harris et al., 1997) to assess the top 5–10 per cent of the world's 9- and 13-year-olds. Unlike the paper-based format of the TIMSS study, World Class Tests are a combination of computer-delivered and paper-based items. The research and development project commenced in autumn 1999 and was a collaboration between the Assessment and Evaluation Unit at the University of Leeds (AEU), the Mathematics Assessment Resource Service at the universities of Durham and Nottingham, and the National Computer Services in Hellaby, which was funded in excess of £1 million by QCA.

The assessment items are a combination of tasks and short questions delivered electronically but marked either manually (to the prescribed mark scheme) or electronically, depending on the task and its format. Each task addresses the higher-order thinking skills typical of gifted pupils aged 9 or 13 years old. Skills such as planning, investigating, interpreting, revising ideas, suggesting options and formulating solutions are targeted within each context for the task. Problem-solving skills such as controlling variables and setting goals or targets for a subproblem to assist in the determination of an overall solution are also emphasised in the more open-ended tasks administered in the computer-based environment. Across both types of assessment, the research team endeavoured to find a balance between subject knowledge to start the task, application of existing procedures for solving problems, the ability to think and reason mathematically within an unfamiliar context and ultimately to solve a given (or chosen) problem.

These pilot items are available for viewing, trial and comment through the QCA website: www.qca.org.uk/ca/tests/wct/.

Automate or informate?

With the increasing power and availability of computers both within schools and to pupils at home, it is only natural that assessment itself will progress to the stage where all tests will be taken electronically or perhaps even on-line. The question remains 'Is the automation of existing forms of assessment appropriate in the information age?'.

Think of the traditional paper-based test where the questions were designed to be displayed in this format and for the purpose of being administered to the same audience on the same day at the same time. If these constraints were not present, how would you change the test? The first, and perhaps most obvious, change would be the introduction of colour into the tests and perhaps the use of simulations (think of the computerised version of the Driving Theory Test). Second, the reliability of the tests could be improved as the test could be tailored to each pupil instead of using a predefined set of questions with difficulty values at or near to the middle of the ability range. Third, the marking of the test could be carried out automatically as the student enters his or her response, thus preventing the two-month delay (typical of GCSE and A-level exams) before receiving the final results. Automated marking allows the testee to obtain their result at the end of the test and therefore make a decision almost immediately on whether it is necessary to re-sit the test to achieve a higher score or even to pass.

But is 'automation' the best use of computers for assessment in the twenty-first century? The results of tests provide 'information' and this information is used to make decisions. So, in designing an assessment system for the future using information technology, researchers need to focus on the concept of 'informate' rather than 'automate'. The assessment system should provide useful information on the pupils' abilities to each individual pupil, to the teacher, to the Head of Department for target-setting, to the Principal or Board of Governors and to the parents. For high-stakes testing such as GCSE or Advanced-level, this information would be important in terms of future plans for study or career opportunities. In terms of summative assessment, the information could be stored electronically in an easily accessible way for reporting and disseminating within and outside the school.

For formative assessment, the feedback from the individual test can be used to offer help targeted to the individual pupil's needs. Ideally, if this help was built into the assessment process, it would be possible for the pupil to receive help at the time of testing rather than later when he or she has forgotten the problem being experienced – deductions for requesting help could be built into the marking rubric. This two-way flow of information would mimic the role of the teacher during classwork activity where he or she asks the pupil leading questions, or Vygotskian prompts, to 'scaffold' the student to the solution rather than just showing him or her the answer or process of reaching the answer.

Conclusion

The process of 'informate' is well underway via a number of research projects. Each pupil sitting a test has a unique login name and password. Every test outcome is recorded and can be accessed by the teacher in a variety of formats:

*   class lists of pupils' National Curriculum levels;
*   individual pupil records over time;
*   problems with particular types of items within a topic can be identified at a class or individual level;
*   feedback on a test – item by item – is available for the pupil;
*   summary information for the whole class is provided for teacher, departmental or school use.

With the current pilots in online assessment being completed at the time of writing, the automated assessment of 'knowledge-rich' subjects such as maths and science is preparing teachers and pupils for the future.

Mathematics Centres

Many universities have centres specialising in assessment and/or mathematics education. The following are some useful websites for further information:

Assessment and Evaluation Unit,
   University of Leeds: http://education.leeds.ac.uk/research/aeu.htm

CEM, University of Durham: http://cem.dur.ac.uk/projects/default.htm

Centre for the Study of Mathematics
   Education: www.nottingham.ac.uk/csme

Classroom 2000 (C2K) in NI: www.c2kni.org/

Heriot-Watt: CALM
                                         www.calm.hw.ac.uk

                                         SCHOLAR
                                         www.scholar.hw.ac.uk

Mathematics in Industry: MEI
                                         www.mei.org.uk

Shell Centre for Mathematics Education:	www.nottingham.ac.uk/shell *or* http://mathshell.com/scp
University of Cambridge:	PRIME maths http://nrich.maths.org.uk/prime/index.html
	Plus+ http://plus.math.org
	NRICH http://nrich.maths.org/index.html

CD compendiums of past paper questions

| ExamPro (GCSE) | PO Box 208, Newcastle-upon-Tyne, NE3 1FX. |
| TestBase (KS2 and 3) | e-mail: info@testbase.co.uk |

Part IV

Personal and professional development

15 Getting your first teaching post

Introduction

The content of this chapter is designed with the mathematics specialist in mind – a person who is likely to be a teacher in post-primary schools. The chapter is subdivided into the three main phases associated with securing a teaching post: the pre-interview stage – applying for jobs and interview preparation; the interview; post-interview acceptance or rejection.

Learning outcomes

By the end of this chapter you should be able to:

- complete an application form well;
- prepare a good CV and covering letter;
- present yourself well at pre-interview meetings and at the interview;
- offer thoughtful and clear responses to interview questions;
- identify areas where you need extra help prior to attending interviews.

Applying for jobs

As you approach the end of your initial teacher training (that is, in your final year of a four-year B.Ed. course or in the second half of a one-year PGCE course), you should start looking in the newspapers and *Times Educational Supplement* for teaching vacancies. Many of the newspapers also have jobs sections on their websites. However, a word of warning – some advertisements do not appear on the website, so be very careful and check the newspapers as well. Job advertisements are brief but precise. For example, if the school is looking for an experienced teacher and does not want a Newly Qualified Teacher (NQT), they will state a minimum requirement of two years full-time teaching experience or alternatively, experience of teaching the A-level Mechanics syllabus, say – something that a NQT is unlikely to have experienced. Other schools are keen to have NQTs and will ask for applications from candidates who possess or are in the process of completing a PGCE or equivalent qualification. In these instances, all mathematics teachers who are interested in the post can apply. More frequently, schools are asking for a Teacher of Mathematics to Advanced-level and ICT to Key Stage 3 (or sometimes GCSE). This is a direct result of the current subject combinations offered at degree level where most undergraduate mathematics courses will encourage their students to take one or two modules of computing, in addition to pure and applied maths in the first year. Historically, the majority of ICT/Computing teachers were trained as maths teachers who, rhetorically speaking, kept a foot in both camps. However, more recently, with the NOF training, the balance between the use of ICT in maths and ICT as a separate subject has led to specialist ICT teachers now being employed to deal with the increasing numbers of pupils opting for ICT as a subject at Advanced-level.

Many schools will also look for 'a willingness to contribute to the extra-curricular life of the school'. As already mentioned, a teacher is more than the person who stands up in front of the mathematics class; he or she must contribute to the running of other aspects of school life such as sport, drama, music/choir, Young Enterprise schemes, Duke of Edinburgh Award schemes, community work, and so on.

Task 15.1 What else can you offer a school?

- Looking back on your teaching placements, what extra-curricular activities were you involved in and which ones would you be willing to do if you were teaching full-time?
- What are your personal interests or hobbies? Could you bring a new 'activity' to the school such as equestrian activities, watersports or golf?
- Do you have any links with businesses or industry that could be used for careers work or to encourage Young Enterprise activity?

Applications for a post

When applying for a job in response to an advertisement in the newspaper, some schools will ask you to write a letter of application, accompanied by a full CV, to the principal of the school. Other schools will direct you to the local Education and Library Board (ELB) or Local Education Authority (LEA) for a standard application form, which is to be completed and returned to them. In both cases, the importance of addressing the requirements as stated in the advertisement or accompanying documentation cannot be highlighted enough. For the purposes of short-listing suitable candidates for interview, a panel scours the application forms or CVs in search of those applicants not fulfilling the minimum requirements. If you omit to mention your degree classification, this can lead to your application being rejected, especially if the minimum requirement is at least a 2:2 Honours Degree in Mathematics or a mathematical discipline. The same applies to your level of experience. If the advertisement states that experience of teaching another subject such as ICT is desirable, remember to include any experience you may have of teaching other subjects such as ICT, RE, Citizenship or Business Studies, even if they were only to Key Stage 3. If you have taught more than one subject, then list them all – make yourself stand out from the other applicants.

Filling out an application form

Before you start filling out the application form, it is advantageous to spend 15–20 minutes listing the minimum requirements for the job and your qualifications or experience that matches each of these requirements. Work through the application form systematically, filling all the spaces and ensuring you have included references to all the essential and desirable criteria mentioned in the advertisement or job description. An incomplete application form may result in you not being short-listed as the panel will have inadequate evidence of your skills, qualifications and/or experience. In some application forms, the final section offers you an opportunity to add any further details regarding the post. Use this space wisely to give an overall impression of yourself and what you could bring to the job.

Make sure you give yourself plenty of time to fill in the application form. Write neatly and check the form for spelling mistakes or grammatical errors and, if possible, ask someone else to double-check it. Photocopy the completed application form before you post it and keep it somewhere safe so that you can read over your application before you attend the interview. Finally, make sure you post the form in good time as late applications are automatically rejected.

Presenting your CV

Templates for a Résumé and Curriculum Vitae (CV) are often included in your word-processing package (MS Word or Claris Works). Résumés tend to be one-page summaries of the main aspects of your qualifications and experience whereas a CV is usually at least two pages long, offering detailed exemplification of your skills and experience in relation to the job description. The generic structure of a CV is as follows:

- Personal details (name, address, date of birth, marital status, telephone/mobile number, fax number or e-mail address, driving licence, photograph of yourself using digital camera).
- Academic qualifications (GCSEs, AS/A-levels, degree, postgraduate certificates or degrees, dissertation titles or topics for project work).
- Relevant teaching experience (include dates, schools, subjects, age groups and ability levels taught).
- Other experience (vacational work, full-time or part-time jobs, tutoring or training, . . .).
- Positions of responsibility (school level, university level, community, summer camps).
- Awards or other qualifications (Duke of Edinburgh, Lifesaving awards, First Aid, . . .).
- Membership of organisations (e.g. Association of Teachers of Mathematics).
- Interests or hobbies.
- Names and addresses of referees.

It is important to tailor your CV to the job you are applying for and not to send a standard CV to all the jobs. If the advertisement or job description states that you will be a form teacher, then use your CV to highlight experience of managing new members of staff in your part-time job, planning activities for summer camps, dealing with 'pastoral' type issues in your job as a Youth Club supervisor, and so on. In terms of a request for extra-curricular involvement, highlight your sporting prowess such as Captain of the 1st XV Rugby team in school, lifesaving certificates, qualified hockey coach or sailing coach; or non-sporting achievements such as Duke of Edinburgh Gold Award, Captain of the Debating Team representing the South-West at the UK finals, member of the U21 University Chess Team, webmaster for the Mathematical Society at university. Be aware of existing clubs and societies as listed in the school prospectus and indicate your willingness to assist with these or how you could introduce a new club such as an Eco Club for environmental issues, a Computer Club to design the school website, a Maths Club to enter challenges and inter-school competitions.

The content of the covering letter

The covering letter should be short, precise and specific to the job. It should be word-processed and should have clearly defined paragraphs addressing the requirements of the advertisement. All the school details must be spelt correctly and the referee information should be accurate and complete. Experience relevant to the post should be outlined and practical teaching should be clearly stated and not generalised. Try to highlight aspects of your CV that indicate that you are likely to fit in with the school ethos – for example, involvement with the community and youth clubs if it is an Integrated or Community school.

Task 15.2 The CV

Create a CV containing all the relevant information and which can be adapted to suit any mathematics post. Try various presentation styles until you find a format that matches your character but remains professional in appearance.

Draft a covering letter that can be used as a template for any job application.

Interviews

One of the first questions a student asks when they receive a letter of invitation for an interview is 'How many people will be on the panel?'. There is no hard-and-fast answer to this question. However, there will usually be a minimum of three – the Principal, Head of Mathematics and a member of the Board of Governors or a representative from the Church. Some panels will also have the mathematics officer from the LEA present, plus additional members of the Board of Governors who do not ask questions but focus on your interpersonal and communication skills. The format of the interview may vary from school to school. Some schools interview during normal school hours, while others wait until late afternoon or early evening to accommodate attendance by the Board of Governors. Depending on the number of applicants, there may be two rounds of interviews either on the same day or you may be called back again for your second interview a week later. In these cases, the first interviews normally last around 10–15 minutes followed by half an hour for the second interview. Other schools may decide to allocate half an hour to each candidate and only interview once.

Visiting the school before the interview

It is important to see around the school prior to the interview so that you are aware of the environment, have a feeling for the school ethos, see the teaching facilities and meet the other members of staff. Some schools will allow you to request a time for visiting the school before you apply for the position, while others invite only the short-listed applicants to attend a tour of the school and the mathematics department on a designated day before the interview. In either case, you are looking at the school as a potential place for employment over the next three or more years, while the staff are surveying you as a potential colleague for the same duration of time. Both situations are dependent on 'first impressions', so make sure you come across well as decisions can be made informally prior to the formal interview. Appearance is as important on this first visit as it is at interview. Dress well and behave in a professional manner at all times. Look interested in what is happening in the classrooms you visit and ask questions about the syllabi taught to the different age groups. Pay attention to wall displays in the rooms – what do they tell you about the children? Look at the textbooks and other resources in view – what does this tell you about the department? What ICT resources are present in each room? How is the maths store arranged? How friendly are the other members of staff? Do you think you would like to work in the school? What extra-curricular activities are offered?

At the interview

Once you have seen round the school, you will be in a better position to determine how committed you really are to securing the position there. It will also give you an insight into the expectations of the department and may influence how you respond to their questions at interview. Clearly, if the school is very traditional in its approach to teaching and learning, it would be wise to adopt a 'traditional' viewpoint when interviewed. This should not be misinterpreted as being old-fashioned – it means you should express some caution when discussing the integration of new teaching paradigms – conveying the positive and negative implications of change and being realistic. An interview is not the time for a debate or to 'make a statement'.

The structure of the interviews tend to follow a generic pattern:

- welcome and introductions to the panel by the principal;
- some general questions about yourself and your teaching experiences;
- formal questions often subject-specific or curriculum-related;
- questions on what you could offer the school;
- an opportunity for you to ask questions.

More recently, some schools have introduced a five-minute presentation to allow the panel to assess your level of preparation, organisation of ideas and communication skills. If this is the case, they will normally give you the title of the presentation in your letter to attend for interview. Remember, a good teacher can capture and hold the pupils' attention and use innovative approaches – try to demonstrate these skills in your presentation. It is worth considering how you can also use this opportunity to demonstrate your other strengths as a teacher. Do you have the opportunity to use an interactive whiteboard, integrate Powerpoint with a maths package or use Excel macros imaginatively?

In terms of the generic questions related to school issues, be honest but thoughtful in your responses. Reflect on your own experiences as a pupil, a student at university or college, a leader or participant in clubs or societies outside school and more recently as a trainee teacher. Think about the people involved in education – the pupils, the parents and the teachers. Where possible, triangulate between these three focus groups. So if you are asked why homework is important, give your reasons in terms of what the pupils gain from doing homework, what the parents gain from their children doing homework and what the teacher gains from receiving homework from pupils.

Sometimes schools will ask you about the importance of a 'good' education or 'what is a "good" education'. There are no right or wrong answers to this. However, try to think of education as developing the person as a whole – socially, academically and physically – and offer a response that encompasses these three aspects.

Other frequently asked questions relate to classroom management and discipline – for example, what would you do if you saw two pupils fighting in the playground at lunchtime? How would you deal with a pupil who persistently arrives late to your classes? Again, there are three aspects to be considered: the school policy on this type of misdemeanour, matching the level of punishment to the frequency and seriousness of the problem, and determining the reason for the behaviour.

Obviously, it is not practical to offer sample answers to all the questions commonly used at interviews as it would mean that everyone would be giving identical and rote-learned replies. However, as preparation for interviews, consider how you would respond to the following questions and make a list of the main points you would address in your reply. Set aside time to reflect on these questions and make notes in advance of the interview and then re-read them before you enter the room.

Typical interview questions

General questions

- Why did you choose teaching as a career?
- What do you feel are the qualities of a modern and effective teacher?
- Tell us about yourself and why you think you are suited to this post?
- Why did you apply for this post?
- What additional qualities can you bring to the school?
- What makes you better than the other candidates who applied for this post?
- How do you rate your PGCE/B.Ed. course? What changes would you make to it and why?
- What have been the high points and low points in your teaching career to date?

- Could you think of a particular problem you encountered in the classroom, briefly describe what it was and how you overcame the problem?
- What would you change about yourself either personally or professionally?
- If you were offered this post, is there any aspect of the job description which would cause you concern?
- If you were a form teacher, what types of activities would you cover during form period?
- What makes a good mathematics teacher?
- What contribution could you make to the extra-curricular life of the school?

School issues

- What are your views on the National Numeracy Strategy/Key Stage 3 Framework for maths?
- What do you understand by 'the basics'? Do you think all teachers can be teachers of numeracy?
- Why is a school policy for discipline important?
- What were the main issues resulting from the Dearing Review of the Curriculum for 16–19-year-olds? How does this impact on mathematics?
- What are your views on Key Skills? Are they of value to students or an unnecessary evil which takes up valuable teaching time?
- Is pastoral care an important part of school life?
- Which examination boards and syllabi are you familiar with and which ones would you recommend and why?
- If you saw two pupils fighting in the corridor, what would you do?
- How would you deal with a student who approached you in confidence for advice on a personal matter?
- How would you deal with a pupil who spoke back when reprimanded by you?
- Suppose some money was taken from a pupil's bag in your classroom, how would you deal with the situation?
- Why do teachers set homeworks?
- What is the difference between formative and summative assessment?
- The UK has been accused of being obsessed with assessing our pupils compared to other European countries. What are your opinions of the current assessment arrangements?

Subject-specific questions and pedagogy

- What is the role of ICT in mathematics?
- How would you integrate Key Skills into your lessons?
- How real is the gap between GCSE and A-level mathematics? How do AS levels impact on your teaching?
- What are your views on GCSE coursework in mathematics?
- What is the best way to teach mathematics?
- How would you motivate reluctant learners?
- Mathematics teachers are often stereotyped as men in tweed jackets with patches on the elbows or wearing woolly cardigans. What impact does this have on the subject and how would you deal with it?

- Why do you think mathematics has a reputation of being a difficult subject to master? How would this influence your teaching?
- Do you think gender differences exist in the mathematics classroom? How would this influence your teaching strategies?
- Why do you think Ma1, Using and Applying Mathematics, was included in the National Curriculum?
- How reliable are the outcomes from mathematics coursework at GCSE?
- How would you incorporate differentiation into your lessons?
- How important are resources in the mathematics classroom?
- What resources do you value most and why?
- Describe what you would consider to be a 'good' mathematics classroom.
- What is good classroom management in a mathematics class?
- Is the ability to communicate verbally important in mathematics?
- What is numeracy? What is the difference between numeracy and mathematics?
- Where does numeracy fit in with the other subjects in the National Curriculum?
- What misconceptions have you met to date in pupils' understanding of mathematical topics?
- How would you introduce [topic] to a group of low/high ability Year [X] pupils?

Future changes

- How would you see the teaching of mathematics in five years' time?
- How can ICT enhance mathematical performance?
- What is the role of ICT in mathematics?
- How would you use video-conferencing in the mathematics classroom?
- Do you feel standards are currently rising or falling in mathematics? Why?
- Describe your vision of a virtual learning environment for mathematics. What would the pupils be doing? What is the teacher's role in this type of learning? What are the key learning objectives? What is the value of this approach?
- How do you view assessment of mathematics in five years' time?
- What do we mean by 'higher order thinking skills' in relation to mathematics?
- What will be the role of the teacher in classrooms in five years' time?

The final few questions at interview

- Is there anything else that you would like to tell us that hasn't already been covered by the interview?
- How could you contribute to the extra-curricular life of this school?
- If you were offered this post, would you accept it?
- Is there anything you would like to ask us?

The most important thing to remember when at an interview is 'be honest'. If you have over-emphasised your role on the application form or if you have said that you have taught topic X and you haven't, then be sure the panel will find out. An experienced teacher will know if you have taught topic X or not by asking what appears to be a simple and relatively easy question but actually pinpoints a major teaching objective that can only be discovered through experience.

Although it is hard to do, try to relax and be yourself during the interview. The members of the panel want to see you as a person, not what you think they want to see. Be polite, cheerful and make good eye contact with everyone on the panel when responding to the questions. Ask for a question to be repeated if necessary or check with them that you have answered all aspects of the question before you move on. Do not rush into your answers, pause slightly and speak clearly when responding. Watch the body language and facial expressions of the members of the interview panel. You will be able to gauge whether they are interested in and agree with your ideas. Keep your answers precise and relevant to the question. If the interviewers wish to hear more detail, then let them ask you a follow-up question.

At the end of the interview, do not feel obliged to ask any questions. It is perfectly acceptable to say that you have read the school prospectus and have no additional questions at the moment. Alternatively, if you have had a tour of the school and have asked the Head of Department questions on a one-to-one basis or as part of a group, then explain this and thank the member of staff for his or her time. You may wish to ask when the successful applicant is likely to hear from the school. No matter how important it is to you, avoid asking questions relating to your salary or holidays. Also, do not ask open-ended questions on generic issues or something that has been in the news, as this will be viewed as time-wasting.

Task 15.3 Draft responses to interview questions

Take each of the questions listed above and make brief notes on the variety and range of responses possible. Jot down occasions when a traditional response would be preferable to 'originality'.

Accepting your first teaching post

The most frequently used method of communication after interview is a telephone call to the successful applicant. Often, the 'reserve' person will also receive a telephone call in case the first candidate does not accept the post or has been offered a job in another school. If you have been unsuccessful this time, consider the interview as valuable experience that will give you the 'edge' at your next interview. Very few people get the first job they apply for and interview panels often have to turn down good candidates in favour of the one who was 'the best on the day'.

Once you have accepted the post informally (by telephone), you will receive written confirmation of the offer and a request to sign the contract. At this stage, any other questions you may have relating to your salary, sickness benefits, holidays, and so on can be clarified before you sign the contract. You may also be asked to attend the school during the final few weeks of the summer term to receive your timetable, organise your resources, find your way around the school and to meet the other members of staff. Sometimes, you will be required to do some substitute teaching to cover classes for the person in charge of timetabling or to assist with the re-organisation of rooms or storing new equipment.

You have now jumped the first hurdle of being a NQT (or a Beginning Teacher (BT) in Northern Ireland). Congratulations!

16 The early years of teaching

Introduction

As with any job, it takes some time for you to settle down and feel in control of all aspects of your life as a teacher. Coming from ITE, where you may have taught a reduced timetable as a PGCE student, to a full-time post with very few non-teaching periods requires a considerable level of adjustment and a certain amount of stamina. It is a good idea to plan ahead over the summer before you start teaching so that you have a range of teaching resources, worksheets and lesson plans already prepared for the first term. This will help you to keep calm and will allow you to focus on your classroom management and teaching without being distracted by the volume of preparation you have to do each evening. The school will have provided you with a Scheme of Work – use it to your advantage. Make a list of any questions you may have relating to the use of software packages or other teaching resources with which you are unfamiliar and sort this out during the in-school non-teaching days before the term begins.

Your first year of teaching is referred to as the Induction Year and from there you progress into Early Professional Development (EPD). These stages are briefly highlighted in the sections that follow. However, more detail can be obtained from your school and LEA or ELB who are responsible for your progress during this period. The final section on Continued Professional Development (CPD) is designed to assist you in obtaining a clear view of the 'whole' picture of teaching as a career. Like any job, changes will be made that will require you to adapt and extend your existing skills. Like all aspects of education, it is lifelong learning.

Learning outcomes

By the end of this chapter you should have a clear understanding of:

- the need for an Induction year;
- the role of early professional development (EPD);
- the importance of continued professional development (CPD).

Induction

Although you have successfully completed your ITE and have qualified teacher status, it will not be confirmed until one year of full-time service has been recorded. This process is called 'Induction' and the arrangements are detailed in *The Induction Support Programme for Newly Qualified Teachers* (DfES, 2003e). All other aspects of your job and your responsibilities are the same as your colleagues who have completed Induction and EPD. You are accountable for your teaching, your pupils' attainment throughout the year, examination results and dealing with parents.

As part of the Induction process, you will receive continued support from the Teacher Tutor or the mentor who is responsible for your personal and professional development within the school. He or she will meet with you on a regular basis and will offer support and advice as necessary. You will also be invited to attend courses organised by the LEA or ELB in which you are working. The courses for teachers completing Induction are usually related to the issues you addressed during the PGCE course, such as Classroom Management, Discipline, Assessment and using ICT in Teaching and Learning. These refresher courses are valuable ways of facilitating discussions between groups of people with the same problems and concerns. By exchanging ideas and experiences with others, you will often find a way of dealing with your own problems. Remember, the VTCs are an alternative support medium.

At the end of the Induction year, the Head of Department, in consultation with the Principal and Board of Governors, will decide if you have made an acceptable level of progress over the year and will then sign off the paperwork surrounding your Induction phase. Depending on the school, you may have an informal interview with the personnel involved in this phase of your development or the Head of Department, and other maths teachers may observe your lessons (similar to during ITE) so that they can make an informed judgement on your level of teaching competence. If you have been receiving an adequate level of support from the department and have demonstrated a successful year of teaching, there is no reason why you would not complete this stage. However, if for some reason your performance is deemed unsatisfactory, do not despair as the school will normally extend your Induction Year for another 12 months and then review the situation again. During this time, you can ask for additional levels of support from the staff responsible for your progress.

Early professional development (EPD)

The EPD phase of your development normally lasts for two years. During both Induction and EPD, the Teacher Tutor will consider issues raised in your Career Entry and Development Profile and will try to assist you in dealing with these aspects of your teaching. As you gain experience, you will also develop interests in other areas of school life, so try to convey these new interests to your mentor or Teacher Tutor. Start thinking about your future. Are there any areas of a teacher's role that you would like to gain more experience of? Who can help you achieve this experience? Do you require additional qualifications to advance in this area (e.g. counselling or pastoral issues)?

Within the context of NI, you will be asked to complete two Professional Development Activities (PDAs): one in a curricular issue, one in pedagogy with ICT as a common strand across both activities. The PDAs are an online package in which you respond to various questions relating to the aims and objectives of the lesson, your teaching methodology, and the outcomes, reflection and evaluation of the lesson. The process must be carried out in at least two cycles to illustrate how you incorporated what you have learned from the first phase into your subsequent teaching delivery. Again, the Teacher Tutor is involved in the completion of the online documentation after discussion with the BT. After two years, these PDAs are submitted to the principal and Board of Governors as evidence of completing EPD. If the work is deemed satisfactory, this group will sign you off as occurred in Induction. Due to the involvement of the Teacher Tutor at every cycle in the PDA, it is unlikely that the final 'board' will challenge the professional judgement of a senior member of staff.

At the end of these years, the compulsory aspects of professional development have been completed and then it will be your decision to progress into Continued Professional Development (CPD).

Continued Professional Development (CPD)

To increase your chances of promotion or to further your professional knowledge of teaching and learning, you may decide to embark on a certificated course delivered by your local university. At present, this type of course is self-funded, so you may wish to spread the financial commitment over three years. In general, all university-based Masters modules are based on research rather than the development of curriculum resources. Each module has an associated assignment that requires the participant to read around the literature in the field and to carry out some action research in the classroom, which is then reported in the evaluation used for submission to the tutor.

A Masters degree normally consists of six taught modules plus a dissertation. The dissertation is an extensive piece of research completed over an academic year. Students must pass all six modules and the dissertation to be awarded a Masters degree. It is possible to follow pathways (or options) addressing areas of interest such as Special Educational Needs, Primary Education, Guidance and Counselling, Leadership and Management. Further details of suitable qualifications will be available via your LEA or on the university's website.

As a result of the recommendations in the report entitled *Making Mathematics Count* (Smith, 2004), changes in the organisation of CPD for maths teachers and its funding are likely to occur in the next few years. The General Teaching Council (GTC) has already introduced a more formal approach to CPD in England through the use of the Teachers' Professional Learning Framework that aims to encourage teachers to map their individual development needs over time. Consideration is also being given to assigning a minimum amount of time to be spent on CPD activities, such as attending courses and completing action research in the classroom, and who should deliver these courses. Due to the shortage of maths teachers in areas of the UK, this report, supported by the findings of the Advisory Committee on Mathematics Education (ACME PR/01), also advocates the development of CPD with a specific focus in the area of mathematical knowledge, skills and pedagogy and the approval of additional remuneration for maths teachers who have successfully completed a series of accredited CPD activities.

Conclusion

As you gain experience in the classroom, you may wish to begin to plan ahead. Subject leaders or Heads of Department have a key role to play within the school assuming positions of middle management. The *Teachers' Standards Framework* (DfES, 2001) describes subject leaders as providing 'professional leadership and management for a subject to secure high quality teaching, effective use of resources and improved standards of learning and achievement for all pupils'. They are responsible for ensuring the implementation of new government strategies in their department and regularly undertake audits of mathematical teaching and learning within the school.

References

Alsopp, S. and Luth, R. (1999). Special needs in the mainstream. In G. Nicholls (ed.) *Learning to Teach*. London: Kogan Page.

Anghileri, J. (2001). *Principles and Practices in Arithmetic Teaching*. Buckingham: Open University Press.

Angoff, W.H. (1971) Scales, norms and equivalent scores. In R.L. Thorndike (ed.) *Educational Meaurement* (2nd edn, pp. 508–600). Washington, DC: American Council of Education.

Askew, M. and Wiliam, D. (1995). *Recent Research in Mathematics Education 5–16*. London: Ofsted.

Askew, M., Brown, M., Rhodes, V., Johnson, D. and Wiliam, D. (1997). *Effective Teachers of Numeracy: Report of a Study Carried Out for the TTA*. London: King's College, University of London.

Assessment Reform Group (1999). *Assessment for Learning: Beyond the Black Box*. Cambridge: Cambridge University.

Baker, E. (1993). Developing comprehensive assessments of higher order thinking. In G. Kulm (ed.) *Assessing Higher Order Thinking in Mathematics*. Washington, DC: American Association for the Advancement of Science.

Bannister, H. (1993). Truths about assessment and the learning of girls: from gender difference to the production of gendered attainment. In J. Blackmore and J. Kenway (eds) *Gender Matters in Educational Administration and Policy: A Feminist Introduction*. London: Falmer Press.

Basic Skills Agency (1997). *Does Numeracy Matter?* London: Basic Skills Agency.

Battista, M.T. and Clements, D. H. (1986). The effects of Logo and CAI problem-solving environments on problem-solving abilities and mathematics achievement. *Computers in Human Behaviour*, 2, 183–193.

Becker, J.P. and Selter, C. (1996). Elementary school practices. In A.J. Bishop, K. Clements, C. Keitel, J. Kilpatrick and C. Laborde (eds) *International Handbook of Mathematics Education*. Dordrecht: Kluwer.

Bell, S., Brown, P. and Buckley, S. (1988). *New York Cop and Other Investigations*. Cambridge: Cambridge University Press.

Black, P. and Wiliam, D. (1998). *Inside the Black Box*. London: King's College.

Bloom, B. S. (1956). *Taxonomy of Educational Objectives: The Classification of Educational Goals. Handbook I: Cognitive Domain*. New York: Longman.

Brophy, J. and Good, T. (1986). 'Teacher behaviour and student achievement.' In M.C. Wittrock (ed.) *Handbook of Research on Teaching*. New York: Macmillan.

Brown, A.L. and Campione, J.C. (1986). Psychological theory and the study of learning disabilities. *American Psychologist*, 14, 10, 1059–1068.

Bruer, T. (1997). *Schools for Thought*. Cambridge, MA: MIT Press.

Bruner, J. (1960). *The Process of Education: A Landmark in Educational Theory*. Cambridge, MA: Harvard University Press.

Bruner, J. (1996). *The Culture of Education*. Cambridge, MA: Harvard University Press.

Butler, R. (1998). Enhancing and undermining intrinsic motivation: the effects of task-involving and ego-involving evaluation on interest and performance. *British Journal of Educational Psychology*, 58, 1–14.

Campione, J.C., Brown, A.L. and Connell, M.L. (1989). Metacognition: on the importance of understanding what you are doing. In R. Charles and E. Silver (eds) *The Teaching and Assessment of Mathematical Problem-solving*, pp. 93–114. Reston, VA: National Council of Teachers of Mathematics.

CCEA (2000a). *GCSE Mathematics Specification*. Belfast: CCEA.

CCEA (2000b). *Strategic Planning and Development of Key Skills. Managing Key Skills Series Booklet 2*. Belfast: CCEA.

CCEA (2002a). *Guttering Task for GCSE Coursework*. Available at: www.rewardinglearning.com/development/qualifications/gcse/gcse_math_internally_ass.html.

CCEA (2002b). *GCSE Investigations and Data Sets*. Available at: www.ccea.org.uk/gmaths_coursework_guidance/index.htm.

Clements, D.H. (1985). Logo programming: can it change how children think? *Electronic Learning*, 74–75.

Clements, D.H. (1986). Effects of Logo and CAI environments on cognition and creativity. *Journal of Educational Psychology*, 78, 309–318.

Clements, C., Kurland, D., Mawby, R. and Pea, R. (1986). Analogical reasoning and computer programming. *Journal of Educational Computing Research*, 2, 4, 473–485.

Cockcroft, W.H. (1982) *Mathematics Counts*. London: HMSO.

Cooper, B. and Dunne, M. (1999). *Assessing Children's Mathematical Knowledge*. Buckinghamshire: Open University Press.

Cowan, P. (2003). *The CAUSES project: Computerised Assessment Units for Special Schools*. Report for the Department of Education, Northern Ireland. Belfast: Queen's University.

Cowan, P. and Lynch, S. (in press). 'Using Multimedia to Incorporate Vygotskian Prompts into an Online Assessment System for Mathematics.' *Interactive Learning Environments*.

Cowan, P., Morrison, H. and McBride, F. (1998). 'Evidence of a spiral curriculum using a mathematical problem-solving tool.' *Interactive Learning Environments*, 6, 3, 205–224.

Curriculum Online (2003). Available at: www.curriculumonline.gov.uk.

Dearing, R. (1996). *Review of the Qualifications for 16–19 year olds*. London: SCAA.

DENI (1992). *Key Stage 3 Programmes of Study and Attainment Targets*. Bangor: Rathgael House.

DENI (1996a). *Northern Ireland Curriculum and Programmes of Study*. London: HMSO.

DENI (1996b). *NI Strategy for Educational Technology*. Bangor: Rathgael House.

DENI (1998). *School Improvement Programme*. Bangor: Department of Education.

DES (1998a). *National Numeracy Strategy*. London: DES.

DES (1998b). *National Literacy Strategy*. London: DES.

DfEE (1998a). *Excellence in Schools*. London: HMSO. Also available at: www.dfee.gov.uk/wpaper/index.htm.

DfEE (1998b). *National Literacy Strategy*. DfEE. Available at: www.standards.dfes.gov.uk/primary/literacy.

DfEE (1998c). *Connecting the Learning Society*. DfEE.

DfEE (1998d). *National Numeracy Strategy*. DfEE. Available at: www.standards.dfes.gov.uk/primary/numeracy.

DfEE (1999). *A Fresh Start – Improving Literacy and Numeracy (The Moser Report)*. Available at: www.literacytrust.org.uk.

DfEE (2000). *Using ICT to Support Mathematics in Primary Schools*. London: DfEE.

DfEE (2001a). Green Paper, *Schools: Building on Success*. Available at: www.dfes.gov.uk/buildingonsuccess/request_brochure.shtml.

DfES (1999). *National Numeracy Strategy*. Available at: www.standards.dfes.gov.uk/primary/numeracy/.

REFERENCES

DfES (2000) *Using ICT to Support Mathematics in Primary Schools*. London: DfES.

DfES (2001a). *Using Assess and Review Lessons*. London: DfES.

DfES (2001b). *Teacher's Standards Framework: Helping you Develop*. Available online.

DfES (2001c). *Mathematics at Key Stage 3*. Available at: www.standards.dfes.gov.uk/keystage3/.

DfES (2001d). *Guidance to Support Pupils with Dsylexia and Dyscalculia*. London: DfES.

DfES (2001e). Green Paper, *Schools: Building on Success*. London: DfES.

DfES (2001f). *National Key Stage 3 Strategy*. London: DfES. Available at: www.dfes.standards.gov.uk/keystage3/.

DfES (2001g). *Springboard 7: A Mathematics Catch-up Programme for Pupils Entering Year 7*. London: DfES.

DfES (2002a). *Key Stage 3 Strategy*. Available at: www.standards.dfes.gov.uk/keystage3/.

DfES (2002b). *Teaching Gifted and Talented Pupils*. Available at: www.standards.dfes.gov.uk/keystage3/.

DfES (2002c). *The Plenary*. London: DfES.

DfES (2002d). *Teaching Gifted and Talented Pupils*. London: DfES.

DfES (2002e). *Guidance on Teaching Able Mathematicians*. London: DfEE.

DfES (2002f). *Framework for Teaching Mathematics: Years 7, 8 and 9*. London: DfES.

DfES (2003a). *Integrating ICT into Mathematics in Key Stage 3*. Available at: www.standards.dfes.gov.uk/keystage3/publications (last accessed June 2003).

DfES (2003b). *Mathematics Transition Units*. London: DfES.

DfES (2003c). *Supporting Progressions through Key Stage 3*. London: DfES.

DfES (2003d). *Securing Progression through Key Stage 3*. London: DfES.

DfES (2003e). *The Induction Support Programme for Newly Qualified Teachers* (reference: DfES/0458/2003). Available at: www.teachernet.gov.uk/professionaldevelopment/nqt/induction/guidance/ London: DfES.

Dick, T.P. (1996). Graphing calculators in secondary school calculus. In B. Waits and P. Gomez (eds) *Proceedings of Topic Group 18*, ICME-8. Available at: http://ued.uniandes.edu.co/servidor/em/recinf/tg18/ArchivosPDF/Dick.pdf

Donaldson, G. (2002). *Successful Mathematics Leadership in Primary Schools*. Exeter: Learning Matters.

Dorans, N.J. and Schmitt, A.P. (1993). Constructed response and differential item functioning: a pragmatic approach. In R.E. Bennett and W.C. Ward (eds) *Construction versus Choice in Cognitive Measurement*, 135–166. Hillsdale, NJ: Lawrence Erlbaum Associates.

Edwards, C., Gandini, L. and Forman, G. (1993). *The Hundred Languages of Children: The Reggio Emilia Approach in Early Childhood Education*. Norwood, NJ: Ablex.

Freudenthal, H. (1968). Why to teach mathematics so as to be useful. *Educational Studies in Mathematics*, 1, 3–8.

Freudenthal, H. (1991). *Revisiting Mathematics Education*. Dordrecht: Kluwer Academic Publishers.

FSA (2000). *Money Counts*. London: Beam Education.

Gardner, H. (1991). *The Unschooled Mind*. London: HarperCollins.

Gardner, H. (1993). *Frames of Mind*. London: Fontana.

Gardner, H. and Boix-Mansilla (1994). Teaching for understanding in the disciplines and beyond. *Teachers' College Record*, 96, 198–217.

Good, T. and Brophy, J. (1991). *Looking in Classrooms*. New York: HarperCollins.

Gordon, N. (1992). Children with developmental dyscalculia. *Developmental Medicine and Child Neurology*, 34, 5, 459–463.

Gottfried, B.S. (1996). *Spreadsheet Tools for Engineers*. New York: McGraw-Hill.

Harris, S., Keys, W. and Fernandes, C. (1997). *Third International Mathematics and Science Study*. Second National Report. NFER: NAACE.

Hart, K. M. (1995). *Children's Understanding of Mathematics: 11–16*. London: John Murray.

Henderson, A. (1998). *Maths for the Dyslexic: A Practical Guide*. London: David Fulton Publishers.

Hunt, E. (1986). Cognitive research and future test design. In *The Redesign of Testing for the 21st Century*. Princeton, NJ: Educational Testing Service.

Jennings, S. and Dunne, R. (1998). *QTS: Teaching Mathematics in Primary Schools*. London: Letts Educational.

Johnston (1997). *LCI: Learning Combination Inventory*. Available at: www.letmelearn.org/ (last accessed February 2003).

Jones, S. and Myhill, D. (in press). *Seeing Things Differently: Teachers' Constructions of Underachievement*.

Katz, L.G. and Chard, S.C. (1989). *Engaging Children's Minds: The Project Approach*. Norwood: NJ: Ablex.

Kelly, A. (1987). *Science for Girls?* Milton Keynes: Open University Press.

Keys, W., Harris, S. and Fernandes, C. (1996). *Third International Mathematics and Science Study*. First National Report. NFER: NAACE.

Kroll, D.L. (1988). Co-operative mathematical problem-solving and metacognition: a case study of three pairs of women. *Dissertation Abstracts International*, 49, 2958A (University Microfilms No. 8902580).

KS3 (2002). Available at: www.standards.dfes.gov.uk/keystage3/respub/mathsframework/foreword.

Kulm, G. (1990). New directions in mathematics assessment. In G. Kulm (ed.) *Assessing Higher Order Thinking in Mathematics*. Washington, DC: American Association for the Advancement of Science.

Kyriacou, C. (1997). *Effective Teaching in Schools: Theory and Practice*. Cheltenham: Stanley Thornes.

Lawlor, G. and Newland, A. (2000) *Your Family Counts*. 4Learning and Maths Year. London.

Learning and Skills Development Agency (2001). *Overview of the Curriculum 2000 (Qualifying for Success) Reforms*. Available at: www.lsagency.org.uk/curriculum2000.

Learning Support Agency (2001). *Does Numeracy Matter?* London: Basic Skills Agency.

Leikin, R. and Zaslavsky, O. (1997) Facilitating student interaction in mathematics in a co-operative learning setting. *Journal for Research in Mathematics Education*, 28, 3, 331–354.

Lerman, S. (1998). Research on socio-cultural perspectives of mathematics teaching and learning. In J. Kilpatrick and A. Sierpinska (eds) *Mathematics Education as a Research Domain: A Search for Identity*. Vol. 1, 333–350. Dordrecht: Kluwer.

Lesh, R. (1990). Computer-based assessment of higher order understandings and processes in elementary mathematics. In G. Kulm (ed.) *Assessing Higher Order Thinking in Mathematics*. Washington, DC: American Association for the Advancement of Science.

Lester, F. K. and Kroll, D. L. (1990). Assessing student growth in mathematical problem-solving. In G. Kulm (ed.) *Assessing higher order thinking in mathematics*. Washington, DC: American Association for the Advancement of Science.

Licht, B. and Dweck, C. (1984). Sex differences in achievement orientations: consequences for academic choices and attainments. In *The English Curriculum: Gender, Material for Discussion*. London: ILEA English Centre.

Linn, R.L. and Gronlund, N. E. (1995). *Measurement and Assessment in Teaching*. Mahwah: NJ: Merrill.

Lochhead, J. and Mestre, J. (1988). From words to algebra: minding misconceptions. In A. Coxford and A. Schulte (eds) *The Ideas of Algebra K-12*. Reston, VA: NCTM.

McLaughlin, M. W. and Shepard, L. A. (1995). *Improving Education Through Standards-based Education Reform*. A report by the National Academy of Education Panel on Standards-based Education Reform.

Marshall, S. P. (1988). *Assessing Schema Knowledge* (Technical Report). San Diego, CA: San Diego State University, Center for Research in Mathematics and Science Education.

Marshall, S.P. (1990). The assessment of schema knowledge for arithmetic story problems: a cognitive science perspective. In G. Kulm (ed.) *Assessing Higher Order Thinking in Mathematics*. Washington, DC: American Association for the Advancement of Science.

Messick, S. (1989). Validity. In R.L. Linn (ed.) *Educational Measurement* (3rd edition). 13–103. New York: American Council on Education/Macmillan.

Minsky, M. (1975). A framework for representing knowledge. In P.H. Winston (ed.) *The Psychology of Computer Vision*, pp. 245–277. New York: McGraw-Hill.

REFERENCES

National Research Council (1989). *Everybody Counts: A Report to the Nation on the Future of Mathematics Education.* Washington, DC: National Academy Press.

National Research Council (1990). *Reshaping School Mathematics: A Philosophy and Framework for Curriculum.* Washington, DC: National Academy Press.

Newell, A. and Simon, H.A. (1972). *Human Problem-solving.* New York: Prentice-Hall.

NFER (1995). *Mathematics and ICT: A Pupil's Entitlement.* London: NFER.

NNS (1999). Available at: www.standards.dfes.gov.uk/primary/publications/mathematics/nns_background/91884/.

NNS (2001). *Guidance to Support Pupils with Dyslexia and Dyscalculia.* DfES 0512/2001.

Numeracy Task Force (1998). *Numeracy Matters.* London: DfES.

Ofsted (1995). *The Ofsted Handbook: Guidance on the Inspection of Secondary Schools.* HMSO: London.

Ofsted (2001). *Inspecting Mathematics 11–16 with Guidance on Self-evaluation.* HMSO: London.

Oldknow, A. and Taylor, R. (2000). *Teaching Mathematics with ICT.* London: Continuum.

Osler, A., Street, C., Lall, M. and Vincent, K. (2002) *Not a Problem? Girls and School Exclusion.* Available at: www.jrf.org.uk/knowledge/findings/socialpolicy/112.asp (last accessed April 2004).

Papert, S. (1971). *Teaching Children to be Mathematicians versus Teaching about Mathematics.* MIT Artificial Intelligence Laboratory, Logo Memo Number 4.

Papert, S. (1980). *Mindstorms: Children, Computers and Powerful Ideas.* New York: Basic Books.

Perry, N. (1998). Young children's self-regulated learning and contexts that support it. *Journal of Educational Psychology*, 90, 715–729.

Piaget, J. (1926). *The Language and Thought of the Child.* London: Routledge & Kegan Paul.

Plummer, G. (2000). *Failing Working Class Girls.* Stoke on Trent: Trentham.

Pollard, A., Triggs, P., Broadfoot, P., McNess, E. and Osborn, M. (2000). *What Pupils Say: Changing Policy and Practice in Primary Education.* London: Continuum.

Polya (1945). *How to Solve It.* Princeton, NJ: Princeton University Press.

Polya (1966). On teaching problem-solving. In E.G. Begle (ed.) *The Role of Axiomatics and Problem-solving in Mathematics*, 123–129. Boston, MA: Ginn.

Popham, W. J. (1990). *Modern Educational Measurement: A Practitioner's Perspective.* Boston, MA: Allyn & Bacon.

QCA (1998). *National Curriculum for England and Wales.* Available at: www.nc.uk.net (last accessed June 2002).

QCA (1999). *Inclusion.* Available at: www.nc.uk.net.

QCA (2000a) *Inclusion.* National Curriculum online.

QCA (2000b). *Adaptable Learning Materials and Practical Guides: Key Skills in A levels: Mathematics.* London: QCA.

QCA (2001a). *Using Assessment to Raise Achievement in Mathematics: Key Stages 1, 2 and 3.* Available at: www.qca.org.uk.

QCA (2001b). *Key Skills for Employability.* Available at: www.qca.org.uk/14–19/11–16schools/downloads/ks_for_developing.pdf.

QCA (2002a). *TestBase: Key Stage 3 and 2 Test Compendium CD.* London: Doublestruck.

QCA (2002b). *ExamPro: The Examination Publishing Package.* London: Doublestruck.

QCA (2003). Available at: www.qca.org.uk/11288/html.

Reynolds, D. and Muijs, D. (1999). The effective teaching of mathematics: a review of research. *School Leadership and Management*, 19, 3, 273–288.

Robertson, J. (1996). *Effective Classroom Control.* London: Hodder & Stoughton.

Rogers, B. (1997). *Managing Behaviour Series.* Videos produced by Quartus, UK.

Rogoff, B. (2003). *The Cultural Nature of Human Development.* New York: Oxford University Press.

Rogoff, B., Goodman-Turkinas, C. and Bartlett, L. (2002). *Learning Together: Children and Adults in a School Community.* New York: Oxford University Press.

Rosenthal, R. and Jacobson, L. (1968) *Pygmalion in the Classroom.* New York: Holt, Rinehart & Winston.

Rothery, A. (1993). *Spreadsheets for Mathematics and IT*. London: John Murray.

Rummelhart, D.E. (1980). Schemata: The building blocks of cognition. In R. Spiro, D. Bruce and W. Brewer (eds) *Theoretical Issues in Reading Comprehension*. Hillsdale, NJ: Erlbaum.

SCAA (1993) *Review of the National Curriculum: Final Report*. London: SCAA.

Schumann, H. and Green, D. (1994). *Discovering Geometry with a Computer – Using Cabri-Géomètre*. Sweden: Chartwell-Bratt.

Schunk, D. (1996). Goal and self-evaluative influences during children's cognitive skill learning. *American Educational Research Journal*, 33, 359–382.

Scottish Executive (1999) *Adult Literacy in the Labour Market: A Literature Review*. Available at: www.scotland.gov.uk/library3/lifelong/alrlr.pdf.

SEAC (1993). *Review of the National Curriculum: Interim Report*. London: SCAA.

Secada, W.G. (1992). Race, ethnicity, social class, language and achievement in mathematics. In D.A. Grouws (ed.) *Handbook of Research on Mathematics Teaching and Learning*. New York: Macmillan.

Shell Centre for Mathematics Education (1984). Available at: www.nottingham.ac.uk/shell or http://mathshell.com/scp.

Skinner, B. (1974). *About Behaviourism*. New York: Vintage Books.

Smith, A. (2004). *Making Mathematics Count: The Report of Professor Adrian Smith's Inquiry into Post-14 Mathematics Education*. Available at: www.mathsinquiry.org.uk.

SMP (1985). *SMP 11–16: Investigations and Stretchers*. Southampton: School Mathematics Project.

Stones, E. (1994). *Quality Teaching: A Sample of Cases*. London: Routledge.

Straker, A. (1997) *National Numeracy Project: Framework for Numeracy 1, 2 and 3*. London: National Project for Literacy and Numeracy.

Theobald, M. (1987). Humanities, science and the female mind: an historical perspective. *Unicorn*, 13, 3.

Thomas, K. (1990). *Gender and Subject in Higher Education*. Buckingham: The Society for Research into Higher Education and Open University Press.

Thompson, I. (1999). *Issues in Teaching Numeracy in Primary Schools*. Buckingham: Open University Press.

Treffers, A. (1987). *Three Dimensions: A Model of Goal and Theory Description in Mathematics Instruction – the Wiskobas Project*. Dordrecht: Reidel.

Treffers, A. (1991). Realistic mathematics education in the Netherlands 1980–1990. In L. Streefland, (ed.) *Realistic Mathematics Education in the Primary School*. Utrecht: CD-b Press/Freudenthal Institute, Utrecht University.

TTA (1999). *The Use of ICT in Subject Teaching: Identification of Training Needs for Secondary Mathematics*. London: TTA.

TTA (2001). *Qualifying to Teach*. London: Teacher Training Agency. Available at: www.tta.gov.uk.

TTA (2003). *In Training: Latest News*. Available at: www.tta.gov.uk/training/ (last accessed July 2003).

Tversky, A. and Kahneman, D. (1981). The framing of decisions and the psychology of choice. *Science*, 211, 453–458.

Underwood, J. and Brown, J. (1997). *Integrated Learning Systems: Potential into Practice*. Oxford: Heinemann.

Van der Veer, R. and Valsiner, J. (1991). *Understanding Vygotsky – a Quest for Synthesis*. Cambridge, MA: Blackwell.

Vygotsky, L. S. (1962). *Thought and Language*. Cambridge, MA: MIT University Press.

Vygotsky, L. S. (1978). *Mind in Society: The Development of Higher Psychological Processes*. Cambridge, MA: Harvard University Press.

Walkerdine, V. (1988). *The Mastery of Reason: Cognitive Development and the Production of Rationality*. London: Routledge & Kogan Page.

Walkerdine, V. (1989). *Counting Girls Out*. London: Virago.

Wertsch, J. (1982). The adult–child dyad as a problem-solving system. *Child Development*, 51, 1215–1221.

REFERENCES

Wittrock, M.C. (1981). Reading comprehension. In F.J. Pirozzolo and M.C. Wittrock (eds.) *Brain, Cognition and Education*. New York: Academic Press.

Younger, M. and Warrington, M. (1996). Differential achievement of girls and boys at GCSE: some observations from the perspective of one school. *British Journal of Sociology of Education*, 17, 3, 299–313.

Index

DISCARD